A Nation Is Born

A Nation Is Born

The Jacob Story

Shaul Bar

WIPF & STOCK · Eugene, Oregon

A NATION IS BORN
The Jacob Story

Copyright © 2016 Shaul Bar. All rights reserved. Except for brief quotations in critical publications or reviews, no part of this book may be reproduced in any manner without prior written permission from the publisher. Write: Permissions, Wipf and Stock Publishers, 199 W. 8th Ave., Suite 3, Eugene, OR 97401.

Wipf & Stock
An Imprint of Wipf and Stock Publishers
199 W. 8th Ave., Suite 3
Eugene, OR 97401

www.wipfandstock.com

PAPERBACK ISBN: 978-1-4982-3935-6
HARDCOVER ISBN: 978-1-4982-3937-0
EBOOK ISBN: 978-1-4982-3936-3

Manufactured in the U.S.A.

January 4, 2016: Permission is hereby granted for Shaul Bar to reproduce the pages stipulated below from his book, A Letter has not been Read.

A Letter That Has Not Been Read: Dreams in the Hebrew Bible
By Dr. Shaul Bar
ISBN: 9780878204243
Pages used in new publication: 19-23, 25-27, 184-189

November 2016: Peter Lang grants you the right to reproduce the chapter:

Shaul Bar, 'The Religious Customs of the Patriarchs', *Daily Life of the Patriarchs* (Oxford: Peter Lang, 2015), pp. 54–59.

Dedicated to:

Don Meredith
Evelyn Meredith
Sheila Owen
Bob Turner

All of whom made me feel at home.

Contents

Acknowledgments | xi
Abbreviations | xiii
Introduction | xvii

1   The Birth of the Twins | 1
      Two Nations Are in Your Womb | 2
      Perez and Zerah | 9
      Different Brothers | 11

2   Deception | 15
      Jacob | 16
      Laban | 21
      Rachel | 26
      Jacob's Sons | 28

3   Jacob's Wives | 34
      Rachel | 34
      Leah | 40
      Bilhah and Zilpah | 44

Contents

4 Religious Practices in the Jacob Cycle | 48
    Altars | 49
    Sacrifice | 50
    Stones | 52
    Vow | 54
    The Thigh Muscle | 55
    Prayer | 56
    The God of Israel and the Alien Gods | 56
    God in the Jacob Cycle | 60

5 Angels | 66
    Angelology in the Hebrew Bible | 66
    Wrestling with an Angel | 69
    Bethel and Peniel | 74
    Hosea | 76

6 Dreams | 80
    Bethel | 81
    Jacob's Dream in the House of Laban | 87
    Laban's Dream | 90
    Incubation | 91

7 The Dinah Story | 95
    And Took Her and Lay with Her by Force | 96
    Justifying the Brothers' Act | 104
    Jacob and Shechem | 107
    An Ancient Story | 108
    Story against Intermarriages | 110

8 Jacob and Joseph | 113
    The Sale of Joseph | 113
    Joseph and His Brothers | 118
    Jacob's Migration to Egypt | 124

9 The Testament of Jacob | 130
    The Maxim's Period | 131
    Reuben | 134
    Simeon and Levi | 135
    Judah | 137
    Zebulun | 140
    Issachar | 141
    Dan | 142
    Gad | 145
    Asher | 146
    Naphtali | 147
    Joseph | 148
    Benjamin | 150

10 Conclusion | 153

Bibliography | 159
Index | 167

Acknowledgments

To start with, I would like to thank my two readers who read the early drafts of the manuscript and offered many perceptive and insightful comments: Anna S. Chernak, who read the initial manuscript and offered valuable advice with continuous encouragement; then Bob Turner, circulation librarian at the Harding School of Theology, who made many suggestions and offered his wisdom. I am grateful as well to Shoshana Cenker, who read the final draft of the manuscript.

I want to express appreciation to the staff of the Harding School of Theology in Memphis, to whom this book is dedicated. Librarian Don Meredith led me to many resources, associate librarian Sheila Owen helped me with research, and Evelyn Meredith supported my investigations with abundant cheer.

Special thanks to Hebrew Union College Library in New York City, where head librarian Yoram Bitton provided me with all the necessary help, wisdom, as well as friendship; and to librarians Tina Weiss and Leonid Gontar, who helped with my research.

Finally, a special thanks to the people at Wipf & Stock for their devotion and expertise in transforming my manuscript into this book, especially copyeditor Noah Crabtree for his attention to detail, masterful work and responsiveness.

Shaul Bar
Memphis, Tennessee
December 2015

Abbreviations

AASOR	*Annual of the American Schools of Oriental Research*
AB	Anchor Bible
ʿAbod. Zar.	*ʿAbodah Zarah*
AJBA	*Australian Journal of Biblical Archaeology*
AJSL	*American Journal of Semitic Languages and Literatures*
Akk.	Akkadian (language)
ANET	*Ancient Near Eastern Texts Relating to the Old Testament*. Edited by J. B. Pritchard. 3rd edition. Princeton: Princeton University Press, 1969.
AnSt	*Anatolian Studies*
Ant.	Josephus, Flavius. *Jewish Antiquities*. Translated by H. St. J. Thackeray. Cambridge, MA: Harvard University Press, 1930.
ASTI	*Annual of the Swedish Theological Institute*
b.	Babylonian Talmud
BA	*Biblical Archaeologist*
BAR	*Biblical Archaeology Reader*
BASOR	*Bulletin of the American School of Oriental Research*
B. Bat.	*Baba Batra*
Ber.	*Berakot*
BethM	*Beth Mikra*

Abbreviations

Bib	*Biblica*
BibOr	Biblica et Orientalia
B. Qam.	Baba Qamma
BTB	*Biblical Theology Bulletin*
BZAW	Beihefte zur Zeitschrift für die alttestamentliche Wissenschaft
CBQ	*Catholic Biblical Quarterly*
CBQMS	*CBQ* Monograph Series
COS	*The Context of Scripture*. Edited by W. W. Hallo. 3 vols. Leiden: Brill, 1997–2002.
ExpTim	*Expository Times*
Heb.	Hebrew (language)
HSM	Harvard Semitic Monographs
HTR	*Harvard Theological Review*
HUCA	*Hebrew Union College Annual*
Ḥul.	Ḥullin
ICC	International Critical Commentary
IEJ	*Israel Exploration Journal*
JAOS	*Journal of the American Oriental Society*
JBL	*Journal of Biblical Literature*
Jdt	Judith
JEA	*Journal of Egyptian Archaeology*
JETS	*Journal of the Evangelical Theological Society*
JNES	*Journal of Near Eastern Studies*
JPOS	*Journal of the Palestine Oriental Society*
JSOT	*Journal for the Study of the Old Testament*
JSOTSup	Journal for the Study of the Old Testament Supplement Series
JSS	*Journal of Semitic Studies*

Abbreviations

KTU	*Die keilalphabetischen Texte aus Ugarit I.* Edited by M. Dietrich, O. Loretz, and J. Sanmartin. AOAT 24. Neukirchener-Vluyn: Neukirchener, 1976
LCL	Loeb Classical Library
LXX	Septuagint
m.	Mishnah
Mak.	Makkot
Meg.	Megillah
Menaḥ.	Menaḥot
Od.	Homer. *The Odyssey.*
Pesaḥ.	Pesaḥim
Rab.	*Midrash Rabbah.* Edited by H. Freedman and M. Simon. 10 vols. London: Soncino, 1939.
RHR	*Revue de l'histoire religions*
Šabb.	Šabbat
Sanh.	Sanhedrin
SBLDS	Society of Biblical Literature Dissertation Series
SJOT	*Scandinavian Journal of the Old Testament*
Soṭah	Soṭah
ST	*Studia theologica*
Syria	*Syria: Revue d'art oriental et d'archéologie*
t.	Tosefta
Tanḥ.	Tanḥuma
TDOT	*Theological Dictionary of the Old Testament.* Edited by G. J. Botterweck and H. Ringgren. Translated by Geoffrey W. Bromiley et al. 14 vols. Grand Rapids: Eerdmans, 1974–2004.
T. Levi	Testament of Levi
Tg. Jon.	Targum Jonathan
Tg. Neof.	Targum Neofiti

ABBREVIATIONS

Tg. Onq.	Targum Onqelos
Ugar.	Ugaritic (language)
VT	*Vetus Testamentum*
VTSup	Vetus Testamentum Supplement Series
Vulg.	Latin Vulgate
WBC	Word Biblical Commentary
WMANT	Wissenschaftliche Monographien zum Alten und Neuen Testament
WTJ	*Westminster Theological Journal*
ZAW	*Zeitschrift für alttestamentliche Wissenschaft*

Introduction

HALF OF THE BOOK of Genesis is devoted to describing the life of Jacob (Gen 25–50). This is not a coincidence, because Jacob became the forefather of the nation called Israel, and his sons were the ancestors of the twelve tribes. Clues about events in Jacob's life also appeared in books outside of the Genesis narrative such as Deut 26:5; Josh 24:5, 32; Pss 105:23; Hos 12:4–5, 13; and Mal 1:1. The reference to Jacob in the book of Hosea has led scholars to believe that this was a different version than the story recorded in Genesis. Hence, it appears that there were different legends connected with Jacob that were not included in Genesis. Thus, it is possible that Jacob's maxim— "And now, I assign to you one portion more than your brothers, which I wrested from the Amorites with my sword and bow" (Gen 48:22)—alludes to a different tradition. More so, later legends about Jacob are found in the apocryphal literature, midrashim, as well as Christian and Islamic literature, which contain traces of earlier traditions. In the rest of the Bible, Jacob is mentioned along with the other patriarchs in reference to the covenant (Exod 2:24; 32:13; Lev 26:42; Deut 29:12; 2 Kgs 13:23). Ezekiel speaks of the connection between the patriarch Jacob and the land. He also refers to Jacob as "God's servant" (28:25; 37:25. Cf. Isa 41:8; 44:1).

The question of the composition of the Jacob stories and their historical value has captured the attention of biblical scholars for centuries. Some treat these accounts as myths or literary epics. Other authors identify historical facts that were expanded with later additions and revisions. Were the stories originally independent of each other? Were they written at different times, in different localities, and for different functions? Who was responsible for their creation? Were the stories combined or morphed by a long literary process of editing?

Introduction

Scholars who adhere to the documentary hypothesis claim that the stories about Jacob were created from the combination of three sources: J and E, with later redactions by P. Therefore, the stories were independent compositions that were patched together by redactors from the tenth to the fifth centuries BCE. These stories were not the earliest. Part of these stories may have originally been transmitted orally. Gunkel attempted to get behind the composite narrative by tracing the smallest units in Israel's earliest traditions. According to him, the basic feature of oral tradition is that each story existed by itself as a separate entity. By examining the forms and cycles of ancient tradition, Gunkel advanced our knowledge of the literary documentary analysis of Wellhausen, who argued that the Pentatuech is comprised of four distinct sources labeled J, E, D, and P. By critical analysis, H. Gunkel identified four main blocks in the Jacob stories. The blocks were stacked on top of one another, so he separated them. The end result was four layers: Jacob and Esau, Jacob and Laban, divine manifestation, and Jacob and his children.[1]

A different approach was taken by M. Noth, who analyzed the stories according to their geographical locations. He separated the stories to East-Jordan and West-Jordan traditions.[2] According to the West-Jordan traditions, Jacob was a cultic ancestor associated with Shechem and Bethel. Although some scholars rejected Noth's division of the Jacob tradition, there are those who adhered to some form of source tradition accepting the northern origin of the Jacob figure, according to which the traditions about Jacob originated at Bethel. After the nation of Israel was conquered by the Assyrians and the northern tribes were taken into exile, Jacob's character grew in stature, and he became the eponymous ancestor of Israel. The exile of the Israelites is reflected in Jacob's exile from his home to Haran. In addition, the later struggle between Israel and Edom led to the development and inclusion of the Jacob and Esau story into the book of Genesis.[3]

Doubts about the three-source approach in the Jacob narrative led scholars to abandon it. Blum followed R. Rendtorff's lead, developing a method that points to succession and expansion of a nuclear story.[4] In

---

1. Gunkel, *Genesis*, 285; A similar path was taken by Rast, *Tradition history and the Old Testament*, 33–56.
2. Noth, *A History of Pentateuchal Traditions*, 89–101.
3. Strange, "Geography and Tradition," 210–22.
4. Blum, *Die Komposition der Vätergeschichte*; and Rendtorff, *The Problem of the Process*, 189–206.

other words, at its core was the Jacob-Esau rivalry (25:21–34; and ch. 27), which he dated to the Davidic-Solomonic period; in addition to the Jacob-Laban story (chs. 29–31), ending with a treaty between Jacob and Laban (31:44–32:2a). To this core (chs. 25–33), a succession of six redactional layers was inserted at the time of the divided monarchy. Later, exilic and post-exilic additions were added (27:46—28:9).

In contrast to the view that the text of Gen 25–36 was developed in several stages, A. de Pury maintains that the Jacob story is a coherent, unified narrative, and its center piece is God's appearance to Jacob in Genesis 28 with its promises and a vow. Unity in the Jacob cycle was also noted by Fokkelman and M. Fishbane, who analyzed the text from a synchronic point of view, setting aside all literary, form, and historical considerations.[5] Fishbane demonstrated that the stories about Jacob are duplicates of one another and appear in chiastic order. The compiler has organized twelve individual units into reverse sequence. Thus, the first and last stories are identical, and so the second and next to the last, etc. More so, the stories share the same vocabulary and thematic similarities, which cement the ties between the parallel episodes.

Examination of the stories shows that they were organized in a systematic way, which excludes any possibility that they were patched together. The stories about Jacob are patterned after the stories about Abraham and are based on the numbers seven and ten. The starting point of the stories is when Jacob steals the birthright from his brother Esau and deceives his father Isaac to receive the blessing. From that point on, we read about the ten trials that Jacob had to endure as a result of his deception. The punishments that Jacob suffered from are equal in numbers to the ten trials of Abraham:

1. Jacob left his father's house to escape the wrath of his brother Esau and to live in danger (Gen 28:10).

2. Instead of his father's blessing that "the elder will serve the younger . . . and people will serve you," the opposite occurred, and he had to serve his uncle Laban. Jacob worked for Laban for seven years and after that for another seven years and then six more years (Gen 29:20).

3. As Jacob deceived his blind father, so Laban exploited the darkness and switched Leah for Rachel (Gen 29:23).

---

5. Fokkelman, *Narrative Art in Genesis*, 83–241; Fishbane, "Composition and Structure in the Jacob Cycle," 15–38; and Fishbane, *Text and Texture*, 40–62. See also Rendsburg, who follows Fishbane: *The Redaction of Genesis*, 51–69.

INTRODUCTION

4. Laban also tried to deceive him with his wages (Gen 31:41).

5. When Jacob escaped from the house of Laban, Laban pursued him for seven days, and Jacob's life was in danger (Gen 31:23).

6. Another danger Jacob faced was his wrestling with the mysterious assailant (Gen 32:25–33).

7. Jacob faced annihilation when his brother Esau came with 400 men (Gen 32:7; 33:1).

8. Dinah, his only daughter, was raped by Hamor (Gen 34:2).

9. His beloved wife, Rachel, died while giving birth to her second son (Gen 35:16–19).

10. Joseph, his favorite son, was sold into slavery, and he thought that a wild animal had devoured him. Hence, for 22 years he suffered (Gen 37:33–35).

The last part of Jacob's life is intertwined with the Joseph story. The stories of Jacob are full of drama and suspense to attract the reader. There are many similarities and parallels within all these stories: Jacob escapes from the house of his father, paralleling his escape from the house of Laban. The angels of God appeared to him when he left Canaan and also when he returned. Joseph lived with Jacob for seventeen years before he was sold into slavery, and for seventeen years with him in Egypt. All of these details add to the artistic flavor of the story.

Each story in the Torah has a didactic purpose; the stories are not collections of ancient fairy tales. The stories describe the unbroken bond between God and his people, the connections between the patriarchs, and the promise of the land and the divine theodicy. The glue of the Jacob cycle is God's guiding hand. More so, the inclusion of the two cultic narrative chapters 28:10–32. and 32:23–33. into the composition adds more significance for the whole Jacob narrative. In this cultic narrative, God is revealed to Jacob, and his words "point far beyond the limits of the individual story and determine the interpretation of the entire Jacob narrative."[6] God is merciful, but he punishes his people. Hence, Jacob suffered exile because he deceived his brother. Nevertheless, God was with Jacob, protecting him and promising to bring him back and to give the land to his descendants. All the trials that Jacob endured prepared him to be a father of a nation. The description of Jacob entering the land of Canaan after his return for

6. Rad, *Genesis*, 316.

Introduction

Padan-Aram and his journeys to Shechem and Bethel are similar to Abraham's journeys and also similar to the conquering of the land by Joshua. In other words, the deeds of the fathers are signs to the sons.

We maintain that the Jacob story can be divided into six units: 1. the stories about Jacob and Esau (25:19–34; 27); 2. Jacob and Laban (chs. 29–31); 3. the return of Jacob to Canaan, and the reconciliation with Esau (chs. 32–33); 4. the Dinah story (ch. 34); 5. the revelation in holy places: Bethel (28:11–22), Mahanaim (32:2–3), Peniel (32:22–32), and the move from Shechem to Bethel (35:1–7); and 6. Jacob and the Joseph story (chs. 37–50). A large part of the stories is devoted to the struggles between Jacob and Esau, Jacob and Laban, and the struggle between Leah and Rachel. Genesis 12–25 describes the relationship between parents and children, while the Jacob stories describe the relationship between brothers. The stories foreshadow the future struggles of Judah with Edom and of Israel with Aram. These struggles reflect the relations during the time of Kings David and Solomon, when Israel overtook Edom and settled its relationship with Aram.

Several monographs have been written on the whole or part of the Jacob cycle. Among the most recent are: Yair Zakovitch, *Jacob: Unexpected Patriarch* (2012); Paul D. Vrolijk, *Jacob's Wealth: An Examination into the Nature and Role of Material Possessions in the Jacob Cycle (Gen 25:19—35:29)* (2011); Kevin Walton, *Thou Traveller Unknown: The Presence and Absence of God in the Jacob Narrative* (2003); C. Recker *Die Erzählungen vom Patriarchen Jakob-ein Beitrag zur mehrperspektivischen Bibelauslegung* (2000); and J. Taschner, *Verheissung und Erfüllung in der Jakoberzählung (Gen 25,19—33,17): Eine Analyse Ihres Spunnungsbogens* (2000). Each of these writers uses a different approach. Zakovitch analyzes the story through a literary prism. Vrolijk examines the nature and role of material possessions in the Jacob cycle. Walton focuses on the presence and absence of God. Recker outlines the different methods that were used in examining the Jacob narrative and stresses the need for multi-perspective interpretation. In addition, through the years a number of important commentaries have been written on the book of Genesis, among them: Skinner, *A Critical and Exegetical Commentary on Genesis*; Speiser, *Genesis*; Westermann, *Genesis 12–36: A Commentary*; and Sarna, *The JPS Torah Commentary: Genesis*.

In this book, our main goal is to rediscover Jacob—to have a better understanding of his personality, his achievements, and his failures. Hence, we will describe Jacob from different angles. In order to achieve this goal,

Introduction

we will use the synchronic method, analyzing the texts in the book of Genesis as they stand and comparing them to the other biblical texts and to the Apocrypha. This in turn will shed more light on the persona of Jacob. It will point to the differences between the stories in Genesis and the later traditions about Jacob. Additionally, I will review material found in the Talmud, the midrashim, and the Jewish medieval commentaries in order to have a better understanding of the Jacob cycle. The Talmud contains a vast amount of *aggadot* (stories). The midrash includes anthologies and compilations of homilies, including biblical exegesis and public sermons. The various sects and currents in Judaism left their mark on it, and almost everything that Jews thought during a period of more than 1,000 years can be found there. Though the interpretative methods of the medieval commentators vary, we still find that, in general, they compromise between the literal and the midrashic interpretation of the biblical text. In addition, they pursue philological-contextual interpretation with a reasoned and scientific perspective.

In chapter 1 we will examine the story of the birth of the twins Jacob and Esau, with an explanation of what stands behind this story. Does it come to explain the relationship between the two brothers? Or maybe the stories were created in order to explain the complex relationship between Israel and Edom in the later periods. In addition, we will compare our story to the birth of Perez and Zerah (Gen 38:27–30). Did the birth narrative of Esau and Jacob influence the story of Perez and Zerah's birth, and is this a variation of the same theme? In Genesis, Jacob is portrayed as a dishonest person who deceived his brother and blind father. Esau, on the other hand, is portrayed as a victim of deception. Does this portrayal of the brothers in the book of Genesis match their descriptions in the later prophetic books? Or did the later authors view and judge the brothers differently?

Trickery and deception are the main motifs that characterize the Jacob cycle. Hence, in chapter 2 we will look into the theme of trickery and deception. All the protagonists take part and play a role in the deception: Jacob, Rebecca, Laban, Leah, Rachel, Simeon and Levi, Hamor and his son Shechem, Jacob's sons, and Tamar (Judah's daughter-in-law). These heroes used tricks, but they themselves were tricked by others.[7] What was behind these deceptions, and what did our heroes try to gain? More so, how were their acts perceived and were they punished for their deceptions?

---

7. Farmer has looked into the folkloristic aspect of stories focusing on tricksters such as Jacob and Samson. See *The Trickster Genre in the Old Testament*.

Introduction

In contrast to Abraham and Isaac, Jacob had an extended family that included several wives and children. Therefore, in chapter 3 we will study the characters of Rachel, Leah, Bilhah, and Zilpah. We will point out their virtues, vices, triumphs, and failures. This analysis will give us a better understanding of who the matriarchs and the maid servants really were.

The book of Genesis has neither laws nor moral responsibilities indicated; only promises of nationhood and posterity were given to the patriarchs by God. Not surprisingly, some scholars claim there is no such a thing as a patriarchal period or patriarchal religion. Indeed, in his *Prolegomena to the History of Israel*, published in 1878, Julius Wellhausen wrote: "We attain [in Genesis] to no historical knowledge of the patriarchs but only of the time when the stories about them arose in the Israelite people; this later age is here consciously projected in its inner and its outward features into hoary antiquity and is reflected there like glorified mirage."[8] In chapter 4 we will examine some religious customs and practices that were already mentioned in the book of Genesis, such as building altars, offering sacrifices, setting up pillars, planting sacred trees, praying, and circumcising. We will compare these customs to later periods in the biblical narrative. This in turn will help us see if the religious customs of the patriarch Jacob were indeed authentic presentations of his faith, or rather presentations of religious beliefs from a later monarchial period. In addition, we will look at the different names for God in the Jacob cycle to see if Jacob was indeed a true monotheist.

In chapter 5 we will study the subject of angels. Stories about angels' appearances to humans are typical of patriarchal narratives and of literature from the period of the judges. Indeed, one of the characteristics of the Jacob cycle is the encounter with angels (Gen 28:12; 32:2). The angels appeared at important junctures in Jacob's life. So what do we know about angels, and what is their function in the Jacob cycle? On the eve of his return to the land of Canaan, Jacob was wrestling with an angel. The wrestling match started at night and ended at daybreak, when, at the end, the angel wrenched Jacob's hip. What stands behind this story? The same story is repeated in the book of Hosea; how different is this version from our story in Genesis, and what purpose does it serve?"

Continuing with the theme of encounters with the divine, in chapter 6 we will examine the subject of dreams. In the ancient world, people believed that dreams contained messages from God. This belief was also shared by the Hebrews. One of the main themes of the book of Genesis is

---

8. Wellhausen, *Prolegomena*, 318–19.

the dream phenomenon. God's first appearance to Jacob was in a dream that took place at Bethel (Gen 28). Later, at the house of Laban, the angel of God appeared to Jacob in a dream (31:10–13). A third dream is related to Laban, who, while in hot pursuit of Jacob, was visited by God in a dream at night (v. 24). Finally, Jacob on his way down to Egypt stopped at Beer Sheba to make sacrifices to God, and God appeared to him in visions of the night (46:1–4). In chapter 6, we analyze the dreams in the Jacob cycle and try to understand what stands behind the dreams and what they convey.

Chapter 7 examines the story of Dinah. According to Gen 34, Jacob's daughter Dinah was violated by Shechem, son of Hamor. Following this act, Dinah's brothers, Simeon and Levi, attacked the city of Shechem in retaliation. They plundered the city to avenge the honor of the family. The rape of Dinah is the first in the list of calamities that befell the patriarch following his arrival in Canaan. Why was this story included in the Jacob cycle, and what was the narrator's message? In addition, we will see how the Bible and later writers viewed the brothers' massacre of the inhabitants of the city of Shechem.

Chapters 37–50 from the book of Genesis are part of the so-called Joseph cycle. These chapters describe the story of Joseph from his youth until his death at the age of 110 years old. Intertwined with the Joseph story are Jacob's last years. In this part of the book of Genesis, the patriarch Jacob is no longer the main character. Instead he is shadowed by his son Joseph and plays only a secondary roll. In chapter 8, we examine the relationship between Jacob and his sons, focusing on Jacob's relationship with his favorite son, Joseph. In addition, we will scrutinize the relationships between Joseph and his brothers to help us see the dynamics that existed in Jacob's family.

In our last chapter, we study the Testament of Jacob. Before his death, Jacob summons his sons and tells them their future. The testament includes ten of Jacob's sayings, which are addressed to each son individually, except Simeon and Levi who are mentioned together. Although Genesis 49:1–28 is often called the Blessing of Jacob, examination of it shows otherwise; it contains curses in addition to praises, as well as geographical and historical details. We will analyze Jacob's proverbs to his sons and see what stands behind his words. The maxims are collections of independent sayings that refer to different events and different situations. Some contain information about past events, while others allude to hundreds of years in the future. We will try to ascertain those events and see if, indeed, they

INTRODUCTION

match our knowledge of the earlier period of the patriarch Jacob. On the other hand, we will see if some of Jacob's predictions about the future of his sons materialized.

We trust that this study will provide a provocative and useful insight into the life of the patriarch Jacob.

1

The Birth of the Twins

THE STORY OF THE birth of Jacob and Esau belongs to the earlier strata of the larger story of the Jacob cycle. Rebecca, Isaac's wife, gave birth to twins from which nations would come. The birth of the twins assured Isaac that the promise of the land and descendants that was given to him and his father, Abraham, would be fulfilled. From the beginning, we read about the brothers' struggle in the womb. This struggle for seniority will continue into adulthood.

So what was the intent of these stories? Were the stories created in order to describe the relationship between Jacob and Esau? This relationship is marked by deception, which is one of the traits that characterizes Jacob's behavior. Or may we say that the stories about Jacob and Esau were probably created in order to explain the complex relationship between Israel and Edom in later periods? Like the Jacob cycle, the Joseph cycle also contains a birth of twins. The twins, Perez and Zerah, are born as a result of Judah unknowingly sleeping with his daughter-in-law Tamar. In this story, Perez stole his brother Zerah's birthright before they emerged from their mother's womb. Evidently there are similarities between the stories. Therefore, the question becomes: did the story of the birth of Esau and Jacob influence the story of Perez's and Zerah's birth, and is this a variation of the same theme? More so, what was the purpose of this story?

In the birth narrative, Jacob is termed as a mild man who stays in camp. His brother, Esau, is a skillful hunter and man of the outdoors. Jacob is portrayed as a dishonest person, who deceives his brother and blind father. Esau, on the other hand, is the victim of a cruel deception and receives the sympathy of the narrator. Hence, did this portrayal of the brothers in the book of Genesis match their descriptions in the later prophetic books? Did the later authors view and judge the brothers differently?

Two Nations Are in Your Womb

Jacob was the younger twin of Isaac and Rebecca. His father was 60 years old at his birth, which took place after 20 years of childless marriage.[1] Rebecca's age, on the other hand, is omitted. We are told that she is a barren woman. Like Sarah, Rebecca is barren, as is Jacob's future wife, Rachel. In other words, all of the matriarchs were barren. This theme is also repeated with Samson's and Samuel's mothers.

Another motif that is common to all these stories is Yahweh's power to open the womb. By opening the womb of the barren woman, God shows his power and signals the arrival of the special child. Gunkel says: "A long infertility of the mother before the birth of the child is a favored legend motif. How passionately the child is desired! The child is a gift of God from the very beginning. It is no wonder that so much becomes of him later."[2] Divine favoritism is also found in the Ugaritic "Legend of Aqhat." The hero's father, Danel, is without an heir; therefore, the birth of his son Aqhat needed divine intervention. This was received through prayers to the deity. Danel also provides the gods with food and drinks for six days; on the seventh day, he is vouchsafed a response from Baal, who in turn petitions El, who conveys to Danel his blessing of the birth of an exemplary son. After the unusual birth, the child Aqhat is to become the hero of the tale that follows.

Like other heroes in the biblical narrative, this one also requires divine intervention. Isaac, although described as a passive man who was led by his father and manipulated by his wife, finally acts. He takes the initiative and beseeches God on behalf of his wife. Isaac prays to God to open his wife's womb. His prayers are answered, and his wife Rebecca conceives. In contrast to Abraham and Sarah who resorted to concubinage, Isaac and Rebecca put their trust in God. The word that describes Isaac praying (*'ātar*) is the same word that was used by Manoah before God removed the barrenness from his wife. How much time passed between Isaac's prayers and God answering his prayers we are not told. The fact that God responded to his prayers shows how powerful his prayers were.

---

1. Isaac was forty years old when he married Rebecca. According to the Talmud, if one is not married by twenty he is cursed by God (see *b. Sanh.* 76b).

2. Gunkel, *Genesis*, 288.

The Birth of the Twins

Isaac's prayers were answered, and Rebecca became pregnant not with one son but with two. However, Rebecca had a difficult pregnancy, and the children struggled in her womb; she suffered from "quickening"—constant movement of the fetuses. To describe the movement of the sons, the Bible uses the verb *wayyitrōṣăṣû*, which means "they crushed/thrust one another." This description is foreshadowing the future, which entails the future relationship between the nation of Israel and Edom, as represented by the two sons to be born. The pregnancy was so difficult that Rebecca says: "If so, why do I exist?" In other words, "there is no point to life." A similar thought is expressed later by Rebecca after the deception episode: "What good will life be to me?" (27:46).

Because of her difficult pregnancy, Rebecca went to inquire of the Lord. The Hebrew word for "inquire" is a technical term for inquiring by means of oracles. The Bible does not tell what kind of method she used. In the ancient world, people usually went to a temple or to a prophet. However, in the patriarchal period there was no cultic personnel, nor was there a specific shrine. Hence, it has been suggested that because the matriarch lived at Beer-lahai-roi, where earlier Hagar had received the divine announcement about the birth of her son, Rebecca possibly went to the same site.[3] No particular details are given about this consultation, because they probably were not important; instead the message itself is described.

The divine name Yahweh appears both in the inquiry as well as in the oracle. The mention of the name Yahweh is not coincidental; it came to remove any suspicion of Rebecca being engaged in a pagan cultic rite. We have to remember that she belonged to a family of idol worshippers. The oracle that Rebecca received from God included a prophetic message stating that she would have twins and that the older would serve the younger.

> Two nations are in your womb.
> Two separate peoples shall issue from your body;
> One people shall be mightier than the other,
> And the older shall serve the younger. (Gen 25:23)

This oracle was very significant because later it justified Rebecca's role in the deception of her husband. More importantly, it showed that Jacob was the true heir to the covenant with Abraham and Isaac. Jacob was chosen in the womb before anyone knew what would become of him. Jacob would surpass his older brother Esau. This forecasts the future of Jacob's

---

3. Sarna, *Understanding Genesis*, 179.

domination of Esau and Israel's subjugation of Edom. The oracle refers to the future relationship between the Israelites and the Edomites. Each of the boys would become a progenitor of a nation. In reality, this oracle started to be fulfilled during the lifetime of the brothers when Jacob gained the upper hand—first when Esau relinquished his birthright to Jacob in exchange for a meal (25:29–34), and second when Esau lost the patriarchal blessing (Gen 27). In the Hebrew Bible, we have many examples of a younger brother who replaces his older brother. Thus, we read of Isaac and Ishmael, Zerah and Pertz, Ephraim and Manasseh, David and his older brothers, as well as Solomon and Adonijah.

Historically speaking, the Edomites became a settled kingdom before Israel. Esau (Edom) was the older brother. The Israelites (the younger) subjugated the Edomites (the older) in the tenth century BCE, during the time of David: "and all the Edomites became David's servants" (2 Sam 8:14). Later, however, this would change, and it was mentioned in Isaac's blessing to Esau: "But when you grow restive, you shall break his yoke from your neck" (Gen 27:40). This reference is to the reign of King Jehoram in the mid-ninth century, when Edom successfully revolted and attained its independence (2 Kgs 8:20–22). Sixty years later, Amaziah defeated 10,000 Edomites and subdued them. He defeated Edom—capturing Sela in the battle—renamed it Joktheel, and annexed it to Judah (2 Kgs 14:7; 2 Chr 25:11–12). The Edomites regained their freedom during the reign of Ahaz (735–715 BCE), who was pressured by Rezin king of Aram (2 Kgs 16:6). As a result, Judah was forced to give Elath to the Edomites who settled there.

The medieval commentators had a different interpretation of the verse, according to which the older will either be served by the younger or will serve the younger. They arrive at this conclusion based on a grammatical issue in the verse. Radak (acronym for Rabbi David ben Joseph Kimḥi, ca. 1060–1235) said: "the word ʾet, which shows which is the object, is not mentioned. The matter is dubious. It wasn't made clear who would serve the other, the older the younger, or the younger older . . ." On the other hand, Rashi (acronym for Rabbi Solomon ben Isaac, 1040–1105) explained the ambiguity of the verse by saying that sometimes one brother will prevail and sometimes the other. It was suggested that the ambiguity of the verse is an indication of the future relationship of the nations of Israel and Edom. It also came to clarify Jacob's behavior in buying the birthright, as well as Rebecca's exploit that causes her husband Isaac to bless Jacob instead of Esau.[4]

---

4. Zakovitch, *Jacob*, 16–17.

The Birth of the Twins

The stories about Jacob and Esau were probably created in order to explain the complex relations between Israel and Edom in later periods. The fact that Jacob and Esau were kin is attested to in numerous biblical texts. In Deut 23:8, Moses commands: "Do not abhor the Edomite, for he is your brother." This verse distinguishes between the Edomites and other nations, such as the Ammonites and the Moabites, who are condemned in the previous verse. In the song of Deborah, which is considered to be one of the oldest pieces of Hebrew poetry, God is described as marching from the plains of Edom to save his people. Evidently, the biblical texts came to convey the idea of the existing linkage between Israel and Edom. A geographical list dating from the period of Amenhotep III contains the name "land of the Shasu Yahwi," and the same name is found in a copy of this list made during the reign of Ramesses II. It is believed that the name of the place was the same name of the deity who was worshiped there.[5] This shows that Yahweh was already an important god in Edom, which further points to the connections between Israel and Edom.

Originally, Jacob and Esau were heads of tribal clans. The biblical story that describes them as brothers came to illustrate the close connections between the two people. They spoke similar dialects and also shared a cultural tie, which is why the narrative in Genesis suggests that they were twins. The hostile relationship between Edom and Israel was attributed to an earlier period, back to the birth of the brothers. The way the brothers fought was later emulated by Israel and Edom.

There are scholars who reject the idea that the relations between Jacob and Esau reflect the future relationship between Israel and Edom. Gunkel, for example, says that we don't know anything about Esau and Jacob, and the traditions of Jacob and Esau as brothers are later traditional stories. He points to the fact that many features of the story are not applicable to Israel and Edom: "In the legend Jacob is not disposed to war; in history Israel conquered Edom in war; in the legend Esau is stupid, in history he is famous for his wisdom."[6] More so, Esau's name does not have much in common with the name Edom, which has a reputation for wisdom in the Hebrew Bible. Gunkel maintains that the conflict of the two brothers is a reflection of the ascent of herders over hunters in ancient Palestine.[7]

---

5. Giveon, *Les Bédouins Shosou*, 26–28. On the Midianite hypothesis, see de Vaux, *Early History of Israel*, 330–338.

6. Gunkel, *Legends of Genesis*, 24.

7. Ibid., 24–26.

Noth followed Gunkel's line of thinking and suggested that the stories about Jacob and Esau were told in the circles of herdsman who enjoyed telling them. The stories were originated among the East Jordanian Ephraimites in the land of Gilead. The stories represent a time when, in Gilead, the huntsman, who was the first and the older, was replaced by the younger herdsman. In this tradition, Esau represents an unknown ethnic group or "a type of huntsman in contrast to Jacob, who represents the herdsman."[8] According to Noth, the main object of the Jacob-Esau story is to exhibit that the herdsman receives preference over the huntsman. The herdsman thinks that he is entitled to receive preference, and he achieves it by the stupidity of the huntsman and by his own cleverness and craftiness.[9]

However, nowhere in the earlier stories of Jacob and Esau is Jacob described as a herdsman. More so, the blessing that he receives from his father better suits a farmer.[10] Hendel does not accept the idea that the stories about Jacob and Esau originally represented the relationship between Israel and Edom, and he maintains that no definitive view can be advanced.[11] According to him, at some point Jacob and Esau "were identified as eponymous ancestors of political groups, and . . . neither the narrative of the two brothers nor the history of the two nations can be discerned with any clarity through the other."[12] Later, he modified his position, suggesting that the Jacob and Esau story is representative of the conflict between civilization and nature. Hence, Genesis 25 and 27 exhibit contrasts between Jacob and Esau. Here, Jacob is identified with civilization, while Esau is wild and uncivilized.[13] Indeed, the relationship between Jacob and Esau is also an expression of cultural and ethnic self-definition, but this was not the intent of the story. The story comes to show how the weaker and the smaller brother succeeded to dominate his older brother.[14]

During the first century CE, Judea was under the rule of the Roman Empire. The Romans controlled large parts of Europe and the eastern part of the Mediterranean. They were known as ruthless and ruled with an iron fist. Any rebellion against them was crushed cruelly, mostly by crucifixion.

---

8. Noth, *History of Pentateuchal Traditions*, 96–97.
9. Ibid., 97.
10. Kugel, *How to Read the Bible*, 710 no. 6.
11. Hendel, *Epic of the Patriarch*, 115.
12. Ibid.
13. McCarter and Hendel, "Patriarchal Age," 27.
14. Kugel, *How to Read the Bible*, 710 no. 6.

The Birth of the Twins

Esau was seen by the ancient interpreters as a hunter who killed animals and men for no reason;[15] he was considered bloodthirsty. Thus, the rabbinic sources transposed the image of Esau onto Rome. Like Jacob struggling with his brother, Esau, so were the Jews during the time of the Romans. The Romans were violent and oppressed the Jews; therefore, the Jews hoped that one day the younger would succeed in overthrowing the Roman rule.

In the birth narrative, we read that Esau emerged first. He was red (*'admônî*). There is wordplay here with the word "Edom," Esau's territory. The other person the Bible mentions as red is King David (1 Sam 16:12; 17:14). Red was associated with being sinister and dangerous, which is found in Egyptian and Ugaritic texts.[16] Some scholars have suggested that prejudice against the redheaded person was widespread throughout the ancient Near East, as well as in Western Christianity. Judah Iscariot is portrayed in medieval art as a red-haired person.[17]

Esau was also a hairy man. The hairiness of Esau will later play a major roll when Jacob poses as Esau to deceive his father, Isaac. There is also wordplay here with the word *śēʿār* (hair)—or *śāʿir* (hairy)—and the land of Seir, the territory of Esau/Edom (Gen 32:4). Esau's hairiness has been compared to Enkidu in the *Gilgamesh* epic.[18] Hairiness was a mark of the vulgarity of a boorish person. The description of Esau's hairiness "like a hairy mantle all over," is very similar to that of Enkidu "shaggy with hair was his whole body."[19] Esau, like Enkidu, is a man of the open fields.

There is no satisfactory explanation for the name Esau. It might connect to the Arabic root *ġ-š-w* (to cover).[20] Thus, the name would mean "the mantled one." Another suggestion is to link Esau with Ousoos, who is mentioned in Phoenician mythology as the hunter who invented the cloak for the human body from animal skin, but this is unlikely. *Targum Jonathan*, Rashi, Rashbam (Acronym for Rabbi Samuel ben Meir 1080–1174), and Bekhor Shor (Joseph ben Isaac, twelfth century), all derive the name from the Hebrew word *ʿ-ś-y* (to make). Therefore, Rashi explains Esau's name: "for (at birth) he was formed."

---

15 See *Jashar* 27:1–13.
16. Sarna, *Understanding Genesis*, 180.
17. Vawter, *On Genesis*, 288.
18. Speiser, *Genesis*, 196.
19. *Gilgamesh*, Tablet 1, column ii, line 36.
20. Eitan, *Contribution to Biblical Lexicography*, 57.

Jacob followed his brother Esau holding onto his heel (ʿāqēb), so he was called Jacob (yaʿăqōb). There is wordplay here between the name Jacob and "heel." Evidently, Jacob tried to prevent the birth of his twin brother. In a second passage, after Esau discovered that Jacob stole his blessing, he asserts that Jacob is rightly named, "for he has supplanted me (wayyaʿqĕbēnî) these two times" (Gen 27:36). Likewise, the prophet Hosea says: "In the womb he tried to supplant his brother" (Hos 12:4). The prophet Jeremiah alludes to Jacob's act of deception: "Trust not even a brother! For every brother takes advantage" (9:3). There is wordplay in the verse on the name Jacob and heel, ʿāqôb yaʿqōb—no doubt this refers to Jacob's crafty dealing with his brother Esau. Here, Jeremiah gives Jacob a bad name. Interestingly, Esau was named according to his appearance, while Jacob was named according to his action. From the moment that he was born, Jacob is grabbing. In other words, from birth the brothers were struggling for the birthright. This was the way the midrash understood it: "What is the meaning of 'struggled'? That they would ascend and descend inside her . . . this one saying, 'I will come first,' and this one saying, 'I will come out first.'"[21]

The name Jacob is well known from the ancient world as a shortened form of יעקב אל yaʿqōb-ēl "may El protect (him)" or "El will protect (him)." Hence, the name was originally theophorous, including the element El, which is now missing. It is proposed that the original name of Jacob is mentioned in Deut 33:28: "Israel dwells in safety; by himself Jacob-el settles."[22] This name is typical to Amorite names from the second millennium. It is found in Upper Mesopotamia—four times in the Chagar Bazar inscription (1800 BCE)—and it appears once at Qattuna on the Khabur River (1700 BCE).[23] Similar names also appear in Egyptian texts from the second millennium: Yʿqbʿr and Yʿqbhr ("Har [the mountain god] shall protect"?). These names were borne by rulers of the Hyksos period.[24]

The name Jacob-El was also the name of a place from the Late Bronze Age. It is mentioned in a list of enemies conquered by Thutmosis III (1749–1425 BCE) and other kings of Egypt.[25] The names that are found in the documents refer not only to cities but also to some tribal groups. Though the exact location of Jacob-El cannot be determined, it appears that the

21. Margulies, *Midrash Haggadol,* ad loc. Gen 25:22.
22. Freedman, "Original Name of Jacob," 125–26.
23. Nougayrol, "Documents du Ḫabur," 207–8.
24. Yeivin, "Yʿqobʾel," 16–18.
25. Aḥituv, *Canaanite Toponyms,* 200; and Wilson, "List of Asiatic Countries," 242.

conquering of the place called "Jacob-El" by Tuthmosis has some connection to the biblical Jacob tradition. The Egyptian list suggests that there was an early hero called Jacob-El who gave his name to the town.[26]

In 1969, a scarab containing the hieroglyphic name *Yʿqb-HR* was found during an excavation at Shiqmona Israel in a Middle Bronze Age II tomb. The archeologist, Aharon Kempinsky, suggested that the second Hyksos ruler of the Fifteenth Egyptian Dynasty was named Jacob-Her and might be the direct descendant of the local Palestinian king of the same name. This Palestinian ruler might be no other than the biblical Jacob.[27] The proposal is speculative—nevertheless, it suggests that the story of Jacob emerged in the second millennium BCE.

As for the Hebrew Bible, although the name Jacob was changed to Israel, we still find the old name Jacob. In poetic forms and also in the prophetic narrative, the name Jacob refers to the people of Israel. The name Jacob is mentioned alongside the name Israel: "I will divide them in Jacob, scatter them in Israel" (Gen 49:7); "How fair are your tents, O Jacob; your dwellings, O Israel (Num 24:5); "They shall teach your laws to Jacob and your instruction to Israel (Deut 33:10); "Let loose a word against Jacob, and it fell upon Israel" (Isa 9:7).

Perez and Zerah

The story of the birth of the twins Esau and Jacob influenced Perez and Zerah's birth story (Gen 38:27–30). The stories are very similar and variations of the same theme.[28] Indeed, the opening statements about the birth of the twins both here and in the story of the birth of Esau and Jacob are almost identical. Rashi, however, noted the discrepancy in the spelling of the word *twins*. Rashi pointed out that the spelling of the word *twins* in the Perez and Zerah story includes the Hebrew letters *alef* and *yod*, but when Rebecca refers to Jacob and Esau, the word *twins* is written defectively, without *alef* and *yod*. This, he explained, was "since one (Esau) was wicked, but both of these were righteous."

The twins Perez and Zerah were born as a result of Judah unknowingly sleeping with his daughter-in-law, Tamar, who had disguised herself

26. McCarter and Hendel, "Patriarchal Age," 26.
27. Kempinski, "Jacob in History," 47.
28. Skinner, *Genesis*, 455.

as a prostitute. In this story, Perez stole his brother's birthright before they emerged from their mother's womb:

> When the time came for her to give birth, there were twins in her womb! While she was in labor, one of them put his hand, and the midwife tied a crimson thread on that hand, to signify: This one came out first. But just then he drew back his hand, and out came his brother; and she said, "What a breach you have made for yourself!" So he was named Perez. Afterward his brother came out, on whose hand was the crimson thread; he was named Zerah. (Gen 38:27–30)

The narrative relates how the twins were born. Like the story of the birth of Jacob and Esau, this story stresses the rivalry between the two brothers, each one wants his priority of birth. When Zerah put out his hand, the midwife tied a crimson thread to it to signify his priority at birth. However, he withdrew his hand and his brother emerged. Because of this, he was named Perez. The name Perez is a wordplay on *pereṣ* (breach). No explanation is given for the name Zerah. The verb *zāraḥ* in Hebrew means "to shine," which suggests an allusion to the crimson thread. It has also been suggested that Zerah is derived from the Aramaic *zeḥorita*, which is a *šānî* scarlet thread. This derivation suits Edom better, which is Esau's other name. Without the vowels, the spelling of Edom is the same as *ʾādōm* (red), which is crimson.[29] An Edomite chief named Zerah is mentioned in Genesis. He was descended from Esau and Ishmael—his father, Reuel, was born of the marriage of Esau to Basemath, the daughter of Ishmael. Zerah was the father of Jobab, an Edomite king (Gen 36:13, 17, 33; 1 Chr 1:37, 44). More so, Zerah was also the name of an Edomite clan (Gen 36:17; 1 Chr 1:37). It is possible that the story alludes to the rivalry between the family of Zerah and Perez in an earlier period.

The birth of the twins came to compensate for Judah's loss of his two sons. Perez, the younger son, belonged to the Judahite clan from which David later descended (Ruth 4:18–22; 1 Chr 2:5, 9–15). Ten generations elapsed between Perez and David, which points to completeness and a new chapter in history. Indeed, 10 generations passed between Adam and Noah, and also between Noah and Abraham. David, like Perez and Jacob, was elected by God as the younger brother over an older one. As we mentioned above, the struggle for the hegemony of the Perezite family among the Judahite clans is probably reflected in the birth narrative of Perez. In the genealogical lists of the tribe of Judah, Perez is always mentioned first (Ruth

---

29. Zakovitch, *Jacob*, 19.

The Birth of the Twins

4:12; 1 Chr 4:1). This is probably because King David's line came through Perez. Later, in the book of Numbers, the Perezite clan was split into the clan of Hezronites and the clan of Hamulites (26:20). Boaz was the ancestor of King David. At his marriage to Ruth, the elders said: "And may your house be like the house of Perez whom Tamar bore to Judah—through the offspring which the Lord will give you by this young women" (Ruth 4:12).

Different Brothers

No information is given about Jacob's childhood except that he emerged from the womb grasping the heel of his brother, Esau. Jacob is described as a mild man who stayed in camp (Gen 25:27). Meanwhile, his brother, Esau, was a skillful hunter and man of the outdoors. Isaac favored Esau because of his hunting and admired him for his skills. Not surprisingly, he asked him to hunt for him and prepare tasty game. In choosing Esau, he elected a son who was the opposite of himself. Esau represents forcefulness and action; he was a hunter and a man of the open field. Isaac was a quiet, peaceful tent-dweller. Perhaps Esau represents everything that Isaac wanted to be. Jacob, on the other hand, was the favorite of his mother. No reason is given for her choice. It may be because of Jacob's lifestyle and because he was easier to manipulate that his mother chose him, but more likely it was because of the oracle that she received. Rebecca liking Jacob, in addition to Isaac's preference for Esau, shows that they also were very different people. It is possible that with the passing of the years, they had grown apart.

Hunting is not mentioned much in the Hebrew Bible. The only hunters who are mentioned are Nimrod, "a mighty hunter" (Gen 10:9); Ishmael, "a bowman" (21:20); and Esau, who is described as going to the field with a quiver and a bow (27:2). Hence, it is possible that we have here a testimony of the tribes of Edom that for their livelihoods they were engaged in hunting. The Bible held hunting in low esteem and has a negative attitude toward hunting as a way of life. Much Near Eastern art portrays kings as engaged in hunting, but not so for Israelite or Judean kings. The animals that the Israelites used for sacrifice were restricted to domesticated animals.[30]

Jacob is the opposite of his brother, Esau. As noted earlier, the Bible describes him as a mild man (*tām*) who stayed in camp. The Hebrew word *tām* is interpreted as a person who is perfect and blameless (Job 1:1, 8; 8:20; Ps 37:37; Prov 29:10). Jacob does not carry arms; he dwelt in a tent

---

30. Sarna, *Understanding Genesis*, 181.

11

that refers, probably, to his involvement in small-scale animal husbandry. Indeed, in Gen 4:20 we read about Jabal: "he was the ancestor of those who dwell in tents and amidst herds." Later, in the house of Laban, Jacob's main occupation was to tend the flocks of his father-in-law.

The contrast in the lifestyles of the brothers was noted by the writer of the apocryphal Jubilees, who accentuated the difference between the brothers by adding derogatory characteristics to Esau:

> And Rebekah bore to Isaac two sons, Jacob and Esau, and Jacob was a smooth and upright man, while Esau was fierce, a man of the field, and hairy; and Jacob dwelt in tents. And the youths grew, and Jacob learned to write; but Esau did not learn, for he was a man of the field, and a hunter, and he learned war, and all his deeds were fierce. And Abraham loved Jacob, but Isaac loved Esau. (Jubilees, 19:13–15)

A similar idea also appears in the Targumim:

> And the two boys grew up, and Esau was a skilled hunter, a man who went out to the fields, but Jacob was a perfect man who frequented the school house. (*Tg. Onq.*, Gen 25:27)

> And Jacob was a man perfect in good work, dwelling in schoolhouses. (*Tg. Neof.*, Gen 25:27)

However, we should point out that in the beginning the sympathy of the biblical narrator was with Esau. After Esau realized that Jacob stole his blessing "he burst into wild and bitter sobbing." The sages, however, later identify Esau with Edom. Here they sympathize with Esau's tears and pain. They were uncomfortable with Jacob deceiving his brother: "Years later, our people will have to shed tears for what the descendants of Esau (the Edomites who helped to destroy the first temple, and the Romans the second temple) did to them, as retribution for the day Jacob made Esau cry."[31] However, in the Hebrew Bible and in the prophetic books, there is a transformation of Esau's character from a harmless person to a person who God hates:

> "I have loved you," says the Lord. But you [Israel] say, "How have you loved us?" "Is not Esau Jacob's brother?" says the Lord. "Yet I have loved Jacob, but I have hated Esau. I have laid waste his hill country and left his homeland to the jackals of the desert." (Mal 1:2–3)

---

31. *Gen. Rab.* 67:4

As Mason points out, God is free to elect and reject, "he does not reject arbitrarily."[32] God rejected Esau/Edom because they created a realm of wickedness. The Edomites worshipped false gods, rejected God, and hated the people of Israel—all these things that God hates (Deut 16:22; Ps 5:6; 11:5; 129:5). Esau's descendants would be excluded as a nation from the special relationship that Israel would have with God. In contrast to Esau, God has a special love for Israel. God chose Jacob and his descendants. He established a permanent relationship with Israel in which he would instruct them with righteousness and would be faithful to them.

In the prophetic books, Esau is also described as a wicked person. In these books we find descriptions of Esau that are not found earlier. Amos, in his prophecy on the nation of Edom, says, "Thus said the Lord: For three transgressions of Edom / For four, I will not revoke it / Because he pursued *his brother* with the sword / And repressed all pity / Because his anger raged unceasing / And his fury stormed unchecked" (1:11). Prophecies from the sixth century—such as in Obadiah; Jer 49; and Ps 137—denounced Edom's treachery and inhumanity toward Judah. Therefore, many scholars suggest that this oracle refers to those later developments.[33] Some see this setting as a description of Edom's actions against Israel following the destruction of the temple.[34] In the text, Edom is referred to as *his brother*. This can be understood as a reference to the ethnic ties between the nation of Israel and Edom. Jacob and Esau, who are the ancestors of these nations, are referred to as brothers. It is possible that we have here allusions to the earlier period of the Jacob-Esau story. In the blessing of Isaac, Esau is promised that he will live by the "sword," and here, in Amos, Edom (Esau) pursued his brother Judah (Jacob) by the sword. Rebekah, who feared for Jacob's life, thought that Esau's wrath would last for a short period (Gen 27:44–45); but here, in Amos, it says that it will exist for all time.

The strained relationship between the two brothers, which is mentioned in the Genesis narrative, is repeated later in the relationship between Edom and Israel. Although many generations had passed, the narrators still refer to Jacob and Esau. The Hebrew prophets frequently designate the people by their ancestors. The wickedness of Esau is also mentioned in the book of Obadiah: "For the outrage to *your brother* Jacob, disgrace

---

32. Mason, *Haggai, Zechariah and Malachi*, 141.
33. Andersen and Freedman, *Amos*, 265.
34. Wolf, *Joel and Amos*, 160.

shall engulf you, and you shall perish forever" (1:10). The prophet Obadiah mentions in his prophecy the two brothers, Esau and Jacob.

Esau's wickedness was determined before his birth, and it was Jacob who God elected as the next patriarch:

> When Rebecca had conceived children by one man our ancestor Isaac—even before they had been born or had done anything good or bad (so that God's purpose of election might continue, not by works but by his call)—she was told, "the elder shall serve the younger." As it is written, "I have loved Jacob, but I have hated Esau." (Rom 9:10–13)

In conclusion, the struggle between the twin brothers, Jacob and Esau, started in the womb. It is a struggle of hegemony. The younger brother tries and succeeds in achieving his goal. This description forecasts the future relationship between the nations of Israel and Edom. In essence, the story comes to show how the weaker and smaller brother succeeds to dominate his older brother. The motif of the younger who wants to achieve priority at birth is also found in the story of the birth of Zerah and Perez. Like the story of the birth of Jacob and Esau, this story stresses the rivalry between the two brothers, where each one wants his priority of birth. Zerah was the father of Jobab, an Edomite king, and was also the name of an Edomite clan. The Perezite family, on the other hand, belonged to the Judahite clans, and King David's line came through Perez. As in the story of Jacob and Esau, which foretells the rivalry between the Edomites and Israel, so too the story of Zerah and Perez does the same. It is also possible that the struggle for hegemony of the Perezite family among the Judahite clans is reflected in the birth narrative of Perez. Following the deception of his brother and his father, the sense is that the narrator's sympathy is with Esau when the narrator describes his wild and bitter sobbing. However, this sympathy will change in later generations and in the prophetic books, where Esau will be described as a wicked person. In these books, we find a description of Esau that is not found earlier. This is the result of hostility that existed between Israel and Edom.

So far, we mainly described the rivalry between the two brothers, Jacob and Esau. In the next chapter, we will examine the motif of deception. All the protagonists take part and play a role in the deception. Jacob, Rebecca, Laban, Leah, Rachel, Simeon, and Levi, as well as Hamor and his son Shechem, Jacob's sons, and Tamar—Judah's daughter-in-law—all deceive one another. Since everyone takes part in deception, the questions become: How did the Bible view these acts? And, were the deceivers punished for their doings?

2

Deception

EXAMINATION OF TEXTS FROM the ancient Near East reveals that deception appears to be a prominent motif. Even the gods engage in deception and trickery. In Mesopotamian literature, Ea, the god of great wisdom and cunning, appears also to be a trickster. In the myth of *Adapa*, the god Ea fears that Anu is apt to offer Adapa the food and drink of eternal life. To prevent Adapa from accepting it, he tricks him into believing that the food and drink are deadly. As advised, Adapa does not accept the food and drink—therefore, humans are mortals. Similarly, in Egyptian literature, four deities are mentioned as engaging in deception: Re, Isis, Horace, and Seth. In one papyrus, Isis's talent for deception is mentioned:

> Now, Isis was a wise woman. Her heart was more devious than millions among men; she was more selective than millions among the gods; she was more exacting than millions among the blessed dead.[1]

The motif of the deception is also found in Greek literature, where humans and gods deceive each other. Athena dresses herself up as an old man. Penelope lies about Laertes's magically shrinking shroud. Odysseus is the king of lies. As for the gods, they do it themselves all the time.

In the Jacob cycle, trickery and deception is one of the main motifs. All the protagonists take part and play a role in the deception: Jacob, Rebecca, Laban, Leah, Rachel, Simeon and Levi, Hamor and his son Shechem, Jacob's sons, and Tamar—Judah's daughter-in-law. What was behind those deceptions and what did our heroes try to gain? How were their acts perceived? Furthermore, were they punished for their deception?

---

1. Ritner, "Legend of Isis," 33–34.

Jacob

The first two episodes portray Jacob in a negative light. In the first story, he takes advantage of his hungry brother, Esau. Jacob is cooking a stew at home. Stew was an important part of the daily diet, mainly because of its nutritious benefit. The stew was made of a kind of lentil or bean, which was softened during cooking. This yellowish-red or dark-brown plant was cultivated in the ancient Near East. When Jacob served it to Esau, he added something that gave it a red color.[2]

Meanwhile, his brother, Esau, went to hunt but returned empty-handed, so he was famished. Since he was hungry and famished, he asked his brother Jacob to give him some of the red stew to eat. To describe his request to eat, the Bible uses the word "gulp down." The word is a *hapax legomenon*, and Skinner says that this is "a coarse expression suggesting bestial voracity."[3] Speiser refers to Esau as "an uncouth glutton."[4] In Rabbinic Hebrew, the word was used for the feedings of animals.[5] From the start, the narrator portrays Esau in a negative light. Responding to his brother's request for food, Jacob answers without hesitation. Jacob wants his brother's birthright, so he asks him to sell it to him. Jacob knows exactly what he wants, and he pursues it with determination and resolve. Did Jacob know about the oracle that his mother received? Or did his mother tell him about it? At this stage, we don't know.

What was behind Jacob's request for the purchase of the birthright? The firstborn was held in great esteem in Israel. He was considered the first fruits of his father's strength (Gen 49:3), and was dedicated to God (Exod 22:28). More importantly, when the inheritance was divided, the firstborn received a double share or twice as much as his other brothers (Deut 21:17). Was it common to sell the birthright? It appears that there are some texts from Nuzi from the fifteenth century BCE with parallels to the exchange between Esau and Jacob. One text mentions a person by the name of Tupkitilla who transfers his inheritance rights for a grove to his brother Kurpazah for three sheep: "On the day they divided the grove (that lies) on the road of the town of Lumti . . . Tupkitilla shall give it to Kurpazah

---

2. Elisha served a similar stew to the disciples of the prophets. After it was boiled in the pot, they were almost poisoned (2 Kgs 4:38–41).
3. Skinner, *Genesis*, 361.
4. Speiser, *Genesis*, 195.
5. *m. Šabb.* 24:3; *b. Šabb.* 155b; *b. Ḥul.* 55b, 58b.

as his inheritance share. And Kurpazah has taken three sheep to Tupkitilla in exchange for his inheritance share."[6] It is not clear, however, if Tupkitilla is the elder brother. Was the grove the entire inheritance or just a portion? There is no mention of hunger by Tupkitilla or any motivation for selling the grove.[7] Nevertheless, the text from Nuzi illustrates that a brother could sell inherited property. Esau's rank is not affected by this transaction, as chapter 27 shows quite clearly.[8]

The firstborn son receives a double share of his father's inheritance; therefore, it is not clear why Esau sold his birthright for almost nothing. The text further says that he despised it (Gen 25:34). In other places, the Bible calls Esau a wicked man. This idea is repeated in the book of Hebrews: "... that no one be immoral and irreligious like Esau, who sold his birthright for a single meal" (Heb 12:16). Not only did he despise his birthright, but he did not see any harm in marrying a Hittite woman, while Jacob and Rebecca thought that endogamy was important in preserving family ties.

Esau sold his birthright because, at that time, Isaac was a poor man, and Esau did not think much of the birthright. Still, if Isaac was poor, why did Jacob want the birthright? It is possible that the rights of the firstborn and the blessings were tied together. Therefore, Jacob went to great lengths to get it. Interestingly, in the Hebrew language, there is a play on the words "firstborn" (*běkōrâ*) and "blessing"(*běrākâ*). What Esau lost here paved the way to a greater loss—the loss of a blessing.

What is surprising is Jacob's behavior. He took advantage of his brother, Esau, and without any shame took from him his birthright for almost nothing. Abravanel (Isaac ben Judah 1437–1508) pointed out that Jacob's behavior was immoral. If Jacob was blameless and upright, he questioned, how could he tell his older brother to sell the birthright for lentil porridge? It is not befitting of a man who fears God and who turns from evil to fix his gaze upon what is not his. It is also curious that he offers a shameful price for the birthright. If Jacob were really righteous and Esau were really foolish, might the righteous Jacob abstain from tricking his foolish brother?

In the second episode, Jacob took advantage of his elderly father, Isaac, who was blind, and he stole the blessing from his brother, Esau. Jacob masqueraded as Esau and misled his father into believing that he was blessing

---

6. Gordon, "Biblical Customs," 5.

7. Van Seters, *Abraham in History,* 92–93; Thompson, *Historicity of the Patriarchal Narratives,* 280–85; and Selman, "Comparative Customs," 97, 116, 123, 135–36.

8. Tsevat, "בְּכוֹר," 126

his older son, Esau. It was immoral to deceive a blind man and a parent (Lev 19:14; Exod 21:17). More so, Deut 27:18 invokes a curse on those who mislead the blind. Hence, Jacob brought upon himself a curse.

In this episode, Rebecca is the force behind Jacob; she dresses him up and pulls the strings that moved him. She does not tell him what to do, but orders him. Jacob recognized the risk that was involved in the plot. The Bible describes his action by three verbs: "He went, he took, he brought." If the plan failed, and his father, Isaac, discovered his identity, he would be the subject of his father's curse. Jacob agrees to his mother's plan only after his mother assures him that the curse will fall on her and not him. Rebecca is the first person who suggests being the recipient of a curse.[9] Jacob knows that a failure to act now will mean forfeiture of the blessing. In this episode, Jacob is cool and calculating; he advances his ambitions at the expense of his brother, Esau. In the end, Jacob received the blessing, but his "victory" is bittersweet because he had to run away from his brother Esau's rage.

The Rabbis tried to justify Jacob's action by attributing the blame to Rebecca. More so, they felt that Isaac and Abraham fathered unworthy sons.[10] They believed that Esau could not be equal to Jacob, who was regarded as a model of virtue and righteousness.[11] More so, they even said that God was helping with the deception:

> When Esau was hunting and tying [his catch], the angel was untying and setting it free. Again the angel would set it free. And why? In order to prolong the hours until Jacob will go and do [what he needed] and goes in to his father and his father will eat and Jacob will take the blessing.[12]

Still, this does not change the reality of the biblical narrative, where Jacob appears as a conniving liar. Indeed, deception is one of Jacob's traits in his feuds with family members as well as with his foes, due to his inferior position (Gen 25:29–34; 27:20; 30:31–43; 32:14–22). Not surprisingly, the sympathy of the narrator is with Esau, and the biblical text describes him crying bitterly. Even in the rabbinic literature, Jacob is criticized. Thus, Esau's "exceedingly great and bitter cry" (Gen 27:34) had been punished in the days of Mordecai who also wailed "with great and bitter cry" (Esth 4:1).[13]

---

9. Allen, "On Me Be the Curse," 159–72.
10. b. Pesaḥ. 56a; Gen. Rab. 68:11.
11. b. Mak. 24a.
12. Tanḥ. (Buber), Toledot 10.
13. Gen. Rab. 67:4.

Deception

In the deception scene, Jacob and Isaac are the only two actors. There is great tension displayed. The reader waits to see if Jacob will succeed in his act of deception. Isaac speaks eight times, while Jacob merely four. Only after Isaac says, "The voice is Jacob's but the hands are Esau's," do we read that Jacob speaks, uttering a single Hebrew word: *hinnēnî*, "I am" (Gen 27:4). Isaac uses his all senses: hearing, touching, tasting, and smelling. It was the skin disguise that saved Jacob; he smelled and felt like Esau to Isaac. The only hurdle was his voice; he could not imitate his brother. Therefore, his father asks him for the third time, "Are you really my son Esau?"

Soon after Jacob leaves, having received the blessing, his brother Esau then arrives. The narrative reaches another climax. The text is full of emotion. When Esau says: "I am your son, Esau, your first-born!" (v. 32), Isaac goes into a state of shock: "Isaac was seized with very violent trembling" (v. 33). He could not imagine that he had been deceived. But more importantly, he could not change the blessing, as it was irrevocable. Because of this, Esau did not ask his father to change the blessing, but also to bless him. Isaac, without hesitation, identifies the deceiver: "Your brother came with deceit and took your blessing" (v. 35). It is noteworthy what *Targum Pseudo-Jonathan* and Onqelos translate here: "Your brother came in with *wisdom*." This is because they thought that Esau was unworthy of the blessing of his father. However, as mentioned above, the sympathy of the narrator is with Esau. In his bitter outburst, Esau says that Jacob cheated him twice. There is the play on the name Jacob (*yaʿăqōb*), as derived from *ʿāqēb* (heel). This is the second time that there is wordplay on the name Jacob. As a description of Jacob's behavior, the root *ʿ-q-b* appears only here and in Jer 9:3 and Hos 12:4. Based on the Ugaritic cognate *ʿqb* (to deceive, impede) it has been suggested that the verb means to deceive. Evidently, at this stage, Esau finally understands the meaning of Jacob's name. Using wordplay again, Esau complains that Jacob took his "birthright" (*běkōrâ*) and "blessing" (*běrākâ*). Still, the question has to be raised here: How can Esau complain that Jacob deceived him after he himself sold his birthright to Jacob and even swore to him?

Questions need to be raised here about Isaac's conduct as well. Did Isaac not see that Esau was unworthy of his blessing and that Jacob was the worthier man? Examination of the following chapter shows that Isaac was aware of his surroundings. He saved the real blessing for Jacob, the blessing of the Abrahamic covenant. The first blessing that he gave to Jacob, while thinking he was Esau, has three parts: 1) assurance of fertility of the soil, which is described as an abundance of grain and wine; 2) political supremacy that people will serve and bow to him; and 3) God's protection, which includes cursing and blessing. Missing in this blessing are the promise of progeny and the promise of the land.

The second blessing was given to Esau. The structure of the blessing is similar to that of Jacob's. In the blessing, Isaac speaks of the fertility of the earth and the relations between brothers and nations. Not mentioned in the blessing is God nor the abundance of new grain and wine, which was already mentioned in Jacob's blessing. Since there is no abundance of grain and wine, it is believed that this is why Isaac says, "by your sword you shall live." Nevertheless, Esau's strength is restricted since "you shall serve your brother." Hence, the blessing here is linked to the oracle Rebecca received: "the older shall serve the younger" (Gen 25:23). Not to end the blessing on a bad note, Isaac says, "But when you grow restive, you shall break his yoke from your neck." It is believed that those words were added later. It probably refers to a later period when Edom broke Israel's yoke during the reign of King Joram (2 Kgs 8:20) or King Ahaz (2 Kgs 16:6).

Isaac's final blessing was given to Jacob. On the eve of Jacob's departure to Paddan-aram, Isaac blessed Jacob as the heir to the Abrahamic covenant. It appears that all along his desire was to bless Jacob and to give him the most valuable of all the blessings. Hence, Isaac saved the promise of progeny and the promise of the land for Jacob. The blessing includes nationhood and national territory and many descendants. In other words, the promises that were given before to Abraham (Gen 12:2–3, 7; 13:15, 17; 15:7–8, 18; 17:1, 6, 8, 16, 20; 22:17; 24:7) and Isaac (26:3–4, 24) are repeated here as those that were given to Jacob.

Jacob was punished severely for his acts of deception. Jacob was elected by God as it was revealed to Rebecca in the divine oracle that she received during her difficult pregnancy (Gen 25:23). Nevertheless, Jacob was impatient by trying to "speed" his predestined right to be Isaac's heir. For his impatience, Jacob paid heavily. Hence, when he appeared before Pharaoh and reported the years of his life, he said, "few and hard" (Gen 47:9). This description is in contrast to Abraham's life where the Scripture says that he died at "a good ripe age, old and contented" (Gen 25:8), or Isaac "at a ripe old age" (Gen 35:29). The description of Jacob's life as "few and hard" is an accurate description. At a young age he had to flee from the rage of his brother and to stay in exile for 20 years. In Laban's house, his father-in-law took advantage of him and substituted Leah for Rachel; more so, he changed his wages time after time. On his way home, Jacob encountered a mysterious assailant, which left him with a strained hip. He was fearful of the upcoming meeting with his brother Esau. His daughter Dinah was raped (Gen 34); his beloved wife Rachel died while giving birth (Gen 35:16–20). Joseph, the son of his beloved wife, was sold into slavery by his brothers. The brothers used an article of his clothing to deceive their father, just as Jacob had used Esau's clothes to mislead Isaac. It is clear that Jacob was condemned for his immoral behavior, and unequivocal condemnation is also found in the prophetic books. Hosea says that the Lord once "punished Jacob for his conduct, requited him for his deed" (Hos 12:3). And Jeremiah warns: "Beware, every man for his friend! / Trust not even a brother! / For every brother takes advantage / Every friend is base in his dealing" (Jer 9:3).

Laban

Jacob's uncle, Laban, was a suitable match for the liar Jacob. In the midrash he is described as "the master of deceivers."[14] According to the midrash, when he kissed Jacob he did it to look for gems hidden on his body or in his mouth.[15] From the start, he took advantage of Jacob and stopped Jacob's freeloading at the end of the month. He recognized Jacob's weakness, which was Jacob's love for his daughter Rachel. He used trickery and deceit, which forced Jacob to labor for Rachel. The trickery practiced by Laban was the retributive counterpart to Jacob's previous acts of deception. As Isaac was blind and could not see, so was Jacob who could not see at night when Laban substituted Leah for Rachel. What we have here is measure for measure; for his deception, Jacob was equally deceived and punished. The sense here is that we have poetic justice.

Jacob has entered Laban's service as a shepherd. To Laban's question regarding wages, Jacob answers that he will serve Laban for seven years for his daughter Rachel. Jacob is not interested in monetary wages. He wants Rachel and tells Laban: "For Rachel thy younger daughter" (Gen 29:18). In his commentary on this verse, Rashi asks: "Why all these signs ['your daughter,' 'the young one']? For he recognized him [Laban] that he is a deceiver. [Therefore Jacob] said to him, 'I shall serve you for Rachel.' But lest you say another Rachel from the street, the text states 'your daughter.' And lest you say, 'I shall change Leah's name, and call her name Rachel,' the text

14. *Gen. Rab.* 75:5.
15. *Gen. Rab.* 70:13.

states, 'the younger.' And nevertheless it was to no avail, for [Laban] deceived him." We should point out that Laban, in response to Jacob's request for Rachel, says, "Better that I give her to you than that I should give her to an outsider" (v. 19). In other words, he does not mention Rachel by name, although he implies it.

Only in the morning does Jacob discover that he was cheated, "and behold she was Leah" (v. 25). Seven years of hard work for Rachel, and now he finds that it was Leah who lay next to him in bed. The trickery succeeded because of a prevailing social custom: The bride was veiled and was brought in darkness. Possibly, heavy drinking was a part of the celebration. Indeed, according to Josephus, Jacob was "deluded by wine and the dark."[16] An interesting interpretation of our verse is found in the Talmud: "But at night it was not Leah. For Jacob had given signs to Rachel, and when Rachel saw that they were bringing Leah in to him she said, "Now my sister will be put to shame." So she arose and gave to her [Leah] those signs."[17]

In the morning, Jacob confronted Laban and asked him, "What is this you have done to me? (v. 25). Jacob is accusing Laban of deception. He uses the same Hebrew stem *r-m-y* that his father Isaac had used to describe Jacob's own act of deception. There is wordplay here with the name "Laban the Aramean." By switching the letters of *ʾărammî* (Aramean), Jacob effectually calls Laban a *rammai* (liar). But more interesting is Laban's reaction to Jacob's accusations: "It is not the practice in our place to marry off the younger before the older" (v. 26). Laban tries to justify his action by shifting the blame to the community. By mentioning the fact that it is not the practice in their place to give the younger before the elder, Laban subtly alludes to Jacob's own act. Jacob, the younger, put himself before his older brother. Jacob does not react and maintains his silence. He tolerates Laban for not informing him about the local custom. The question remains that if it was the local custom, why then did Laban not tell this to Jacob and save him from this agony? Why didn't he marry his daughter Leah to another man? Was Leah so unattractive? Were her weak eyes so unappealing that no one wanted to marry her? It appears that Laban planned all along to marry his two daughters to Jacob, so he set traps for Jacob.

In spite of Jacob's accusations, Laban did not lose any time and came up with a new plan. He promised Jacob that as soon as the seven days of Leah's wedding feast were over he could marry Rachel. This seemingly

---

16. Josephus, *Ant.* 1.19.6.
17. *b. Meg.* 13b.

generous offer included a harsh demand that Jacob had to work for Rachel for another seven years. Evidently, Jacob did not have any other choice and agreed to it. Laban controlled the situation from the start. In the end, Jacob married Rachel as well. He was married to two sisters, which was forbidden by later law (Lev 18:18)—this points to the antiquity of the narrative. Marrying the two sisters was a punishment for deceiving his brother and father. Laban's trickery was not only motivated by his desire to marry off his two daughters, but it was also motivated by greed. He wanted to exploit Jacob as much as possible.

Laban's greediness and exploitation surfaced again following the birth of Joseph. Jacob expressed his desire to return home after fulfilling his obligations to Laban, but Laban ignored Jacob's request. He admitted that he had grown rich and that he had been blessed by Yahweh because of Jacob. We have here the fulfillment of God's words to Abraham: "And all the families of the earth shall bless themselves by you" (Gen 12:3). In contrast to previous times when Laban had dictated the conditions, here Jacob made the demands. Although at their first meeting Laban had used similar language, saying, "Tell me, what shall your wages be?" (29:15) and "Name the wages due from me, and I will pay you" (30: 28), this time Jacob was prepared and set a trap for Laban. The old cunning Jacob surfaced again—he used trickery to increase his flock. According to his agreement with Laban, the multicolored animals, which were the irregular ones, would be his payment. The pure white sheep and the dark goats were Laban's. Multicolored sheep and goats were very rare. Sheep were mostly white, and goats were all black or dark brown. More so, to increase his chances, Laban removed all the multicolored animals. So how did Jacob get the multicolored animals? According to one explanation, he manipulated the pigmentation of the flocks through visual stimulus. Jacob took various trees from which he peeled the dark bark, and underneath was white. He took the rods and placed them in watering troughs where the goats came to drink. The goats saw their reflections in the water, which were speckled because of the reflections of the sticks. When the monochrome goats came to drink, they mated and the results were streaked, speckled, and spotted kids. This method was done by popular belief in magic without the intervention of God.

The sages, on the other hand, believed that the rods were irrelevant, or were instruments of divine intervention. Thus, we read in the midrash:

> You might ask how it was that Jacob could do this, setting the peeled rods at the troughs so that they [the flocks] would breed

in front of the rods, since this would appear to be stealing. The answer is that this was not, Heaven forbid, anything like stealing, for the angel had already spoken to him [as Jacob later says, Gen 31:11–12]. What Jacob did, he did on the angel's instructions.[18]

Similarly, we read in *Genesis Rabbah*:

> R. Ḥunia said: the ministering angels would take [animals] from Laban's flocks and put them into Jacob's flocks.[19]

A similar interpretation is also found on the eve of Jacob's escape from Laban's house. While consulting with his wives Rachel and Leah, he attributes the increase of the flock not to magic but to divine intervention. His success was a result of a revelation he received in a dream where an angel of God appeared to him. Nevertheless, there is also a scientific explanation to Jacob's manipulation of the flock. The vigorous animals were hybrids; their coloring came from recessive genes that emerged when they bred together. As a result of it, Jacob obtains healthy, multicolored sheep and goats, while Laban had weak, black or white animals.[20]

Jacob spent twenty years in the service of Laban. In spite of Laban's trickery, Jacob was blessed. He ended up with a large family. In those years, most of Jacob's sons were born. The information about the tribes reflects an early history of the tribes and their formation. Most of his adult years were spent in the house of Laban. In those years, he encountered people who would shape his life and character. Constant pain and a hard life were Jacob's companion while he was in the house of Laban. He served Laban faithfully, but his father-in-law deceived him. At first it appears as though he did not mind. But in the exchange between the two on the eve of his journey back to Canaan, Jacob spells out all of his frustrations with his father-in-law:

> These twenty years I have spent in your service, your ewes and she-goats never miscarried, nor did I feast on rams from your flock. That which was torn by the beast I never brought to you; I myself made good the loss; you exacted it of me, whether snatched by day or snatched by night. Often, scorching heat ravaged me by day and frost by night; and sleep fled away from my eyes. Of the twenty years that I spent in your household, I served you fourteen

18. *Midrash Leqaḥ Tov*, ad loc. Gen 30:39.
19. *Gen. Rab.* 73:10.
20. Sarna, *Understanding Genesis*, 212.

> years for your two daughters, and six years for your flocks; and you changed my wages time and again. Had not the God of my father, the God of Abraham and the Fear of Isaac, been with me, you would have sent me away empty handed. But God took notice of my plight and the toil of my hands, and He gave judgment last night. (Gen 31:38–42)

For twenty years Jacob served Laban faithfully. Here, for the first time, he stands up to Laban and expresses his frustration and anger. For twenty years Laban was blessed because of Jacob, as he himself admitted (Gen 30:27). According to the ancient Near Eastern law, a shepherd was liable only for lost or stolen sheep. The book of Exodus states: "If it was torn by beasts, he shall bring it as evidence; he need not replace what has been torn by beast" (Exod 22:12). Nevertheless, Jacob paid for the losses that Laban suffered, so he did beyond what the law required. He repeats his complaint that Laban changed his wages ten times. This accusation appeared first in his conversation with his wives Rachel and Leah, when he accused their father of cheating him. Not surprisingly, they agreed with him and complained about their father too. They felt like strangers in their own home. They agreed with Jacob that their father had cheated him of his dues and so cheated them too.[21] A father was supposed to give part of the *mōhar* to his daughter, but Laban did not give Leah or Rachel a dowry or presents.

Jacob's main complaints are the length of his work for Laban and the recurring changes of his wages. According to the law in Deuteronomy, "When you set him free, do not let him go empty-handed: Furnish him out of the flock, threshing floor, and vat, with which the Lord God has blessed you" (Deut 15:13–14). In his outburst against Laban, Jacob uses the same words: "You would have sent me away empty-handed" (Gen 31:42). It is only because of God's intervention that Jacob escapes Laban's deceitfulness. Although Jacob paid for his wives and his possessions, Laban felt that they still belonged to him: "The daughters are my daughters, the sons are my sons, the flocks are my flocks, and all that you see belongs to me" (31:43). At the end of the story, when Laban and Jacob conclude a pact of

---

21 According to Rachel and Leah, their father did not provide inheritance for them, but women did not inherit property (Num 27:7–11). It was customary to give dowry at the time of marriage. The bridegroom gave presents to the bride's father which later was passed to the bride as dowry. But Jacob's dowry was his fourteen years of service. So it appears that they refer to the fact that their father cheated Jacob of his due and thus cheated them too.

non-aggression, only then does Laban recognize Jacob as constituting an independent social entity of equal rights.

Rachel

Like father, like daughter. For the fraud that her father Laban used on her wedding night by deceiving her and Jacob, it is now Rachel's turn to pay her father back. Rachel stole her father's idols (*těrāpîm*) without Jacob's knowledge. She placed them in the camel cushion and sat on them. Laban blamed Jacob for the theft of his gods. He started his search for the stolen idols in his son-in-law's tent, moving to Leah's and secondary wives'. He ends his search at Rachel's tent. In this way, the narrator increases the tension and the suspense. Laban searches the tent but cannot find the idols. To describe his search, the narrator uses the Hebrew word *māšaš*. Ironically this is the same word that was used to describe Isaac's attempt to identify his son by feeling him (27:22).[22]

Rachel fools her father. She tells him that she cannot rise before him and greet him because of the pain from a menstrual cycle. According to the biblical law, a woman was considered unclean at the time of her menstrual period (Lev 15:19). More so, a person who came into contact with her during that period was considered unclean (ibid.). However, these regulations have no relevance for Laban. Sitting on the idols shows us what Rachel was thinking of the idols—they were futile and unclean. In the ancient world, there was a belief that women having their menstrual period were possessed by evil spirits; thus, people avoided approaching them.

Scholars have labored to explain why Rachel stole her father's teraphim. Some cite legal documents from Nuzi: possession of the teraphim would guarantee Rachel or her husband the right to inherit her father's estate or to function as the head of the family. Draffkorn notes that the household gods are the guardians who symbolize the family's holdings. Therefore, the possessor of the teraphim is the legitimate owner of the property.[23] Greenberg rejects these assumptions, noting that nowhere in the story is there any suggestion that Rachel or Jacob had any claim on Laban's estate that they might assert through possession of the teraphim. All

---

22. Fokkelman, *Narrative Art in Genesis*, 170.
23. See Draffkorn, "Ilani/Elohim," 219.

Jacob wanted to do was to get away with utmost haste and to put as much distance as possible between himself and Laban.[24]

One of the functions of these household gods seems to have been protecting the members of the family when they were traveling. Moshe Greenberg cites evidence of this from Josephus, who writes about a Parthian widow who secretly brought to the home of her second husband, a Jewish general in Babylonia, "the images of those gods which were their country gods, common to her husband and to herself: now it was the custom of that country for all to have the idols they worship in their own houses, and to carry them along with them when they go into a foreign land."[25] Rachel, fleeing her father's house, could not take the household gods with her openly, so she stole them so that they would protect her on her journey.

The Greco-Roman world also had its household gods, or *Penates*. Aeneas, fleeing burning Troy, takes the civic Penates with him. An Etruscan vase of the fifth century BCE depicts Aeneas's wife carrying a pillow-shaped object with straps, which evidently contained the sacred vessels of Troy. According to Plutarch (Camillus 20:6), Aeneas stole the "Samothracian images" and guarded them closely until he settled in Italy. The common element in the stories of Rachel and Aeneas is that both are people who, when embarking on a voyage to a new country, take the household gods to protect them. Recall that the Danites, on route to their new territory in the north, steal the teraphim from Micah's house (Judg 18:14–20).

Another possibility is that teraphim were used to obtain knowledge of the future and were taken on important journeys to indicate the routes to be taken. According to *Midrash Tanḥuma* and *Targum Yerušalmi*, Rachel stole the teraphim to prevent her father from learning what road they were traveling and so that she herself could inquire as to the path ahead.[26] That is, she believed taking the teraphim would confuse Laban and help Jacob get away.

There is an interesting parallel between the theft of the idols by Rachel and the story of Michal's deception of her father, Saul. King Saul tried to kill his arch enemy David; thus, he sends messengers to his daughter's house to seize David. Michal, on the other hand, tries to save her husband, David. To achieve her goal she used trickery. According to the biblical account, Michal took the household idols (*tĕrāpîm*) and laid them in the bed with

---

24. See Greenberg, "Another Look," 245.
25. Josephus, *Ant.* 18.9.5.
26. Gevaryahu, "In Clarification of the Nature of the Terafim," 84.

goat's hair to make it look as if David were still in bed. The teraphim were probably the size of a human head. The reason for the presence of teraphim in David's house is not clear, since they are denounced vehemently in the Hebrew Bible.

When Saul sent his messengers to take David, Michal lied and said that he was sick. Michal did not allow the messengers to enter the house. She was stalling, giving David time to escape. The messengers believed that David was sick and did not enter the room to check. Saul, unlike his messengers, was not convinced; clearly he did not trust his own daughter, since he was very suspicious. Therefore, he sent the messengers again, but this time they were to enter the house. Their mission was to examine David to ascertain his illness. If, indeed, he was very sick, they were instructed to bring him in a bed so that Saul could slay him. On the second trip to David's house, the messengers discovered that they had been totally fooled. Instead of David, they found the teraphim. We can see how the stories are very similar in both trickery and deception. It is the daughters who deceive their fathers and used the teraphim in the deception act. The daughters betrayed their fathers' trust.

Nevertheless, there are notable differences between the stories. In Genesis the teraphim disappear, while in Samuel it is David who disappears. The act of deception goes undiscovered in Genesis, while in Samuel it is Saul who discovers his daughter's deception. The author of Sam 19 evidently was familiar with our story and approved of Rachel's act of deception. He used the image of Rachel as a model for Michal. However, Rachel was punished for the deception of her father. When Laban accused Jacob of the theft of his gods, Jacob pronounced a death sentence on the person who stole Laban's gods. Jacob's words resonate with Joseph's words about the person who stole his cup: "with whomever of your servants it is found, let him die" (Gen 44:9). Jacob was convinced of the innocence of the people in his camp. He unknowingly pronounced a death sentence on his beloved wife. This death sentence was delayed, and Rachel died while giving birth to Jacob's son Benjamin.

Jacob's Sons

Like their father, Jacob's sons also used trickery and deception. It appears that the sons learned something from their father. Following the rape of Dinah (Gen 34:1–2; see also above, chapter 7), the brothers spoke to Shechem and his father Hamor with guile. Dinah, their sister, was raped, which made them distressed and very angry. To convince Jacob and his sons to accept a marriage between his own son, Shechem, and Dinah, Hamor offered some land for Jacob and his sons to dwell in and acquire holdings in as a part of the marriage proposal. To this suggestion, the sons of Jacob responded with the prerequisite of circumcision as a requirement. Although the narrator says that they spoke with guile, indeed it was the practice among the Israelites. On the other hand, while speaking with their townsmen, it appears that Shechem and Hamor were also dishonest and used double-talk. First, they did not disclose their own selfish reasons for the circumcision. Second, because they needed to convince their townsmen to be circumcised, they changed their original proposal. They omitted the part about property rights for Jacob and his sons; instead they suggested that all of Jacob's and his sons' belongings—their cattle, and substance—would be theirs.

Jacob's sons Simeon and Levi were full brothers of Dinah. They took advantage of the situation when the townspeople were recovering from the circumcision and were in severe pain. They came and slew the entire male population in the city and took their sister. In addition, they seized all their flocks and herds, their children, and wives. It is interesting to note that in the targumim, such as *Neofiti*, this act of the brothers is not described as guile, but rather as the *vastness of their wisdom*. Similarly, targums *Pseudo-Jonathan* and *Onqelos* describe their act as "with wisdom." Evidently, *Neofiti*, *Pseudo-Jonathan*, and *Onqelos* avoid mentioning the fact that the brothers spoke deceitfully or with guile, but approved of their actions. This is also mentioned in *Genesis Rabbah*, which justifies the brothers' proposal and says that the brothers were not guilty of deceit, because Shechem had defiled their sister.[27]

In the *Testament of Levi*, we have a different interpretation of this story.[28] According to this testament, Jacob and his sons proposed circumcision and intermarriages with the Shechmites, but Levi was against this idea. Levi tried to persuade his father and his brother Reuben to change their offer of circumcision; he did not want to use circumcision as a trick. Since the Shechmites were circumcised, Levi was left with no choice, so he and his brother Simeon went and slaughtered the Shechmites. This also explains Jacob's reaction: "And [our] father heard of it and was angry and distressed, because they had accepted circumcision and had been killed after that."

27. *Gen. Rab.* 80:8.
28. Kugel, *Ladder of Jacob*, 47–49.

At first, there is no mention of punishment for slaughtering all the males in the city of Shechem. Jacob only rebuked his sons for jeopardizing the safety and the survival of the clan. More so, he did not even raise the question of why the innocent people were killed for the crime of one person. Only later, on his deathbed, will Jacob punish his sons for their actions. In his last words to Simeon and Levi, he curses their anger and predicts that they will be scattered in Israel (see more on that in chapter 9).

Deception was also used by Jacob's sons against their own father. Joseph was the favorite son of Jacob. He was the son of his beloved wife Rachel and was born to him in his old age, so Jacob transferred his love to Joseph. The preferential treatment is expressed by the coat of many colors. Giving Joseph the coat of many colors provoked and increased the resentment toward Joseph in the family. The biblical narrative is very laconic, and very rarely do we find a description of people's looks or clothes unless it serves a purpose in the story. Hence, the reader knows already that the coat will play an important role in the story. The brothers hated Joseph for this parental favoritism. By showing favoritism toward Joseph, Jacob committed the same "sin" that his father did when Isaac loved Esau more than Jacob. This favoritism appears several times in the Jacob family: Rebecca loved Jacob more than Esau, and Jacob loved Rachel more than Leah. Leah is twice described as "hated" (Gen 29:31, 33); so now it is her children who hate. In the Talmud, Jacob's favoritism toward Joseph is condemned; this is what a father should avoid: to prefer one son over the other.[29] It leads to disastrous consequences. The resentment and hatred would increase with the dreams that Joseph had. Jacob took his son's dreams seriously, and thus he berated him for them. The brothers hate was so deep and intense that they could not speak civilly or peacefully with him.

One day, Joseph's brothers traveled from Hebron to Shechem, the place where Jacob's sons had massacred the son of Hamor, to pasture their father's flock. We do not know why Joseph failed to travel with his brothers. Fearing that his sons and flocks were near Shechem, Jacob sent his son Joseph on a reconnaissance mission. When Joseph arrived to visit his brothers, just seeing him from afar ignited the brother's hatred and murderous plans. They decided to kill him then throw him into one of the pits and say that a savage beast devoured him. However, they changed their plans after seeing a caravan of Ishmaelites passing by. Judah suggested selling Joseph to the Ishmaelites. By selling him, they would avoid the danger of blood guilt. The

---

29. b. Šabb. 10b; b. Meg. 16b; Gen. Rab. 84:8.

brothers accepted Judah's proposal and sold Joseph into slavery. To conceal their conduct and deceive their father, they slaughtered a *kid* and dipped the coat of many colors in the blood of a kid. In doing so, they emulated their father Jacob. What we have here is "measure for measure." When Jacob fooled his father and deceived him, he covered himself with the skin of a kid. Now it is his sons who turn the table on him. The trick worked, and when the brothers brought the tunic to their father covered with the kid's blood, Jacob, recognizing the tunic, surmised that his beloved son was torn by a wild beast.

The motif of a *kid* will surface again in the story of Judah and Tamar. Judah's daughter-in-law, Tamar, deceived him since he did not fulfill the law of levirate marriage. Shelah, Judah's son, was grown up and was not given to her as a wife as the biblical law required. Thus, Tamar tricked Judah and disguised herself as a cult prostitute. Not suspecting that it was his daughter-in-law because of her covering, Judah slept with Tamar, because he thought she was a harlot. When she asked him for payment, he promised to send a kid from the flock. Again, we have here "measure for measure." Judah and his brothers deceived their father Jacob—now it is Judah who is deceived by Tamar. The brothers used the blood of a kid—now it is a kid that Judah has promised to send.

Following the deception of their father, Judah left his brothers. According to the midrash, the brothers were angry at him because of his bad advice to sell Joseph.[30] Hence, Judah, like his father Jacob, is separated from his family because of his act of deception. Judah's isolation from his brothers is also mentioned in the pre-monarchic times, when the tribe of Judah was separated from the other tribes because of Canaanite enclaves. This isolation is mentioned in Deuteronomy: "Hear, O Lord, the voice of Judah, and restore him to his people" (33:7). Another interpretation is that Judah went down from his brothers because he was demoted from his high status as the leader of the brothers after failing to convince them to rescue Joseph,[31] or because Judah's attempts to rescue Joseph were not successful.[32] Judah persuaded his brothers to sell Joseph rather than leave him in the pit to die, but more was expected of him. As the leader of his brothers, he was supposed to do more for his younger brother Joseph. The isolation of Judah from his family was not the only punishment that he endured. He was also punished by the death of his two sons Er and Onan, in addition to the de-

30. *Tanḥ.* (Buber), *Ber.* 183.
31. *Tanḥ.* (Buber), *Vayeshev* 12.
32. *b. Soṭah.* 13b.

ceit by his daughter-in-law Tamar. However, later, Judah was compensated for the death of his sons by the birth of the twins Perez and Zerah.

The other brothers were punished by Joseph, who exerted psychological pressure on them by various tests. In his dealing with his brothers, Joseph appears as a person who is bent on revenge. He first tested them by three days of incarceration. During that time, their feelings of guilt erupt. They believed in retribution, feeling that they were being punished for what they did to their brother. Furthermore, Joseph tested his brother's solidarity and integrity by incarcerating Simeon before their eyes, sending them home without him. Now they had to face their father with another brother missing, like many years earlier when they had returned without Joseph. He exerted additional pressure on his brothers by returning the money for the grain to their sacks. When the brothers found the money they were fearful, which was an expression of guilt and divine judgment, as they had expressed before (Gen 42:21–22, 28).

Joseph also insisted that the brothers had to bring Benjamin with them, and then he deceived them. He ordered his attendant to put his silver goblet in Benjamin's bag and accused the brothers with the theft of the goblet. When their bags were searched, the brothers pronounced a death sentence on the guilty person. They were convinced of their innocence. The whole story is similar to the story of Laban's pursuit of Jacob, when he searched Jacob's tents for the missing teraphim. On that occasion, Jacob had pronounced a death sentence on the guilty person, not realizing that it was his beloved wife Rachel. Unlike his mother, who succeeded in her deception, the cup was found in Benjamin's bag. When the goblet turns up in Benjamin's bag, the brothers tear their clothes. Before, at the disappearance of Joseph, it was Jacob who tore his clothes, now it is all the brothers who tear their clothes as a sign of mourning and solidarity.

Joseph further tested his brothers by telling them to return home without Benjamin, who was to stay in Egypt as his slave. Again, this is a flashback to twenty years ago when the brothers returned home without Joseph. It was a trial of their integrity; they could return home and save their lives and leave their brother Benjamin behind, which would be disastrous to their father. Or, if they stayed with Benjamin, they would not be able to bring food back home to their families, who would die from starvation.

The story reaches its climactic moment when Judah speaks with Joseph. Judah pours his heart out in the longest speech in the book of Genesis. He appeals to Joseph's sense of humanity and fairness. As noted above in his dealing with his brothers, Joseph appears bent on revenge. Abravanel, in his interpretation, says that Joseph's intention was to provide his brothers with the opportunity to demonstrate their full repentance. Joseph had to be convinced of his brothers' change of heart. Therefore, he puts them through this series of tests. Forgiveness and reconciliation are possible only after the brothers show remorse. The brothers repeatedly proved their integrity and family loyalty. Finally, when Judah suggests that he replace Benjamin, would Joseph be convinced of their change of heart? The answer is yes, as demonstrated by his crying over them.

An alternate theory is that Joseph hated his brothers so much that he put them through a series of tests. This might also explain why he did not make any attempt to contact his family in Canaan after he became viceroy of Egypt.[33] But what is not clear is why he caused his father Jacob to suffer so much! His father loved him—he gave him the coat of many colors, mourned for him after he thought that he was dead, and refused to be comforted. Hence, Joseph was acting according to the divine plan. Jacob must suffer for his deception of his father and brother.

In conclusion, deception was a way of life in the ancient world, and in this respect the Hebrews were no different from other people. Jacob, Laban, Rachel, Jacobs son's, and Tamar, Judah's daughter-in-law—all of them deceived one another. The aim of these deceptions was to gain the advantage of being in control. But the Hebrew Bible, with its high moral standard, did not approve of this kind of action, as we read in the Ten Commandments (Exod 20:7). Hence, not surprisingly, each person was punished for their deception. In the current chapter, we noted that the marriage of Jacob to the two sisters Rachel and Leah was partly a result of the deception that was played by Laban on Jacob. In the next chapter, we will examine the characters of Jacob's wives and concubines and explore the rivalry between the wives.

---

33. Soller, "Why No Message?," 158–67.

3

Jacob's Wives

THE BIBLICAL NARRATOR EMPLOYS a technique to describe heroes by comparing and contrasting them. Using this technique, the narrator directs the reader to the virtues and weaknesses of his hero. Characters can be revealed through their actions, lack of actions, appearances, gestures, and comments. In the narrative, characters are revealed both by statements made by them or by other characters, in addition to descriptions given by the third-person narrator.[1] In this chapter, we will examine the characters, Rachel, Leah, Bilhah, and Zilpah. We will point to their virtues, vices, triumphs, and failures. This analysis will give us a better understanding of who the matriarchs and the maidservants really were.

Rachel

Rachel was the wife of Jacob and the mother of Joseph and Benjamin. She was the younger daughter of Laban. Her name means "a ewe lamb."[2] Rachel was a shepherdess, which was a rarity among the women of Israel. This was not the case among the bedouin in Sinai, as seen in the story of Jethro's daughters (Exod 2:16). The first time she is mentioned is when Jacob arrived at the well near Haran. It was love at first sight. Jacob kissed Rachel and broke into tears. It is the only place in the Bible where a man kisses a woman who is neither his mother nor his wife. Outside the book Song of Songs, not much is mentioned of a love between a man and a woman.

---

1. Alter, *The Art of Biblical Narrative*, 116–17.
2. Cf. Gen 31:38; 32:15.

Jacob's Wives

The meeting at the well has a close resemblance to the meeting between Abraham's servant and Rebecca. At first, Rachel was passive. It was Jacob who rolled the stone from the mouth of the well and watered the flock of his uncle Laban. Only after Jacob told her that he was her father's kinsman did Rachel, like Rebecca, run to tell her father Laban about the arrival of his sister's son, Jacob.

Rachel is a beautiful and lovely woman. This description is redundant, but it is probably to stress her beauty and character. Later, the same Hebrew words are used by the narrator to describe Joseph as well-built and handsome (Gen 39:6). Evidently, Joseph received his good looks from his mother, since no other male is described like this. The text tells us that "Jacob loved Rachel . . . So Jacob served seven years for Rachel and they seemed to him but a few days because of his love for her" (Gen 29:18, 20). His love for Rachel is also evident in his meeting with his brother, Esau, upon his return home. Before this meeting, he placed Rachel and Joseph last in line, to ensure that if the meeting turned hostile they would have the chance to escape. More so, when he presented his wives and children to Esau, he placed Joseph and Rachel at the end. Interestingly, Joseph preceded Rachel in line, and here he is the only child who is mentioned before his mother. Jacob's special love for Rachel is also manifested in Judah's speech to Joseph. He quotes his father as saying, "As you know, my wife bore me two sons" (Gen 44:27). This sounds as though he had only one wife. Indeed, in the genealogy of Jacob, which appears in Gen 46:8–26, Jacob's other spouses are not referred to as wives. It is only Rachel who is called a wife. Jacob's love remained undiminished even after Rachel's death. This love was transferred to her sons, Joseph and Benjamin. Later, Jacob's love caused jealousy among his sons, which is manifested in the hatred of the brothers toward Joseph.

Jacob was a poor man when he arrived at the house of his uncle Laban. Therefore, he had to work for seven years in lieu of the bride price. He had already worked one month for nothing. What is interesting is that Laban took the *mōhar* for himself, as mentioned in Leah and Rachel's complaint about their father: "now that he has sold us and has used up our purchase price" (Gen 31:15). The *mōhar* was a financial gift given to the bride in order to secure her future, in case she lost her husband or was cast out. The groom deposited the *mōhar* with the bride's father or a guardian. In this case, Laban used the equivalent bridal price and did not save it for his daughters. The *mōhar* was part of the dowry. Documents as late as the fifth century BCE found in Elphantine reveal that the *mōhar* was handed over to the girl's father or guardian.[3]

Like previous matriarchs, Rachel was a barren woman. The fact that her sister gave birth caused her to be jealous. Leah had already given birth to four sons: Reuben, Simeon, Levi, and Judah. Her anger and jealousy were manifested in an outburst to Jacob: "Give me children or I shall die" (Gen 30:1). This exchange is the only quarrel between the two lovers. It was the suffering of the childless wife, which grew with each son that Leah had. Rachel demanded multiple sons, so that she could match Leah—only then could she be an equal to her sister Leah. A similar situation is mentioned with the matriarchs Sarah and Rebecca, but their reactions are mild in comparison (16:2; 25:21), although they had waited many more years than Rachel. Jacob rebuked Rachel and said, "Can I take the place of God?" (30:2). The exchange between the two demonstrates how desperate Rachel was, as well as Jacob's loss of patience. This is the only time that Jacob reprimanded one of his wives. From Jacob's words we can see that he knew that only God could open a woman's womb. He reminded Rachel that it was God who had prevented her from childbearing.

Like Sarah, Rachel resorted to the device of concubinage. She gave to Jacob her maid, Bilhah, who gave birth to two sons, Dan and Naphtali. It appears that this custom was for the sake of the wife and not the husband, since Jacob already had four sons. More so, Jacob already had a second wife. Therefore, not surprisingly, Rachel saw Dan and Naphtali as her own children. Unlike Sarah, she was happy with the new baby, which is made clear when, upon naming Dan, she proclaims, "God has vindicated me" (Gen 30:14–16). This might also reflect a liturgical formula: "by Your power vindicate me / O God, hear my prayer" (Ps 54:3b–4a). Rachel believed that God approved of her action. However, as we shall see later, God judged her unfavorably. Since Rachel demanded sons, Bilhah gave birth to a second son. The second son she named Naphtali. The meaning of the name is unclear. It comes from the root *p-t-l*, which means "twist, struggle." It is possible that it refers to "struggles in prayer" for divine favor.[4] Many years later, the Rabbis stated: "who brings up children is called the parent, not who gives birth."[5] Rachel is depicted here as competing with her sister

---

3. Cowley, *Aramaic Papyri*, 44–50 no. 15; Yaron, "Aramaic Marriage Contracts," 4–5.

4. Dillman *Genesis*, 241; Fokkelman, *Narrative Art in Genesis*, 135; Andersen, "Note on Genesis 30:8," 200.

5. *Exod. Rab.* 46:5.

Leah. Although her husband Jacob loved her more than Leah, this was not enough for her. This portrayal is similar to the rivalry between Peninah and Hannah, the wives of Elkanah (1 Sam 1:2). Hannah was the beloved of Elkanah but was barren; Peninah, on the other hand, had children.

Rachel, yearning for a child of her own, appears also in the story of the mandrake (Gen 30:14–16). Accordingly, she gives her conjugal rights to Leah in return for the mandrake that Reuben had collected. This plant played a great role in ancient times, and it was believed to have magical powers. Its fruit smelled strong, and it looked like a small apple. It was associated with aphrodisiac powers. Aphrodite, the Greek goddess of love, beauty, and sex, was given the nickname "Lady of Mandrake." The Bible does not tell us the reason for the interest of the two sisters, but evidently they shared folkloric beliefs about the power of mandrake. This magic fruit did not help Rachel, and when she did give birth, it was not because of the mandrake but because "Yahweh remembered Rachel" (Gen 30:22).

There is a flaw in Rachel's character: she resorted to the use of the mandrake and to superstition instead of trusting God. She falls for the temptations of the mandrake in exchange for Jacob. This story reflects how desperate Rachel was, willing to go to such lengths as to remove herself from the shame of childlessness that she resorted to artificial means. There are similarities between the story of the mandrake and the exchange of the birthright for lentil stew. Accordingly, the story of the mandrake is a mirror image of the purchase of the birthright. In one story, Jacob took advantage of his brother's hunger and purchased the birthright for an insignificant fee. In the second story, Leah purchased the right to spend the night with her husband for a minor fee—the mandrake. The story of the mandrake indirectly criticizes Jacob for the purchase of the birthright, and it is measure for measure punishment.[6]

Only after Leah gave birth to seven children was it Rachel's turn to give birth. She named her son Joseph. By giving that name, she proclaimed that God had taken away (*'āsap*) her disgrace, and expressed her desire that the Lord might give her an additional (*yôsēp*) son (Gen 30:23–24). The fact that Rachel was barren and gave birth to a son shares a theme that her son is destined for greatness. This, indeed, is found among other stories in the Hebrew Bible, such as Samson (Judg 13) and, in particular, the birth of Samuel (1 Sam 1:3). The story alludes to Joseph's importance through the fact that his birth is the last of the birth stories of Jacob's sons born in Mesopotamia.

---

6. Zakovitch, *Jacob*, 75; Ben-Reuben, "Buying Mandrakes," 230–31.

Rachel gave birth to her second son while she was dying, and she named him Ben-Oni, which means "son of my sorrow." However, Jacob changed the baby's name to Benjamin because he wanted to give his son a positive name. The name has several interpretations, such as "son of my right hand." The Hebrew word, *yāmîn* (right) also means strength (Exod 15:6); therefore, we can explain the name as "son of my strength." Another interpretation, "son of the south," is based on the association of the tribe of Benjamin with a tribe mentioned in a text from Mari called *Dumu-yamina*, "son of the south." However, this connection is unproven. A third suggestion is "son of my old age." Indeed, in Gen 44:20, Benjamin is called "son of my old age." This interpretation is also found in the *Testament of Benjamin* 1:16.

Benjamin is the only son who was born in Canaan and not in Mesopotamia. The story of his birth is an independent story and is not included among the other stories of the births of Jacob's sons. The story has its own characteristics and includes details such as Jacob's journey, the birth place of Benjamin, the death of Rachel, and her burial. Nevertheless, this story is an integral part of the stories that describe the births of Jacob's sons. This seemingly independent story is explained by the fact that Benjamin was the youngest and was born later. Indeed, one of the main motifs of the Joseph story is Benjamin's young age and the love of Joseph and Jacob for him. The other link to those stories is the interpretation of the name Joseph: "So she named him Joseph, which is to say, 'May the Lord add another son for me'" (Gen 30:24). Giving birth to Benjamin signals the beginning of the fulfillment of Isaac's blessing for Jacob that included a promise of kingship. This fulfillment is found in the person of King Saul, a Benjaminite.

The flaw in Rachel's character is revealed once again in the story of the theft of her father's household gods. The Bible refers to it as thievery; even her father's mistreatment does not justify it. What is not clear is why Rachel stole the household gods. One reasonable explanation is that she wanted to conceal Jacob's escape from her father. If this is true, she was still an idol worshiper, since she believed in the household gods. As a result of the theft, she became the object of Jacob's curse: "Anyone with whom you find your gods shall not live" (31:32). According to the midrash, "It was like a verbal slip of a ruler."[7] She was saved for a short time from the curse, again, by deception. Rachel sat on the idols when her father searched for them. She told him that she had her period; therefore, he could not approach her.

---

7. *Gen. Rab.* 74:9.

Jacob's Wives

However, as mentioned before, Rachel dies on the journey home to Canaan after giving birth to her second son. The death of Rachel and the birth of Benjamin marks the end of childbearing in the Jacob cycle.

The traditions about the birth of Rachel's sons reflect the Israelite tribal history. Rachel gave birth to Joseph and Benjamin, while her maid Bilhah gave birth to Dan and Naphtali. Two other tribes came through Joseph—Ephraim and Manasseh. It is believed that in the formation process of the league of twelve tribes, the tribes that were associated with Rachel constituted a separate confederation. Tribes that belonged to the concubine Bilhah were of inferior status in the confederation. The story of Benjamin's birth is very ancient. Since Joseph and Benjamin are brothers, they belong to the Rachel tribes. Later, after the settlement, Benjamin was tied with the tribe of Judah rather than with the fraternal Joseph tribes. Noth and others have suggested that Rachel and Leah were originally "eponymous ancestors" of semi-nomadic tribes that settled in the area that would later become Israel, during a different period and during several waves of migration.[8] It was hypothesized that Rachel's tribes were the last wave that came out of Egypt, which destroyed Jericho, Ai, and the coalition of kings near Gibeon. Those traditions were embraced by the other Israelite tribes and found their way into the literary writings of Exodus and Josh 1–10. However, we must stress here that there is no proof for these speculations.

As Jacob had a special love for Rachel during her lifetime, he also marked his love for her in death. He placed a commemorative pillar on her grave to mark her tomb. Nevertheless, Rachel was not buried next to him in the Cave of Machpelah, but she was buried on the road to Ephrath. This was probably because Leah was still alive. Jacob did not want to humiliate Leah and her sons, as she was the first wife. Therefore, Rachel was buried on the road. It is Leah who was buried next to Jacob for eternal sleep. Jacob asked to be buried in the Cave of Machpelah, while, according to the midrash, Jacob buried Rachel at Ephrath because he foresaw that the exiles would pass this way on their way to the exile in Babylon. When they passed, Rachel asked God for mercy on them.[9]

Outside of Genesis, Rachel is mentioned twice in the biblical literature—once, together with Leah, in the marriageable blessing of Ruth (4:11) a second time in Jeremiah, where the prophet describes her as weeping in Ramah for her children who are in exile (Jer 31:15). As the symbolic

---

8. Weippert, *Settlement of the Israelite*, 5–46, esp. 42–46.
9. *Gen. Rab.* 82:10.

mother of Israel, she is mourning her dead children, and no one can give her comfort. Therefore, God speaks to her with the command to not mourn for her children, who are not dead but shall return from exile.

Rachel is the mother who understands pain and anguish, as was reflected in her own life. Her tomb became a place for pilgrimage for all those who mourn and pour their hearts out. Rachel symbolizes unfulfilled dreams; she was supposed to be the first wife but became the second wife. It was her sister who gave Jacob son after son. The two important tribes, Judah and Levi, came through her sister, Leah. Rachel was left dreaming a dream, and when she was close to achieving it as a mother, it was taken away from her. She gave birth to Joseph, but she died when the other son, Benjamin, was born. Rachel was always close to achieving happiness, but in the last moment, it was snatched away from her.

Leah

Leah was the first wife of Jacob. In the Bible, she is described as Rachel's sister. Her name has several interpretations: "cow," "strong woman," or "mistress." It is possible that the interpretation of the name as "cow" points to the cultural and historical memory of the Leah tribes, which were in Canaan longer and had already become cattlemen.[10] Leah does not appear independently, but always next to her sister. She is mentioned along with Rachel in the stories of Jacob's escape from Laban (Gen 34:4–16); in the meeting that follows the escape (34:17–32:1); in the encounter with Esau (32:23–33:7); in the genealogical list of Jacob's family (46:8–27); and in Jacob's Testament, where he requests to be buried in the Cave of Machpelah (49:30–31). The first detail about Leah is that her eyes are weak. It is possible that this refers to their paleness and lack of luster. This, evidently, does not flatter her. Indeed, by contrast, Rachel is described as shapely and beautiful. The midrash has a very interesting interpretation: "Because she expected to fall into Esau's lot, and she wept, because everyone was saying, Rebecca has two sons, and Laban has two daughters. The older [daughter] for the older [son], and the younger [daughter] for the younger [son]."[11]

Leah was married to Jacob as a result of trickery. Her father Laban substituted her for her sister Rachel on the wedding night. Jacob probably felt resentment toward her for taking part in the deception. Indeed, in

10. Rad, *Genesis*, 286.
11. *b. B. Bat.* 123a.

the midrash we read that Jacob reproached her, saying, "O thou deceiver, daughter of a deceiver, why did you answer me when I called Rachel's name?" Leah responded, "Is there a teacher without a pupil? I learned from your example. Did you not answer your father when he called Esau?"[12]

Jacob's feelings toward Leah are not clear in Gen 29:30, "he loved Rachel more than Leah." In another words, he still loved Leah, but not as much as he loved Rachel. We have to remember that she gave him six sons—Reuben, Simeon, Levi, Judah, Issachar, Zebulon—and one daughter, Dinah. Her maidservant, Zilphah, bore another two sons—Gad and Asher. Leah had to fight for Jacob's affections; it is evident from the names she gave her children that she wanted to be the preferred wife: "Leah conceived and bore a son, and named him Reuben; for she declared, 'It means: "The Lord has seen my affliction" it also means: "Now my husband will love me"'" (Gen 29:32). Leah also recognizes God's role in her pregnancy and hopes that the end of her suffering is near. She conceived again, bore a son, and declared, "'This is because the Lord heard that I was unloved and has given this one also'; so she named him Simeon. Again she conceived and bore a son and declared, 'This time my husband will become attached to me, for I have borne him three sons.' Therefore he was named Levi" (Gen 29:33–34). It is noteworthy that Leah changes her language from "Now my husband will love me" to "my husband will become attached to me." She now believes that her husband will appreciate her because she has given him three sons. When the fourth son arrives, she names him Judah: "'This time I will praise ['ôdeh] the Lord,' therefore she named him Judah. Then she stopped bearing" (v. 35). As before, Leah praises the Lord. Nevertheless, we are informed that she stopped bearing. No reason is given for this stoppage, but according to the next chapter, Jacob stopped fulfilling his conjugal duty (Gen 30:14). It is noteworthy that the first three names that Leah gave her sons were connected with her desire and yearning for the love of her husband. This is not the case with her fourth son, Judah, where she only praises God. At this stage, it appears that she has had enough of him and, for a while, stops trying to win him. Interestingly, wives assume the responsibility for naming children in the Jacob cycle, for Leah's (29:32–35; 30:11–12, 18, 20) and for Rachel's (30:6–8, 24; 35:18). Benjamin's mother named him Ben-Oni, but his father called him Benjamin. In contrast, in the stories about the patriarchs Abraham and Isaac, it is the fathers who gave names to their children.

---

12. *Gen. Rab.* 70:19.

This longing for her husband's love is also manifested in the story of the mandrake. The mandrakes are identified with the *Mandragora afficinarum*. It is believed that this fruit has aphrodisiac powers and even the power to increase fertility. Rachel was aware of the mandrake powers; therefore, she asked Leah to give her the mandrake that belonged to her son Reuben. Leah gave the mandrake to Rachel in exchange for conjugal rights. According to the custom, Jacob was required to alternate between his wives, spending one night with one wife and the next with the other one. However, Jacob probably spent more time in Rachel's bed than in Leah's. This is, indeed, clear when Leah complains bitterly that Rachel sought to take away "my husband" and also the mandrake of her son. Leah was ready to trade the mandrake for Jacob. The sages pointed out that Rachel was willing to give up Jacob for one night. She belittled his bed; thus, she was not buried next to him. More so, she did not even consult with him if he agreed to the new situation. Leah was willing to suffer humiliation for the suggestion to her husband: "You are to sleep with me, for I have hired you with my son's mandrakes" (30:16).

Out of the union between Leah and Jacob a fifth son was born. Leah named him Issachar: "And Leah said 'God has given me my reward [*śĕkārî*] for having given my maid to my husband.' So she named him Issachar" (30:18). The meaning of the name Issachar is *yēš śākār* "There is a reward," a phrase that is found in Jer 31:16 and 2 Chron 15:7.[13] Although God helped Leah, she interpreted his intervention incorrectly. She sees Issachar's birth as a repayment for her giving Zilpah to Jacob and not as an example of anticipating God's will.[14] Leah conceived a sixth son and called him Zebulun. There are two explanations for this name: One is connected to the stem *z-b-d* "to give, to grant," which appears in our verse. The second one is based on the stem *z-b-l*, which means "to dwell," or, in other words, "my husband will dwell with me."[15] Again, Leah sees the birth of her children as a means of winning her husband's love. Lastly, the narrator tells us that she bore him a daughter and named her Dinah. There is no explanation of this name. The sense is that this fact is mentioned here to prepare the readers for the ensuing events in the future when Dinah will play a major role in chapter 34.

Leah struggles to win Jacob's love. Because of her misery, God rewards her with children. The priesthood and the monarchy—the two hereditary institutions—are traced to her sons Levi and Judah. Leah's love for her

---

13. Isbell, "Initial 'Alef-Yod," 229.
14. Zakovitch, *Jacob*, 72.
15. Sarna, *Understanding Genesis*, 210.

husband is constant. She works, struggles, and bears most of his children. It is possible that the feud between the two sisters is a prelude to and justification of the law that appears later in Lev 18:18: "Do not marry a woman as a rival to her sister and uncover her nakedness in the other's lifetime." Marrying two sisters creates an unhealthy situation. The fact that Jacob married two sisters shows that this story comes from an earlier period when such marriages were permitted.

The stories of the matriarchs follow a literary paradigm.[16] The legitimate wife is contrasted with a second wife who possesses different characteristics. The stories display a constant rivalry and jealousy between the two, which was a result of a polygamous society and barrenness. By contrasting the two women, the author could point to the strengths and weaknesses of the two characters. The clash between the two was resolved when one woman expelled the other or when one of them died. In our case, Rachel died while giving birth to Benjamin. However, in our story, the clash between the two sisters does not end with the death of Rachel.

This rivalry between the sisters had an enduring influence on the Jewish nationhood. It continued with the rivalry between Leah's sons and Rachel's son Joseph. More so, it intensified with the enmity between Leah's tribes, led by Judah, and Rachel's tribes, led by Joseph's son Ephraim. This rivalry repeated itself in the conflicts between the kingdom of Judah and Israel. It ended only with the disappearance of the tribe of Ephraim.

In his prophecy, Ezekiel speaks about the union of the tree of Ephraim and the tree of Judah. This rivalry will continue until the End Days, where it is prophesized that there will be one Messiah from the house of David (Ezek. 37:17–25).

In contrast to her portrayal in Genesis, Rachel is the weeping mother, and Leah is the happy mother. Leah's relationship with Jacob is more permanent and more complete. It was Leah who was Jacob's full partner in life, and the true wife. The bond between the two was manifested in the bearing of the sons, which was a lasting connection. This lasting connection goes from Leah to the house of David, through her son Judah. It was Leah who showed love, fidelity, and continuity, and she was the true wife, therefore, not surprisingly, she is the one who was buried next to Jacob.[17]

---

16. Brenner, "Female Social Behavior," 257–73; Cohen, "Sibling Rivalry," 331–42.
17. Steinsaltz, *Biblical Images*, 59–61.

Bilhah and Zilpah

Sarah provides her husband, Abraham, with a handmaid, while Laban, the father-in-law of Jacob, gives his daughters handmaids. Thus, Leah receives Zilpah, and Rachel, Bilhah. When Rachel discovers that she is barren, she gives Bilhah to her husband Jacob so that she might bear children in her place. Jacob already had many children when Rachel presents Bilhah to him. This evidently hurt Rachel, who could not conceive. Rachel is unhappy being childless and is envious of her sister Leah. It was a grave matter for a man to be childless, because it left him with no heirs. This was also devastating for a woman; to have children was to be a success in life, while having none was considered failure. Indeed, this kind of feeling was expressed by Rachel to Jacob: "Give me children, or I shall die" (Gen 30:1). Since she could not conceive, she resorted to concubinage.

The meaning of the name Bilhah is unclear. Noth connected it to the Arabic *baliha* without explaining it; however, this means "stupid, unconcerned."[18] It is possible that the name is connected to the Horite clan *Bilhān* mentioned in Genesis 36:27.

Out of the union between Jacob and Bilhah (Rachel's handmaid), two sons, Dan and Naphtali, were born. The names of the sons, Dan and Naphtali, reflect vindication and a belief in divine favor. After the death of Rachel, Reuben, the firstborn of Leah, went and laid with his stepmother, Bilhah. Reuben came to the aid of his mother by making sure that no one could displace her as the chief wife. In the Talmud, we read, "He resented his mother's humiliation. Said he, 'If my mother's sister was a rival to my mother, shall the bondmaid of my mother's sister be a rival to my mother?'"[19] Interestingly, this is the second time that Reuben came to the aid of his mother. Before, he came to her aid with the mandrake. In both stories, Reuben's activities include the words "and Reuben went" (30:14; 35:22). But this time, his actions have grave consequences.

Stories about a son who has a sexual relationship with his father's concubine in order to protect his mother's honor are also found in the literature of the ancient world. In the Iliad, we read how Phoenix lay with his father's concubine as a result of his mother request:

> I left Hellas, the home of fair women, fleeing from strife with my father Amyntor, son of Ormenus; for he waxed grievously worth

---

18. Noth, *Die israelitischen Personennamen*, 10 no.3.
19. b. Šabb. 55b.

against me by reason of his fair haired concubine, whom himself he ever cherished, and scorned his wife, my mother. So she besought me by my knees continually, to have dalliance with that other first myself, that the old man might be hateful in her eyes. I hearkened to her and did the deed, but my father was ware thereof forthwith and cursed me mightily, and invoked the dire Erinyes, that never should there sit upon his knees a dear child begotten of me; and the gods fulfilled his curse, even Zeus of the netherworld and the dread Persephone.[20]

In contrast to the biblical narrative, which is very laconic in describing the Reuben and Bilhah story, a more detailed description is found in the *Testament of the Twelve Patriarchs* and the book of Jubilees. In the *Testament of Reuben*, he confesses his transgressions to his sons and implores them to learn from his mistakes:

> ... for had I not seen Bilhah bathing in a secluded place I would not have fallen into so great sin ... For while our father Jacob was away on a visit to his father Isaac, when we were in Eder, near the house of Ephrath, Bilhah had been drinking; and she was lying asleep in her bedroom with nothing over her. And I went in and saw her nakedness and did the wicked deed; and I left her still asleep and went away. And immediately an angel of God told my father Jacob about my wickedness; and he came and mourned over me. And as for Bilhah, he had no further relations with her. (3:9–15)

A more detailed description of the story appears in the book of Jubilees:

> And Jacob moved and settled to the south of Migdal-Eder Ephrate. And he went to visit his father Isaac, he and his wife Leah, on the new moon of the tenth month. And Reuben saw Bilhah, Rachel's maid, his father's concubine, bathing in water in a secluded place, and he became enamored of her. And he hid himself and went into Bilhah's house at night and found her asleep alone on her bed in her house; and he lay with her. And she woke up and looked round, and behold Reuben was lying with her in the bed; and she lifted the edge of her coverlet and took hold of him, and when she realized it was Reuben she cried out aloud. And she was ashamed because of him, and she let go of him and she fled. And she was much upset by what had happened and said nothing to anyone about it. And when Jacob returned and asked for her, she said to him, "I am not clean for you, for I have been defiled: Reuben

20. Homer, *Iliad*. 9.448–57.

defiled me and lay with me in the night, when I was asleep, and I did not realize who it was until he had uncovered my shame and had intercourse with me." And Jacob was very angry with Reuben because he had lain with Bilhah—because he had uncovered his father's shame. And Jacob did not approach her again because Reuben had defiled her. (33:1–10)

The resemblance between the two versions is very clear. In the story, Reuben sees Bilhah bathing, which is a reminder of David looking at Bathsheba when she was bathing (2 Sam 11). The author of the book of Jubilees stresses the fact that Bilhah was an innocent victim; she bathed in a secluded place. Later that night, she did not realize it was Reuben in her bed—a reminder of Jacob and Leah on the wedding night. Bilhah confesses to Jacob that Reuben defiled her. This resulted in Jacob never sleeping with her again.

Only here is Bilhah called a concubine (Gen 35:22). The term has sociological implications; sleeping with the father's concubine signaled legitimacy and validated succession. In a later period, Ish-boshet rebuked Abner for sleeping with his father's concubine (2 Sam 3:7–8). Absalom slept with his father's concubine when he was planning to seize the throne. Similarly, Adonijah requested to sleep with Abishag the Shunammite. Solomon interpreted it as an intention for treason (1 Kgs 2:13–25). In this story, Reuben challenged his father's authority and was trying to promote his mother's rights. He probably also tried to prevent Bilhah from succeeding Rachel as his father's favorite wife.

For his act, Reuben lost his hegemony. First Chronicles 5:1 mentions that Reuben was the firstborn of Israel, but when he defiled his father's bed, his birthright was given to the sons of Joseph. Interestingly, Jacob is silent; he just "heard about it" (Gen 34:5). The narrative does not report any reaction, only that he was angry. Or maybe, was it that he could not control his oldest son? The answer to these questions is found only at the end in Jacob's Testament. When Jacob summons all his sons to hear his last message, he mentions that Reuben defiled his bed; therefore, he will not excel any longer. In other words, he lost his supremacy.

Laban gave his handmaid Zilpah to Leah on the occasion of her marriage to Jacob. The meaning of the name is unclear. Noth connected it with the Arabic *zalfun, zalfatun*, which means "dignity," while Bauer suggested to connect it with *dhulifa*, which is "to be small."[21] When Leah stopped

---

21. Noth, *Die israelitischen Personennamen*, 10; Bauer, "Die hebräischen Eigennamen als sprachliche," 78.

bearing, she resorted to concubinage, thus giving Zilpah to her husband Jacob. At this stage, Leah had four sons: Reuben, Simeon, Levi, and Judah. Evidently, Leah wanted to outdo her sister; she was jealous of Rachel. Leah was yearning for Jacob's love, which is clear in the names that she gave to her sons. As a result of the union between Jacob and Zilpah, two sons were born—Gad and Asher. When Zilpah gave birth: "Leah said, 'Luck has come [bāʾ gād]!' And she named him Gad" (Gen 30:11). The name Gad appears as a name of the god of luck in some Near Eastern cultures. It is similar to the Greek *Tyche* and Latin *Fortuna*. This pagan god is mentioned in Isa 65:11, where it is paired with "Destiny." Leah attributes this luck to her own actions and not to God. When Zilpah gave birth to her second son, Leah declares, "'I am happy, [bĕʾošrî] for women have praised me [ʾišrûnî].' So she named him Asher (Gen 30:13)." The name Asher is derived from the stem ʾ-š-r, "happy." Leah is full of joy since she produced many sons.

When Jacob migrates to Egypt, the Genesis genealogies list sixteen descendants of Zilpah (46:16–18). Gad had seven children (46:16), while Asher had four sons, one daughter, and two grandchildren, who were the sons of Beriah (46:17). Speiser tried to link Laban giving Zilpah to Leah with a Hurrian marriage practice. According to him, it was customary among the upper class to give a slave girl to the bride on the occasion of her marriage.[22] However, this view was refuted by Van Seters, who pointed out that giving a maid to a bride was a common practice in Mesopotamia.[23]

In conclusion, although rivalry existed between the two sisters, Rachel and Leah, there is no hatred between them. This is in contrast to the intense hatred in Genesis among brothers. Rachel and Leah were different from Sarah as well. The first matriarch expelled Hagar and her son, Ishmael; she insisted that Ishmael would not have a part in the paternal estate. Not so with Rachel and Leah. The wives of Jacob did not abandon the children of the handmaids; they accepted them as their own sons. The sisters were devoted to their children as well as the children of the handmaids. This is probably why we read in the blessing that was bestowed on Ruth, "The Lord make the woman who has gone into thy house like Rachel and like Leah" (Ruth 4:11). So far we have examined the complex relationships that existed in the Jacob cycle. In the next chapter, we will look into the religious customs and beliefs that are mentioned in the Jacob cycle to see if Jacob was a monotheist.

22. Speiser, *Genesis*, 227.
23. Van Seters, "Jacob's Marriages," 377–95.

4

Religious Practices in the Jacob Cycle

THE BOOK OF GENESIS prescribes neither laws nor moral responsibilities; only promises of nationhood and posterity were given to the patriarchs by God. Not surprisingly, some scholars claim there is no such thing as a patriarchal period or patriarchal religion.[1] Scholars maintain that the stories in Genesis are late retrojections composed during the monarchial period.

The Rabbis were also aware of the lack of moral responsibility and the lack of law. Therefore, they believed in the existence of a divine covenant with the whole human race. According to them, God made a covenant with Adam and Noah. These came to be known as the Noachide Commandments. Nevertheless, examination of the book of Genesis reveals that some religious customs and practices were already mentioned, such as building altars, offering sacrifices, setting up pillars, planting sacred trees, praying, and circumcising. In order to identify the religious customs and practices of the patriarch Jacob, we will use a diachronic approach and examine the biblical text. In other words, we will try to identify the patriarch's historical beliefs by examining the different religious customs described in the book of Genesis. In addition, we will compare them to later periods in the biblical narrative. This in turn will help us to see if indeed the religious customs of Jacob were authentic presentations of his faith, or rather presentations of religious beliefs from the monarchial period. We will also examine the different names of God in the Jacob cycle. Hence, we will study names such as El Shaddai, El Bethel, El the God of Israel, Mighty One of Jacob, as well as "the God of my Father." This will help us to answer the question, was Jacob a true monotheist?

1. Wellhausen, *Prolegomena*, 318–19; Hoftizer, *Die Verheissungen an die drei Erzväter*, 6–30; Thompson, *Historicity of the Patriarchal Narratives*; Van Seters, *Abraham in History and Tradition*, 220–33.

Altars

One of the main religious characteristics of the patriarchs was their building of altars. The altars were a place to commune with God. Therefore, the patriarchs invoked God's name. The altars were built on the occasion of epiphanies—not for sacrifice, but as enduring signs. They served as signs of gratitude for God's promises. Segal explains the building of altars as the attachment of spiritual context to the place. Accordingly, the patriarchs built altars where they prayed to God, but removed the pagan elements.[2] The custom of naming the altars or invoking God's name continued with Moses (Exod 17:15) and Gideon (Judg 6:24), but is not mentioned afterward. There is only one instance, at the binding of Isaac, when Abraham makes a sacrifice on an altar that he erected (Gen 22:13). Thus, not surprisingly, the patriarchs did not have priests. Priests will appear in Israel only after the Exodus, with the dedication of Aaron and his son by Moses (Exod 28–29; Lev 8–10). Before the existence of the priesthood, it was the head of the family who brought sacrifices and blessed the members of his family (Gen 28:1–4; 48:9–20; 49:3–28). In the book of Exodus, the firstborn leads the community (Exod 22:28). In Exod 24:5, they are referred to as the "young men of the people of Israel." But they lost their important role after the story of the golden calf (Exod 32:26–29; Num 8:2–26). This change is echoed in Num 8:18: "Now I take the Levites instead of every first-born of the Israelite."

Setting up an altar is mentioned in the Jacob cycle for the first time when Jacob arrived to Shechem. Hence, Jacob sets up an altar and calls it "El the God of Israel" (Gen 33:20). In contrast to the previous building of altars by the patriarchs, this one does not respond to theophany. But it is connected to the promise Jacob made at Bethel: "if God will be with me ... then Yahweh shall be my God" (28:20–21). Therefore, Jacob calls the altar El Elohei-Israel (i.e., Jacob). The naming of the altar "El Elohei-Israel" also points to the connection between the place and the God of Israel. In Genesis, the verb that is used for building altars is *b-n-y*. Here, the Hebrew verb is *wayyaṣeb*, which is connected with *maṣēbâ*, a pillar. Since the *maṣēbôt* were later forbidden, it is suggested that a later hand substituted "altar" (*mizbēaḥ*) for *maṣēbâ* in this place.[3] Returning back to Bethel in the land of Canaan, Jacob built a second altar and named the place El-Bethel

---

2. Segal, "The Religion of Israel before Sinai," 220–21.
3. Pury, *Promesse divine*, 442.

(35:7). Here, however, God instructed Jacob to go to Bethel and to build an altar there (35:1). This is the only place where God instructs a man to build an altar. We should point out that Jacob had already erected a pillar there to commemorate God's promises (Gen 28:18). However, according to the biblical narrative, Jacob had vowed to change the memorial stone to a "house of God." Thus, the building of an altar where, until now, only a pillar stood is the fulfillment of Jacob's vow. Not clear, however, is why God had to instruct Jacob to erect the altar, which Jacob had vowed nearly 22 years earlier to build. The medieval commentators Rashi and Radak said that God commanded him to return there, implying he must fulfill the vow without delay because had he done it sooner he would not have been punished by the abduction of Dinah. Rashi says: "Since you delayed fulfillment of your vow, you were punished, and this came to you from your daughter." The fact that God roused him shows that Jacob was procrastinating. The word קום *qûm* (arise) indicates that God considered Jacob to be "sitting," i.e., delaying.

Jacob is credited with the construction of the two altars in Shechem and Bethel, so it is noteworthy that Abraham also built altars there. Upon his arrival, he built an altar in Shechem when God promised to give the land to his descendants (Gen 12:6–7). Following his travels, he built a second altar at Bethel (v. 8). Evidently, the mention of the construction of the two altars in Shechem and Bethel came to stress the sanctity of these places. Hence, not surprisingly, Moses commanded the Israelites to erect an altar upon their arrival there. Eventually, Joshua fulfilled this command (Josh 8:30). No doubt the existence of these traditions testifies to the sanctity of Shechem within the circle of the author who created them.

Sacrifice

Sacrifice is mentioned after the pact between Jacob and Laban (Gen 31:54). Jacob offers a sacrifice on the height, before sharing a meal with his kinsmen. There is no mention of an altar or a priest. This kind of offering was made where people camped. It has the characteristics of nomadic origin. The animal was taken from the flock, and it was not burnt but eaten by the person who offered it and his family. In the ancient world, treaty-making was sealed by a meal.[4] When a superior recognized the power of an inferior party, he would seek a treaty from the inferior. The two parties took

---

4. Exod 24:5–11; Deut 27:6–7.

an oath of non-aggression, which was sealed by eating a meal together.[5] Indeed, Gen 26:30 records a treaty between Isaac and Abimelech, followed by a feast that includes eating and drinking. Thus, Beno Jacob pointed out that the story of Jacob offering a sacrifice does not speak of a sacrifice, but of fraternization after peacemaking—a common meal uniting the two parties."[6] We should note that this peacemaking meal also had a religious element; each side swore by his own deity and called him to act as a judge if one of them violated the treaty.

The second time sacrifices are mentioned is when Jacob was on his way to Egypt. He stopped at Beer Sheba and offered sacrifices to the God of his father Isaac (Gen 46:1). Apart from Gen 31:54, this is the only case of the verb "to offer sacrifice" in the book of Genesis. It does not mention an altar, however, he probably used the altar that Isaac constructed (Gen 26:25). The sacrifices are termed as זבחים *zĕbāḥîm*. This type is different from "burnt offerings" because only a small part of the slaughtered animal was burned, while the larger part was eaten at a festive family or communal meal. It could be offered in making vows or as an act of thanksgiving, but here it has an additional meaning. Jacob offered his sacrifices before the Lord appeared to him, rather than afterward, which suggests that it might have been for the purpose of incubation. Incubation was a well-known phenomenon in the ancient world. The subject went to a sacred place, offered sacrifices to God, and fell asleep, hoping he would be visited by him in a dream. The content of the dream was supposed to provide advice and guidance. Jacob offered sacrifices and requested divine assistance; as a result, the Lord appeared to him and encouraged him. Indeed Josephus's description of the incident echoes this view:

> Halting at the Well of the Oath, he there offered sacrifice to God; and fearing that by reason of the prosperity prevalent in Egypt his sons would be so greatly enamored of settling there . . . and furthermore that having taken his departure into Egypt without God's sanction his race might be annihilated; yet terrified withal that he might quit this life before setting eyes on Joseph—these were the thoughts which he was revolving in his mind when he sank to sleep. Then God appeared to him and called him twice by name . . . Encouraged by this dream, Jacob with greater ardor departed for Egypt along with his sons and his son's children.[7]

5. McCarthy, "Three Covenants in Genesis," 182.
6. Jacob, *The First Book of the Bible*, 216.
7. Josephus, *Ant.* 2.170–76.

Stones

In the Jacob stories, one of the cultic motifs that is repeated is the setting up of pillars. In the morning after God appeared to him in a dream at Bethel, Jacob took the stone that had been under his head "and set it up as a pillar and poured oil on the top of it" (Gen 28:18). This is unlike Abraham and Isaac, who built altars in response to a theophany. The pillar was an upright piece of stone. In antiquity, there was widespread belief that the stones were the dwelling places of gods and spirits; the veneration of pillars may represent a survival of that belief. Later, stones symbolized the presence of the deity in a temple and afterward still served as a memorial to the deity's appearance in a particular place. These pillars became a symbol of Baal and were associated with the high places of Canaanite religion. Thus, the Bible condemns their use (Exod 34:13; Deut 7:5; 12:3; Hos 10:1; Mic 5:12).

In the older traditions of the patriarchs, the legitimacy of the pillars is not in question. The stone that was under Jacob's head marks the place of the encounter with God. It serves as a witness to Jacob's dream and to God's promises to him. Similarly, a pillar is used as a testimony to the pact between Jacob and Laban (Gen 31:45–54). A large stone also served as a memorial of the covenant between Israel and the Lord at Shechem (Josh 24:27).[8] When Laban made a pact with Jacob, he instructed his kinsman to gather stones and to make a mound. This is the only instance in the Hebrew Bible that a pile of stones served as part of a treaty agreement. Usually a pile of stones indicates that the space is a burial site and is useful for locating ruins of an ancient city.

In addition to setting up the pillar following his dream at Bethel, Jacob also poured oil on top of the stone. Skinner believes this is a trace of a primitive belief of stone worship, where the anointing of the stone was originally a sacrifice to the indwelling numen. He cites an example from Pausanias (x. 24. 6): "on a small stone in a sanctuary of Delphi oil was poured every day." Pouring oil over a stone is frequently associated with the consecration of cultic items (Exod 40:9–13; Lev 8:10–12; Num 7:1). Thus, it is not a witness, but it is a cult object endowed with divine powers and representing God himself.[9] However, the parallels to Pausanias's description are from a later period with a different religious matrix, so it is unwise to make any comparisons. More

---

8. See Skinner, *Genesis*, 378; Houtman, "What Did Jacob See?," 343. "Sacred Stones Sometimes Considered as the Dwelling of the God or even the God Himself," see Fitzmyer, *Aramaic Inscriptions*, 90.

9. Houtman, "What Did Jacob See," 343; Sommer, *Bodies of God*, 49–50.

likely, the pouring of oil over the stone signals a bond between Jacob and God. There is extensive evidence from the ancient Near East for the use of oil in international treaties. It served as a token of friendship and peace. In our story, it connects Jacob with a vow that he has to fulfill.

Jacob experienced a second theophany at Beth El when he returned to Canaan. He set up a stone pillar to commemorate the experience. This event also featured the offering of a libation and the pouring of oil upon the stone (Gen 35:14). It is not clear if this is a rededication of the pillar of 28:18 or the erection of a new one.[10] In contrast to the earlier story of Beth El, Jacob offers a libation. In the Hebrew Bible, a libation is a wine offering. This is the only time that a libation is mentioned in Genesis. The libation is poured on the pillar but not on the altar. In the ancient world, a libation was, at first, an offering for the dead, as it is attested among the Egyptians, Persians, Greeks, and Arabs.[11] However, it is not mentioned in the Hebrew Bible, though food offering is mentioned in Deut 26:14. Sarna suggests that we don't have a reduplication of the earlier ceremony of 28:18, but simply an added dimension. Hence, Jacob is "rehabilitating the original stela, which is now invested with new meaning."[12] To bolster his study, he points to an inscription about Sennacherib: "When the palace shall have become old and ruined, may some future prince restore its ruins, look upon the stele with my name inscribed [on it], anoint it with oil, pour out a libation upon it, and return it to its place."[13]

Contrary to Sarna's suggestion, however, the text presents Jacob as erecting a new stone pillar. The author knew about the Bethel story in Gen 28 but assumed the pillar that Jacob erected did not exist anymore. Thus, the pouring of oil has the same meaning as the rite in chapter 28; it came to establish a contractual bond between God and Jacob.[14]

In Gen 35:20, a different meaning for a pillar appears. In this instance, Jacob sets up a pillar over Rachel's grave, where the stone serves as a memorial marker. Much later, Absalom sets one up for himself, since he had no children (2 Sam 18:18). This use of stones as memorial markers survives until this day, as evidenced by the practice of people marking the graves of their loved ones with stones.

10. Sarna, *Understanding Genesis*, 242.
11. Skinner, *Genesis*, 424.
12. *Understanding Genesis*, 242.
13. Luckenbill, *Annals of Sennacherib*, 130.
14. Pagolu, *Religion of the Patriarchs*, 169.

As we have already mentioned, the setting up of pillars was forbidden later, and they were considered illegitimate (Deut 16:22). The last time that the Bible mentions the erection of pillars is with Moses, who sets up twelve at Mount Sinai (Exod 24:4). In this account, they symbolize the twelve tribes of Israel. It appears that the distinction between legitimate and idolatrous practices was difficult, therefore the pillars were outlawed.[15] Rashi noted: "Although [the pillar] was pleasing to Him in the days of the Patriarchs, now He hates it because it was made into idolatrous practice."

Vow

Another religious custom that is mentioned in the Jacob cycle is the taking of a vow. In the morning following his dream at Bethel, Jacob took a vow. His vow resembles others described in the Bible such as those of Jephthah the Gileadite (Judg 11:30–31), Hannah (1 Sam 1:11), and Absalom (2 Sam 16:8). In each case, someone makes a commitment that, if not fulfilled, will entail certain other actions on his/her part. The conditions of Jacob's vow is symmetrically parallel to his commitments. It should be emphasized, however, that Jacob's vow is unique because God has already promised him everything he is asking for (v. 15). The vow, which is a reaction to the verbal content of his dream, refers to the divine promises to him personally, but not to God's promises to the nations as a whole. Fokkelman, who noticed this, maintains that in general, the patriarchs do not respond to divine promises focused on the distant future.[16] The fact that Jacob's conditions were already promised to him by God was noted in *Genesis Rabbah*:

> R. Aibu and R. Jonathan disagree. One maintained that this passage is disarranged, while the other holds that it is all in order. The view that the account is disarranged [is based on the argument: God had already promised] *And, behold, I am with thee* (Gen 28:15), yet he actually said, If God will be with me! But how does he who holds that the narrative is in order explain If God will be with me? Jacob declared thus: If He will be with me, all the conditions which He stipulated being fulfilled, [then will I fulfil my vow].[17]

---

15. Tigay, *Deuteronomy*, 162.
16. Fokkelman, *Narrative Art in Genesis*, 75.
17. *Gen. Rab.* 70:4.

Two different explanations were given here: The first is that the events were disarranged—in other words, the theophany in v. 15 came in response to Jacob's vow in v. 20. The second explanation is that Jacob is pledging himself to complete certain actions after the promises are fulfilled, as an act of gratitude to God.

The Thigh Muscle

There is one religious prohibition from Jacob's time that has lasted to our day. The prohibition is against eating the thigh muscle. It is mentioned after the angel wrenches Jacob's hip at its socket. Nowhere else does the Hebrew Bible reference this, and it is not part of the later Jewish law. Evidently, this ancient custom existed among the Israelites, and the book of Genesis is giving an etiological explanation for it. Explaining the prohibition, the Talmud expounds: "It consists of two nerves, the inner, next the bones is forbidden and one is liable on account of it; the outer next to the flesh is forbidden but one is not liable on account of it."[18] A second view in the Talmud says: "The Torah forbade only the branch nerves of it."[19] Rashi interpreted it as only the nerves that branch from the main sciatic nerve are prohibited because they are tender and could give flavor into the substance it is cooked with. However, the actual sciatic nerve is hard like a wood and is not forbidden. The sciatic nerve must be removed and the Israelites are not allowed to eat it. According to Wenham, by avoiding eating the thigh muscle the Israelites were reminded of Jacob's encounter with God and the promise of ultimate victory and blessing he received from God.[20] It is possible that this part of the body was subject to a taboo because it was thought to belong to the reproductive area. The Hebrew word *nāšeh* has been associated with the Akk. *nišū* (people) and *nīšu* (life), Ugar. *nšm* (man), and the Heb. *'ĕnôš* (man). Therefore, it is believed that *gîd hannāšeh* refers to the membrum virile, the life-producing sinew.[21] Frazer has compared our story to a custom of an Indian tribe in America. The thigh muscle was removed and disposed of; it was not eaten because of the fear that if a man would eat this, it would harm the way he walks.[22]

18. *b. Ḥul.* 91a.
19. Ibid., 92b.
20. Wenham, *Genesis 16–50*, pp. 297–98.
21. Gevritz, "Of Patriarchs and Puns," 53.
22. Frazer, *Folklore in the Old Testament*, 2:423.

Prayer

Before the encounter with his brother Esau, Jacob turned to God in prayer (Gen 32:11–13). The prayer starts with an appeal to God. Jacob invokes the "God of my father Abraham, and God of my father Isaac, O Lord." Then he reminds God of his order, "Return to your country and to your kindred, and I will do you good." This is exactly what God told Jacob in 31:3. Jacob tells God that he is in this present situation because of his obedience. He then mentions what God has done for him, saying he is not worthy of all the mercies and faithfulness. The petition is preceded by self-deprecation. Similarly, Saul and David both expressed their unworthiness at their selection as king. Verse 12 is the heart of the petition, where Jacob asks "Please rescue me from my brother" so he will not kill the women and children. Jacob begs God to avert his brother's attack when he cites his fear of being annihilated. The prayer ends with a reminder about God's promise to be with him and to make his descendants numerous (28:14). This prayer is "a model of rhetoric—a principle of which is to persuade the one appealed to that his interests and one's own coincide."[23] It is also notable that this prayer lacks any confession of guilt. This corresponds well with the patriarchal era when there was no moral code. This ultimately changes in the covenant at Sinai.

The God of Israel and the Alien Gods

In the covenant between Jacob and Laban, it is Laban who invokes "the God of Abraham and the god of Nahor—their ancestral deities," saying, "Judge between us" (Gen 31:53). It was customary for each party in a non-aggression pact to swear by their own god. The gods were considered to be the guardians of the covenant. Interestingly, Laban invoked two gods, "the god(s) of Abraham and the god(s) of Nahor," which shows that he was a polytheist. Laban referred to the god of Terah, the father of both Abraham and Nahor. But as we know, Terah practiced polytheism. Jacob, on the other hand, swears by the fear of Isaac. It is noteworthy to mention that Laban was familiar with the god(s) of Abraham. This treaty between the two parties determined the boundaries between the two nations. According to Mazar, this covenant reflects the relationship between Aram and Israel before the

---

23. Greenberg, *Biblical Prose*, 14.

beginning of David's war against Aram–zobah—it reflects the early historic course of events.[24]

The first mention of tension between the God of Israel and that of alien gods appears in Jacob's return to Bethel.[25] Jacob orders the people of his household: "Rid yourself of the alien gods in your midst, purify yourself, and change your clothes" (Gen 35:2). The alien gods were probably part of the spoils found in Shechem or carried by the captives. It might be that they refer to the teraphim that Rachel stole from her father (31:19). Verse 4 mentions the "rings that were in their ears"— those objects, along with the alien gods, were buried. The rings were not ordinary pieces of jewelry; they were amulets, objects of superstition that were used in false worship (Hos 2:15; Judg 8:24).[26] Vawter believes that the author had in mind crescent earrings that symbolized moon worship in the ancient Near East.[27] Later, earrings were used for the making of idolatrous, cultic objects such as the golden calf and an ephod (Exod 32:2–4; Judg 8:24–27). The demand for the renunciation of the foreign gods and renewed devotion to God is also attested later in the biblical narrative (Josh 24:14, 23–24; Judg 10:16; 1 Sam 7:3–4). We have here the first step toward the idea that is expressed later in the Ten Commandments, "You shall have no other gods before me" (Exod 20:3).

Jacob does not destroy the foreign gods; instead he buries them. According to the Talmud, one is required to pulverize or scatter idols to the wind or cast them into the sea.[28] Thus, the question is, what is the significance of burying the idols? Several proposals have been raised, such as that it is a black-magic ritual of internment of guardian figurines.[29] Another proposal is that it is not burial that is portrayed, but a setting aside of the religious figurines in preparation for a holy war in which the terror of God will be used against the enemy.[30] An alternative option is that the act of burial meant the forsaking of the father gods. Gunkel pointed to the Greek tradition where the buried statues were directed toward the land of the enemies to repel the attack. Similarly, in our story, the buried idols intended

---

24. Mazar, "The Historical Background of the Book of Genesis" 78–79.
25. Sarna, *Understanding Genesis*, 239.
26. Skinner, *Genesis*, 423.
27. Vawter, *On Genesis*, 362.
28. *b. 'Avod. Zar.* 43b and 51b.
29. Nielsen, "The Burial of Foreign Gods," 103–22.
30. Keel, "Das Vergraben der 'Fremden Götter,'" 305–36.

to repel the attack of the Canaanites.³¹ Sarna suggests a different interpretation: "the internment of the idols intact under the tree may be an intention to neutralize veneration of the terebinth."³²

We should point out that the biblical narrator used the verb טָמַן *ṭāman* and not קָבַר *qābar* to describe the burial of foreign gods. This is not a coincidence, because *ṭāman* appears with the meaning "hide by burying."³³ Therefore, when Moses covers the body of the Egyptian with sand, his aim was not to bury the corpse but to hide it. Similarly, in Job 3:16, Job wishes he were like *nēpel ṭāmûn* (a buried stillbirth); the miscarriage is not so much buried as hidden in shame. Not surprisingly, the narrator did not use the verb *qābar*, which has the connotation of honorary burial and instead used *ṭāman*, which has the meaning of "hide by burying." Indeed, later in verse 8, we read about the death of Deborah, Rebecca's nurse. There, the narrator used the verb *qābar* to describe her burial.

At first glance, it is not clear if the removal of the alien gods, the command to purify, and the change of clothes belong together. Ramban (Rabbi Moses ben Naḥman, known as Naḥmanides, 1194–1270) pointed out that immersion and changing of clothes were not required for the purification because the idolatrous aspects of these items had been annulled; thus, burial was sufficient for them. However, it is possible that the contact with the alien gods caused pollution; therefore, those acts were necessary. It is noteworthy that in many ancient world religions, the ritual of purification and change of clothing came before a cultic act. Indeed, purification appears in preparation for an experience with God (Exod 19:10) and also before the crossing of the Jordan (Josh 3:5). Similar conditions appear in Genesis 35, where the Israelites had just entered the land of Canaan and were on the verge of meeting God. Those circumstances required a change. This was manifested with the burying of alien gods, purification, and the changing of clothes.

The purification rite of Bethel serves as a response to the defilement mentioned in chapter 34, which is dominated by the theme of defilement. Thus, one of the key words in the chapter is defile (טמא), which appears in vv. 5, 13, 27. In contrast, chapter 35 starts with the subject of purification. Therefore, we find the word purify (טהר) in verse 2. The pairing of the terms "defile" and "purify" appears in the biblical narrative in ritual

---

31. Gunkel, *Genesis*, 367.
32. Sarna, *Understanding Genesis*, 240.
33. Kellerman, "טָמַן" 5:342–44.

prescription (Lev 11:47; 20:25). Interestingly, the term "purify" appears only in the patriarchal narrative here with Jacob. Before, it appeared in the flood narrative in Gen 7:2, 8; 8:20.

The burial of foreign gods by Jacob is very similar to the story of the covenant Joshua made with the Israelites at Shechem. Therefore, in Gen 35:2 we read, "Rid yourselves of the alien gods in your midst"; in Joshua, "Then put away the alien gods that you have among you" (Josh 24:23). The command "Rid yourselves" appears elsewhere only in a Deuteronomistic context (Josh 24:14, 23; Judg 10:16; 1 Sam 7:3). Similarly, it is also found in the concealment of an object under the tree—in Genesis we read, "Jacob buried them under the terebinth that was near Shechem" (Gen 35:4), while in Joshua, "He took a great stone and set it up at the foot of the oak in the sacred precinct of the Lord" (Josh 24:26). The message of the author of Genesis is that the place that the Israelites thought as a legitimate temple of God (Josh 24:26) is no other than a defiled contaminated place.[34] What was buried under the oak tree were foreign gods that Jacob buried; therefore, the place was not holy. The negative aspect of the concealment of the foreign gods is also prevalent in the LXX, which added, "and he destroyed even to this day." In other words, the place is still contaminated. It appears the author wanted to convey that Shechem is an illegitimate place while glorifying Bethel.[35] This anti-Shechem tradition was later used by the Rabbis against the Samaritans for whom Shechem was the holiest city:

> R. Ishmael son of R. Yossi went up to pray in Jerusalem. He passed a terebinth grove and was seen by a Samaritan who asked him, "Where are you going?" He said: "To go up to worship in Jerusalem." He said: "Would it not be better to pray at this blessed mountain than at that dunghill?" He said: "I will tell you what you resemble, a dog eager for carrion. Because you know that idols are hidden beneath it, for it is written, 'And Jacob hid them,' therefore you are eager for it . . ." (*Gen. Rab.* 81:3)

The negative view of Shechem is also mentioned when Joseph was sent to look for his brothers who were at Shechem at the time. According to the midrash, "'he arrived to Shechem' (Gen 37:14), a place marked for wrongdoing. In Shechem they abused Dinah, in Shechem they sold Joseph, in

---

34. The story in the book of Genesis was used also by the sages in their polemics against the Samaritans and their belief in the sacredness of Shechem. See *Gen. Rab.* 81:3.

35. Zakovitch, *Jacob*, 132.

Shechem was divided the kingdom of the House of David, 'Jeroboam fortified Shechem in the hill country of Ephraim . . .'" (1 Kgs 12:25).[36]

God in the Jacob Cycle

When Jacob spoke about his God, he referred to him by different titles. Besides Yahweh and Elohim, he uses other names such as: El Shaddai (Gen 28:3; 35:11; 43:14; 48:3; 49:25) *El Elohei Israel (33:20)*; El-Bethel (31:13; 35:7); "Mighty One of Jacob"(49:24); In addition, the phrase "God of your father" with the name of the patriarch appears in Jacob's dream at Bethel: "I am the Lord, the God of your father Abraham and the God of Isaac"(28:13). Hence, the question that needs to be raised here is: was Jacob a true monotheist, or can we say that he worshipped different deities, which means he was a polytheist?

In the patriarchal narrative, there are several names or appellations of a deity beginning with the element ʾēl. The term *El* appears to be the general appellative meaning "god, deity." The meaning of the name is "to be strong" or "to be preeminent." The mention of the different *ēlîm* in Genesis points to an earlier phase of worshipping God. When the first Hebrews moved into Canaan, they found altars and sanctuaries where El was worshiped. Since El had many traits in common with their own clan deity, they identified him with their own God. Indeed, Genesis shows that the characteristics of the biblical El are very similar to those of El in the Canaanite epics from Ugarit. We believe that the Canaanite El was assimilated into the biblical concept of God at an early stage in the patriarchal narrative.

Since this fusion between El and Yahweh took place at an early stage, this is the reason why there is nothing negative about El, even though he was worshipped by the Canaanites. Conversely, Baal, the Canaanite god of storm and fertility, is condemned time after time in the Hebrew Bible. Baal is the chief rival of Yahweh who led the Israelites astray from their covenant with God.

In Gen 33:20, Jacob builds an altar in Shechem and calls it El Elohei Israel; the narrator evidently identifies this El with Yahweh. While Exodus indicates, "I appeared to Abraham, to Isaac, to Jacob as El Shaddai, but by my name Yahweh I was not known to them" (6:3). According to the book of Exodus, the patriarchs knew God mainly as El Shaddai. El Shaddai is the most common name constructed with the initial *ēl*. The epithet

---

36. *Tanḥ.* (Buber), *Vayeshev* 2.

Šaddai appears alone or in combination with *ēl*. The term El Shaddai appears mostly in poetic texts, which testifies to its antiquity, since Hebrew poetry tends to preserve early forms of the language.[37] The term appears several times in the Jacob cycle (Gen 28:3; 35:11; 43:14; 48:3; 49:25). The sages interpreted the name *Šaddai* as a combination of particle *ša* with *dai*, meaning "sufficiency."[38] Modern scholars connect it with the Akkadian *šadû* (mountain), frequently used as a divine appellation. Hence, the name meant "The One of the Mountain," corresponding to the divine epithet "The Rock."

The expression "El Bethel" appears twice in Genesis. When Jacob recounts to his wives his dream about the rams who are mounting the sheep, he says that the angel of God told him, "I am the God of Bethel, where you anointed a pillar" (Gen 31:13). In the account of his return to Canaan from Padan Aram we read: "There he built an altar and named the site El-Bethel" (35:7).

The question is whether the expression "El Bethel" should be taken as alluding to a Canaanite deity worshipped under the name "Bethel."[39] There is, in fact, abundant evidence for the cult of a deity named Bethel, whose name was derived from the holy site. In Jer 48:13, for example, the prophet parallels the Moabite deity Chemosh with Bethel. The verse indicates that the Israelites prayed to that deity. In a treaty between the Assyrian king, Esarhaddon, and King Baal of Tyre from the seventh century BCE, in which the gods are called upon to curse anyone who violates the pact, Bethel appears among the list of deities invoked.[40] As a theophoric element, it is also found in personal names in Babylonia from the time of Nebuchadnezzar to that of Darius II. Later, around the year 400 BCE, the Jews of Elephantine in Egypt were familiar with deities like Eshem-Bethel, Herm-Bethel, and Anath-Bethel.[41] Among their personal names are Beth-el-Nathan, Bethel-Aqob, and so on. In Ugaritic texts, the expression *bt il*

---

37. Sarna, *Exploring Exodus*, 51.

38. Gen. Rab. 46:2.

39. Gen 28:17, 22; 32:20; 1 Sam 10:3; Amos 3:14, 5:5; Hos 10:8, 15; and Zech 7:12. In the last of these we should read it as a personal name. See Hyatt, "A Neo-Babylonian Parallel," 387–94.

40. See "Treaty of Esarhaddon with Baal of Tyre," in *ANET*, 534: "May Bethel and Anath-Bethel deliver you to a man-eating lion." See also Hyatt, "Deity Bethel," 82.

41. Hyatt, "Deity Bethel," 84–85. According to Hyatt, Eshem-Bethel, Herm-Bethel, and Anath-Bethel are to be taken as names of double deities.

appears a number of times, but in several places it is clear that the meaning is merely "the house of El."

Whether it is ever the name of a particular deity is a matter of scholarly debate.[42] Additional evidence has been uncovered in the Greco-Syrian text from the dedication of an oil press in 223 CE, found at Kfar Nebo. It includes the name of a god named *Sumbétylos* along with two other gods.[43] Hence, there is no doubt that the Semitic pantheon in general, and the Canaanite pantheon in particular, included a deity known as Bethel. We may conjecture that it was the veneration for temples that led people to consider the sanctuaries to be deities in their own right. The house of the father of the gods, El, was a prime example.

On the basis of this evidence, some scholars have hypothesized that Gen 31:13 refers to a deity called "Bethel" and indicates that the cult of this god existed among the Israelites' ancestors. Accordingly, they have emended the text to read, "I am the God El-Bethel,"[44] or "the god *who appeared to you* in Bethel."[45]

We should note, however, that the divine name used in the story of Jacob's dream at Bethel is "Elohim" or "Elohei (the god of) your father." In addition, the idea that Bethel is the name of a god can be rejected because the relative adverb "where" occurs twice in Gen 31:13: "I am the God [of] Bethel, *where* you anointed a pillar and *where* you made a vow to Me," proving that "Bethel" is the name of a place. Noteworthily, El Bethel (31:13; 35:7) and El Elohei-Israel (Gen 33:20) are connected to certain locales—*El Bethel* to Bethel, and *El Elohei-Israel* to the vicinity of Shechem. On the other hand, *El Shaddai* does not correspond to a place.

The patriarchs also worshiped a personal god. Each patriarch had personal ties with that God—"the god of Abraham"[46] (Gen 28:13; 31:42, 53), the "Fear of Isaac" (31:42; 53), and "Mighty One of Jacob" (49:24).[47]

42. Ibid., 87; Albright, "North-Canaanite Poems," 136; Ginsberg, *Ugaritic Texts*, 82. In contrast, see Pope, *El in the Ugaritic Texts*, 59, who denies any reference to Bethel in the Ugaritic pantheon.

43. Hyatt, "Deity Bethel," 86.

44. Ibn Ezra, Kimḥi, Luzzatto.

45. See the Aramaic versions and the Septuagint; the same approach is followed by Skinner, Speiser, and Westermann in their commentaries on the verse.

46. It was suggested that the name was "the Shield of Abraham" on the basis of Gen 15:1. See Hyatt, "Yahweh as 'The God of My Father,'" 130.

47. "Mighty One of Jacob" appears elsewhere only four times and in poetic text (Isa 49:26; 60:16; Ps 13:2, 5; Isa 1:24).

The "Mighty One of Jacob" is similar to the Akkadian divine title *bēl abāri* (endowed with strength). It symbolized protection and security for the community that is identified with Jacob, the same way the "Fear of Isaac" represented assurance and protection for the community that bore Isaac's name. God was the patron deity of the clan. Therefore, when Laban and Jacob formed a pact, each side invoked his own deity. Laban swore by the God of Nahor, while Jacob by the Fear of Isaac. Alt suggested that the patriarchal gods did not bear their own names but were named for their cult founder. To bolster his claims, Alt pointed to the Nabatean and Palmyrean inscriptions from the first century BCE to the fourth century CE. The inscriptions describe nomadic people who worshipped "the god of *x*," where *x* was the name of the founder of the cult. However, we should note that the patriarchal period is too remote from the Nabatean period to make a valid comparison. Alt further says that the cults of theses deities were restricted to certain locals and sanctuaries. He concluded that the cult of the "Mighty One of Jacob," was worshipped among the tribe of Joseph, "the Fear of Isaac" among the tribes of Judah and Simeon, and "the god of Abraham" in the clan of Caleb and the tribe of Judah. But as noted by scholars, there is no basis for this theory.[48] Later, these deities were morphed by the literary editors into the God of Israel. Their epithets disappeared and they are found under names such as "the God of your fathers," and "the God of Abraham, Isaac and Jacob."

The phrase "the God of [my/your/his] Father," with the names of the patriarchs, points to the close relationship between the patriarch and God. This epithet is used when God appeared to Isaac, "I am the God of your father Abraham" (26:24), and to Jacob in his dream at Bethel, "I am the Lord, the God of your father Abraham and the God of Isaac" (28:13). This formula is also mentioned in God's revelation to Moses: "I am, he said, the God of your father, the God of Abraham, the God of Isaac, and the God of Jacob" (Exod 3:6). The use of the formula here comes to stress continuity between the patriarchs and Moses. There are some instances where the formula "the God of [my/your] father" is mentioned without the name of the patriarch (Gen 31:5, 29; 43:23; 46:3; 49:26). Lewy was the first to point out that the phrase "God of the father" was well known in the ancient Near East over a long period, from the nineteenth century BCE on.[49] Evidently,

---

48. Haran, "Religion of the Patriarchs," 51 no. 34; Wenham, "Religion of the Patriarchs," 172–73.

49. Lewy, "Les textes paléo-assyriens," 29–65.

the phrase, "the God of [my/your/his] Father," which is attested in the patriarchal narrative and in the ancient Near East, came to indicate the close relationship between the individual and his god, who was his patron and protector. It was typical for a nomadic society to look for an intimate god who would guide and protect them.

We have to remember that when the patriarchs and the first Israelites came to Canaan they made "the language of Canaan" their own (Isa 19:8). Thus, not surprisingly, the terms that they used to describe their God were similar to that of the Canaanites. For the sages, the ancestors of Israel were true monotheists. Most telling is a midrash that grapples with the different names of God. According to this midrash, the different names of God point to different attributes of God:

> R. Abba. b. Mammel said: God said to Moses: 'Thou wishest to know My name. Well, I am called according to My work; sometimes I am called "Almighty God", "Lord of Hosts", "God", "Lord". When I am judging created beings, I am called "God", and when I am waging war against the wicked; I am called the Lord of Hosts." When I suspend judgment for man's sins, I am called "El Shadday" (Almighty God), and when I am merciful towards My world, I am called "Adonai" for "Adonai" refers to the attribute of Mercy, as it is said: The Lord, the Lord (Adonai, Adonai), God, merciful and gracious.[50]

In conclusion, examination of the Jacob cycle shows no regular patterns of worship. A liturgical calendar and specific places for worship did not exist yet. Religion developed as a reaction to a developing situation. There were no temples and no priests. Instead, Jacob, like the previous patriarchs, built altars to God as a form of worship and invoked his name. Sacrifices are mentioned as a form of fraternization after peacemaking, such as sharing a meal. One instance mentions sacrifice as a part of dream incubation. Prayers are a simple, spontaneous outpouring of the heart and are not connected to a site or a cult. They were individual and tailored for a specific purpose. In the Jacob stories, one of the cultic motifs that is repeated is the setting up of pillars. It served as a witness to Jacob's dream as well as God's promises to him. Another occasion uses a pillar as a testimony to the pact between Jacob and Laban (Gen 31:45–54). Grave markers are yet another example of the usage of pillars. In later periods, the setting up of pillars was forbidden and they were considered illegitimate (Deut 16:22).

50. *Exod. Rab.* 3:6.

Religious Practices in the Jacob Cycle

There is one religious prohibition from Jacob's time that has lasted to our day. The prohibition is to not eat the thigh muscle. Nowhere else in the Hebrew Bible is this mentioned, and it is not part of the later Jewish law. In other words this is an ancient custom that existed among the Israelites only.

The first mention of tension between the God of Israel and that of alien gods appears in Jacob's return to Bethel. Jacob orders the people of his household, "Rid yourself of the alien gods in your midst, purify yourself, and change your clothes" (Gen 35:2). The different divine names do not point to different gods worshiped by Jacob. On the contrary, the different names for God point to different attributes of God. Since the Canaanite god El had many traits in common with their own clan deity, the patriarchs identified him with their own God. The Canaanite El was assimilated into the biblical concept of God at an early stage in the patriarchal narrative.

The difference of beliefs between the Israelites and their neighbors will become more apparent only after the covenant at Sinai. From that point on, Israelites inhabit one side of the world, with Gentiles on the other side. The religious customs in the Jacob cycle point to a distantly primitive stage of Israelite religion, which was similar to the Israelites' neighbors'. In the Jacob's stories we have the first steps toward monotheism, which developed fully only after Israel received its laws and commandments.

Continuing with the theme of God in the Jacob cycle, in the next chapter we will examine the appearance of angels and the story of Jacob wrestling with the angel of God.

5

Angels

ONE OF THE CHARACTERISTICS of Jacob's stories is the appearance of angels. The angels appear at important junctures in Jacob's life. First, in Jacob's dream at Bethel, the angels are going up and down on the stairway (Gen 28:12). Angels are also mentioned in Jacob's return from Laban's house: "Jacob went on his way, and the angels of God encountered him" (32:2). In Laban's house, an angel of the Lord appeared to Jacob in a dream. Finally, on the eve of his meeting with his brother Esau, he had a wrestling encounter with an angel. So what do we know about angels, and what is their function in the Jacob cycle? What's behind Jacob wrestling with the mysterious assailant who wrestles with him until daybreak when, in the end, he wrenches Jacob's hip? Who was the mysterious assailant, and what was the purpose of the story? The prophet Hosea repeats the story of Jacob wrestling with an angel—how different is this version?

Angelology in the Hebrew Bible

Stories about angels' appearances to humans are typical of the patriarchal narrative and of the judges' period. Indeed, one of the characteristics of the Jacob cycle is his encounters with angels. When the Bible needs to describe divine encounters with humans in a dramatic fashion, it uses angels. After the period of the judges, the appearance of angels diminishes. The last person who received a revelation from an angel was the prophet Elijah. With the development of classical prophecy, the prophet came instead of the angel. Only later, in prophetic vision, do we again encounter not only angels, but a new type of angels. The angels no longer appear to humans, but are seen in visions. The Hebrew word for an angel is *mal'āk*, derived from the stem *l-'-k* (to send). In Genesis, it is also used for ordinary humans (32:4). Later, a prophet or a priest might also be called "an angel of the Lord" (Hag 1:13; Mal 2:7). There is not much we know about them. They are nameless, they have no individuality or free will, and no hierarchy exists among them. Their main function is to deliver God's words—to be emissaries. In Israel, as in the ancient Near East, the angels were part of the royal court. Yahweh was envisioned as a king, and the angels served in his royal court (Gen 32:1–2). There are incidents where angels are perceived in human form; therefore, the people to whom they appear are not aware of their divine presence. Abraham's three visitors are described as "men" (Gen 18:1, 16, 22; 19:5, 10, 12, 16). Later, they are described as angels (19:1, 15), but the people of Sodom perceived them to be human (19:5, 9). A similar incident is described in the Samson story where an angel of the Lord appears to Samson's mother. She describes him as a man of God who "looked like an angel of God, very frightening" (Judg 13:6). Her husband, Manoah, does not recognize him as an angel at first, but only after he disappears in flames on the altar (vv. 20–21).

There are some texts where the distinction between God and the angels is not clear. In some narratives, the angel appears to be a distinct figure, but later in the narrative, it appears as though it is Yahweh and not an angel. The angel speaks to Hagar (Gen 16:7–8, 9, 11), but Hagar in return responds to God (v. 13). The same is true in the story of the binding of Isaac. God commanded the sacrifice of Isaac; however, later Abraham is addressed by the angel of the Lord from heaven (Gen 22:1–2, 11–18). The angel of the Lord appears to Moses in the burning bush (Exod 3:2), but Moses speaks directly with God throughout the rest of the story. In the Exodus story, it is first God who leads the Israelites (13:21), then it is his angel (14:9). So, too, in the Gideon story: Gideon sometimes speaks with God and sometimes with the angel (Judg 6:11–23). From this, scholars infer that the angel was not an independent being, but a manifestation of divine power and will. Since the angel is partly identified with God, he is his messenger; therefore, he uses God's name while speaking. Another possibility is that the phrase "angel of God" is an addition. At first, only the name of God appeared in the stories, but the fear that the stories would be perceived as too corporeal caused the addition of the phrase "angel of the Lord." However, since this was not done consistently, there are difficulties. Indeed, this view was held by the Maghārrīya—a Jewish sect that flourished in Egypt—and by the Karaites. Accordingly, all the anthropomorphic passages in the Bible are referring to angels, rather than to God. More so, it was an angel who created the world and addressed the prophets.

In the Jacob cycle, we read about encounters with angels. However, it is not clear what the angels' roles are in these encounters. In Jacob's dream at Bethel, the angels are going up and down on the stairway (Gen 28:12). The angels don't have any role in the dream. The ladder and angels are only stage props, whose main function is to lead up to the climax—the appearance of the Lord. Perhaps the angels are scouting out the land and then returning to heaven to report to God. Or, perhaps they represent Jacob's hopes and fears and his prayers that the Lord will protect him. These prayers ascend to heaven where they are answered. Rashi, on the other hand, tries to explain why the angels ascended first and then descended. According to his interpretation, "The angels that accompanied him in the land (of Israel), do not go outside of the land, and they ascended to the heavens. Then descended the angels of outside the land to accompany him."

Angels are also mentioned upon Jacob's return from Laban's house: "Jacob went on his way, and the angels of God encountered him" (32:2). How Jacob saw them—in a vision, in a dream, or face to face—we are not told. It appears that Jacob's journeys are marked by the appearance of angels, on his way out of Canaan as well as on his return. This suggests that they accompanied Jacob during his travels. It is possible that their presence points to divine protection, which is mentioned in Ps 91:9–11: "Because you took the Lord—my refuge / the Most High—as your heaven / no harm will befall you / no disease touch your tent / For He will order His angels / to guard you wherever you go." The divine messengers encounter Jacob, but they do not say anything to him. This encounter with the angels is similar to Jacob's experience at Bethel. Both speak of the meeting as an encounter (*pāgaʻ*), and both mention "angels of God." Both deal with the departure and entry to the land of Canaan. In both incidents, the name of the place is changed because of Jacob's experience there. In the first encounter, Jacob changes the name to Bethel, and in the second encounter, to Mahanaim.

Jacob named the place "God's camp," Mahanaim.[1] Houtman pointed out that the word "camp" conveys a temporary settlement in contrast to the permanent, stable "house of God" at Bethel.[2] The Hebrew word means "two

---

1. The place Mahanaim appears prominently in later Israelite history. It was one of the Levitical cities of refuge. Ish-boshet the son of King Saul ruled over Israel from there (2 Sam 2:8). Fleeing from his son Absalom, David found refuge there (17:24–29). In Solomon's day it was a district capital.

2. Houtman, "Jacob at Mahanaim," 39.

camps"—so why two? It is possible that an allusion was made to the camp of messengers and the camp of Jacob. According to Rashi: "(Mahanaim is to be interpreted as the dual form, i.e.,) two camps, (one) outside of the land (of Israel), that came with him until here, (and the other) of the land of Israel that came toward him." However, Jacob had still not reached the land of Israel, and he was, in fact, far away from there. Hence, Ramban, in his interpretation, suggested that the place is called Mahanaim, in the dual form, because it is common in proper names to have a plural ending.[3] Alternatively, it is possible that the place named Mahanaim is foreshadowing the future when, in verses 8–9, Jacob divides his family and flock into two camps to avert total distraction and to minimize his loss. More so, it is possible that Mahanaim is derived from *minḥâ* (tribute); thus, again it serves as a hint about the future encounter between Jacob and Esau.

Jacob's encounters with the angels, the heavenly messengers, served as communication channels between heaven and earth. Their presences came to protect Jacob and are the fulfillment of God's promise to Jacob: "Remember, I am with you: I will protect you wherever you go and will bring you back to this land" (Gen 28:15). The encounter at Mahanaim served as a reminder of God's promises to Jacob to protect him. This meeting at Mahanaim is a prelude to the approaching meeting with Esau, as it came to encourage Jacob. The patriarch should not be afraid; he can depend on God. Indeed, following the encounter, Jacob appears to be encouraged. He takes the initiative and sends messengers (*mal'ākîm*) to contact his brother Esau. Interestingly, the Hebrew word for messengers is the same word used for angels.

Wrestling with an Angel

A third encounter with an angel is recorded in Gen 32. Jacob is on the eve of his meeting with his brother, Esau, and he is seized with fear. He prays to God and asks him to save him from his brother, Esau. Jacob is afraid that his brother will come and strike him down with all his family. Thus, he reminds God of his promises of posterity—promises that still need to be redeemed. In order to soften the possibility of hostility from his brother and to propitiate him, he sent him a gift that as an expression of friendship and subordination. The gift included 550 beasts. Another measure that Jacob

---

3. See for example: Yerushalaim (Esth 2:6); Mizraim (Gen 10:6); Kittim (10:4); Hushim (46:23).

took was to transfer his family and all his belongings to the other side of the river. The crossing of the river took place at night. Why Jacob did this at night is not clear. More so, why did Jacob return alone to the other side of the river with this family staying behind? If Jacob did it out of concern for their safety, why does he leave them without protection? Was Jacob afraid for his life, so he left his family as a shield between himself and Esau? It was suggested that his irrational behavior represents his disturbed state of mind. Jacob was afraid and worried. He could not sleep, so he decided to press on.[4] Another possibility is that Jacob crossed the river with all his family to be closer to Esau's path. By doing so, he wanted to take advantage of the immediate psychological advantage gained from Esau receiving the gifts. He wanted to create the impression that he was on his way to meet his brother Esau—not that he was trying to avoid meeting him.

A different interpretation explains why Jacob was left alone by reading לכדו (for his jar) instead of לבדו (by himself). According to Rashi, "He forgot small jars and returned for them." Similarly, in the Talmud we read, "R. Elazar said: For he remained behind on the account of some small jars."[5] Evidently, the vessels were used for drinking. Jacob was concerned that his young children should have a chance to drink from them on the journey.

Jacob is left alone. He is separated from his camp and suddenly finds himself wrestling with a man. Jacob is attacked by a man and has to fight for his life. There is wordplay here in the proper names, Jacob (*yaʿăqōb*) and the river Jabbok (*yabbōq*). In addition, there is a wordplay with the Hebrew word "to wrestle," which comes from the root *ʾ-b-q*, and the name of the river, *yabbōq*. Another interpretation, which is found in the midrash, derived *wayyēʾābēq* (he wrestled) from *ʾābāq* (dust). The men were engaged in wrestling, kicking up the dust, and when thrown, they rolled in the dust. Therefore, the midrash translates: "who was covered with dust? The man who (strove) with him."[6]

The mysterious assailant who attacked Jacob is called *man* at first, then *ĕlōhîm* (Gen 32:24, 28, 30); however, Hosea refers to him as an angel (Hos 12:4). Sommer argues that "an angel and the God Yhwh could overlap or . . . a small-scale manifestation or fragment of Yhwh can be termed *malʾakh*."[7] When the dawn broke, the mysterious attacker asked Jacob to

---

4. Wenham, *Genesis 16–50*, p. 292.
5. b. Ḥul. 91a.
6. Gen. Rab. 77:3.
7. Sommer, *Bodies of God*, 41.

let go. Why did the man demand this from Jacob? It has been suggested that it was a demon whose powers evaporated at dawn.[8] Night in the Hebrew Bible is associated with evil and death; therefore, the plague that was inflicted on the firstborn in Egypt took place at night (Exod 12:13, 23, 29). The midrash has a different interpretation, according to which the angel wanted to be in time to sing with a heavenly choir. A similar request was made by Jupiter: "Why do you hold me? It is time. I want to get out of the city before daybreak."[9]

Commentators such as Rashbam, Hizkuni (Hezekiah ben Rabbi Manoah, mid-thirteenth century), and Abravanel suggested that when the man asked to leave, this indicates that he wanted to conceal his identity. It is also possible that this alludes to the idea that no man can see God and remain alive (Exod 33:20). Evidently, the man could not overcome Jacob. Jacob's herculean strength was mentioned already when he removed the stone from the mouth of the well. The shepherds could not do it by themselves. Similarly, here, the man himself could not overcome Jacob. To avoid defeat, the man wrenched Jacob's hip at its socket—literally, the "hollow of his thigh." Still, Jacob refused to release the adversary, despite having been injured. As dawn was breaking, Jacob realized the divine nature of his adversary. He requested to be blessed. The man asks Jacob's name, since to bless a person, one needs to know the name of the person whom he is blessing. This is a rhetorical question since the man knew with whom he fought. In divulging his name, Jacob discloses his character. The name Jacob is associated with deceit and deception.

The mysterious assailant changed Jacob's name to Israel. By changing the name, it signals a new beginning and is a form of blessing. It changes the fate of the bearer of the new name. The name Jacob, as mentioned, had a negative connotation and was associated with deceit and lies. Now Jacob is on the eve of his entrance to the land of Canaan as the father of the twelve tribes-to-be and the father of the future nation of Israel. Thus, he needed a change—a new name, which indicates a new beginning. This was noted by Rashi, who says, "It will no longer be said that the blessing came to you through deviousness ['oqbâ—a Hebrew word that means crookedness and shares its radicals with the name Jacob] but instead through lordliness [śĕrārâ—an Aramaic word, the root of which can be taken out of the name Israel] and openness." Although Jacob's name is changed to Israel, the

---

8. McKenzie, "Jacob at Peniel," 73.
9. Plautus, *Amphitryon*, 532–33.

narrative continues to refer to the patriarch as Jacob. In other words, the name Israel becomes synonymous with Jacob. Therefore, the correct translation of Gen 35:10 should be, "your name will no longer be Jacob exclusively, but your name will (also) be Israel." Indeed, this is what the prophet Isaiah said: "Listen to Me, O Jacob, Israel, whom I have called" (48:12).

In the biblical text, the new name Israel is explained as a wordplay on the verb "to struggle, fight." In other words, Jacob struggled with God and man and succeeded. The same meaning occurs in Hos 12:4, where the prophet refers to Jacob, saying, "he strove with God." The ancient translations interpreted the verb in a different way. According to the LXX, Vulgate, and Peshitta, it derives from *śārar* "to rule." Thus, it seems that the name Israel means "El will rule." Another interpretation, which is found in Ramban's commentary on Deut 2:10 and 7:12, explains the name as "He who is upright with God." The epithet "Jeshurun"—Hebrew *yĕšurûn* (the upright), from *yāšār* (upright)—alludes to Israel in Deuteronomy (32:15; 33:15, 26) and Isaiah (9:5, 6).

The name Israel in the Bible is associated with struggle and triumph. Documents outside of the Bible attest to Israel prevailing against the odds. In the victory hymn of King Merneptah of Egypt (ca. 1207 BCE), it reports that "Israel is laid waste, his seed is not." The second document, the victory inscription of King Mesha of Moab (ca. 830 BCE), declares, "Israel has perished forever."

Following the change of his name, Jacob asks the mysterious assailant for his name. Earlier, it was the angel who asked Jacob a rhetorical question—"What is your name?" Now it is Jacob's turn to inquire as to the identity of the man—"Pray tell me your name!" Before the Babylonian exile, all the angels are anonymous. They are mentioned by name only later in the book of Daniel. This was because of the fear that they would become objects of worship. A similar story is mentioned in Judg 13:17–18. When Samson's father, Manoah, tried to discover the identity of the divine being, he said to him: "Why do you ask my name, seeing it is wonderful?" (Judg 13:17–18). In both instances, Jacob and Manoah are rebuffed, which leads them to the realization of the identity of the mysterious man.

Jacob names the place Peniel, which literally means "Face of God." Jacob refers to the event by saying that he saw a divine being "face to face." The expression "face to face" is used in the Bible to describe divine-human encounters. Although the struggle took place at night, Jacob still was able to see the divine being "face to face." Until now, the main point was on the wrestling, which took place at night; now the focus is on seeing the divinity. Despite having seen God, Jacob says that his life has been preserved. In Exodus (33:20), God tells Moses, "Man may not see Me and live!" In other words, man cannot understand the ultimate mystery of God; only a glimpse of divine reality is possible. When Moses saw the burning bush, he hid his face, "for he was afraid to look at God." Gideon and Manoah were afraid of dying after experiencing God's self-manifestation. What Jacob describes here was the intensity of the encounter with the divine presence.

Jacob wrestled with the divine being at night; now the sun rises upon him, which means a new day and a new life after a struggle. When Jacob left, fleeing, from his home, it was marked by the setting of the sun. Now with his return to the promised land, the radiance of the sun greets him as he is ready to enter.

In the midrash, we find the view that the mysterious assailant was the guardian prince (angel) of Esau.[10] The midrash tries to convey the idea that Jacob, before he overcame a "man" (Esau), defeated *ĕlohîm*, which is the angel who protected Esau. It was customary in ancient times for the two rivals to fight against each other before god; it was considered an ordeal. Similarly, we find rivalry between Rachel and Leah. When Rachel finally overcomes Leah, she uses similar language to that which Jacob used: "A fateful contest I waged with my sister; yes, and I have prevailed" (Gen 30:8).

The story of Jacob wrestling with a mysterious being evidently has several layers, which include mythical imagery. It has been suggested that originally the story was a tale about a hero who, before entering and possessing a new land, had to fight against a god or a demon who guarded the boundary of that land.[11] Many fairy tales from the ancient world tell of a god who is forced by humans through deceit, or who is forced to tell a secret of something divine. In the *Odyssey*, Menelaus held Proteus, the old man of the sea, until he revealed his knowledge to him.[12] King Numa seized Faunus and Picus Martius and obtained from them the rites and sacrifices that enabled him to entice Jupiter to come down to earth.[13] In another tale, Hercules challenged anyone to a wrestling match. No one dared, so Zeus came in human form and wrestled evenly with him until

---

10. *Gen. Rab.* 77:3, 78:6; *Song. Rab.* 3:6.
11. McKenzie, "Jacob at Peniel," 71–76.
12. Homer, *Od.* 4.380–390.
13. Cornell, *Fragments of the Roman Historians*, 2:548.

he revealed his identity to his son.[14] It appears that the story belongs to a very primitive form of Israelite belief. The story was refined later to suggest that the adversary was Yahweh. At the center stands Jacob, who is on the eve of meeting his brother Esau. The story is a reflection of Jacob's life and his struggles with people and God.[15] The "man" with whom Jacob struggles with symbolized Esau, Isaac, and Laban. The "man" in the beginning and the end of the story is also God. Jacob faces a moral crisis: he has to face his brother, whom he has deceived. He goes to meet his brother, not as a victor, but as a humble man who limps as a result of his fight. His brother, Esau, is also portrayed sympathetically, as he runs to embrace Jacob and kisses him. The story is a combination of psychological and theological elements. Jacob will enter the promised land as the father of the Hebrew nation. Since his old name Jacob is connected to deceit, his name is changed to Israel. It is a new beginning for the father of the Hebrew nation. Not surprisingly, fear seizes him with all the thoughts of deception and struggle surfacing at this crucial moment.

Bethel and Peniel

There are many similarities between the Bethel story and the Peniel story. Both stories occurred at night—first Jacob's dream at Bethel, and second the wrestling with the mysterious assailant at Peniel. God always revealed himself to Jacob at night. Fear seized Jacob after the dream at Bethel and before his encounter at Peniel. Angels are mentioned in the two stories. In both stories Jacob is left alone. In the Bethel story he is fleeing from his brother Esau to the unknown, and here he is on the eve of meeting his brother Esau. Jacob receives divine blessings, which are the same that were made to Abraham; thus, he becomes the third patriarch. At Peniel, Jacob's name change is the essence of the blessings, and Jacob becomes the father of the Israelite nations. Following his dream, Jacob names the place Bethel, and after fighting the mysterious assailant, he names that place Peniel. Hence, a question needs to be raised: since Bethel was a dream setting, was Peniel a dream setting as well? Indeed, it was noted already by the Rambam (Maimonides, Moses ben Maimon, 1135–1204) in his book, *Moreh Neuvechim,* where he deals in one chapter with the nature of prophecy. He

---

14. The scholia on Lycophron (Sheer), 41.
15. For further study, see Kodell, "Jacob Wrestles with Esau," 65–70.

interprets the story of God's theophany to Abraham as a prophetic vision. Rambam applies the same principle with Jacob's wrestling with the angel:

> The same, I hold, is the case when it said in reference to Jacob, "And a man wrestled with him" (Gen 32:25); this took place in a prophetic vision, since it is expressly stated in the end (v. 31) that it was an angel. The circumstances are here exactly the same as those in the vision of Abraham, where the general statement, "And the Lord appeared to him," etc., is followed by a detailed description. Similarly the account of the vision of Jacob begins, "And the angels of God met him" (Gen 32:2); then follows a detailed description how it came to pass that they met him; namely, Jacob sent messengers, and after having prepared and done certain things, "he was left alone," etc. "and a man wrestled with him" (ibid. ver. 24). By this term *"man"* [one of] the angels of God is meant, mentioned in the phrase, "And angels of God met him"; the wrestling and speaking was entirely a prophetic vision. That which happened to Balaam on the way, and the speaking of the ass, took place in a prophetic vision, since further on, in the same account, an angel of God is introduced as speaking to Balaam. I also think that what Joshua perceived, when "he lifted up his eyes and saw, and behold a man stood before him" (Josh v. 13), was a prophetic vision, since it is stated afterwards (ver. 14) that it was "the prince of the host of the Lord."[16]

Abravanel, in his commentary, ponders whether Jacob's wrestling with the angel was in a dream, as Rambam maintains, or whether Jacob was awake the whole time as the Ramban says. Abravanel, who cites the Ramban, differs sharply with the Rambam regarding our episode. Abravanel asks the simple question: if this is a prophetic vision, why does Jacob limp on his thigh when he is awake? Further, Abravanel wonders why Jacob would say, "I have seen the Divine, face to face, yet my life was spared" (32:31), since prophets are never afraid that they will die as a result of their visions. More so, Jacob had previously seen a more powerful vision: the presence of God.

Genesis 35:10 contains a second, parallel tradition of the blessing and the change of Jacob's name. Here, the events take place at Bethel and not in Peniel. More so, it is God who blesses Jacob and not the angel. The first time that the change of name occurred, it took place on the other side of the Jordan River. Now that Jacob finds himself in the promised land, the

---

16. Maimonides, *Guide of the Perplexed*, 2:42.198.

name Israel needs to be confirmed by God himself. No explanation for the name Israel is given here, which shows a dependence on the earlier story. With the change of name, God bestows on Jacob the blessings of fertility, nationhood, kingship, and territory. Jacob receives the same blessings that were given to the previous patriarchs, Abraham and Isaac. By receiving the blessing, Jacob becomes the heir to the Abrahamic covenant. According to the Ramban, God was saying, "now you are still called Jacob, even though the angel of Esau changed your name to Israel (32:29); for he was not sent to you with the authority to change your name. But from now on, your name will not be called Jacob, but Israel shall be your name. That is the meaning of, Thus He called his name Israel." What the Ramban says is that at this time Jacob's name was changed, and not earlier by the angel. Rashi, on the other hand, says that when the angel told Jacob, "No longer will it be said that your name is Jacob, but Israel" (32:29), he was not changing Jacob's name; he was merely informing him that his name would be changed by God at some time in the future. Another interpretation that is given by the Ramban is that by saying, "'Your name is Jacob,' He was alluding to the fact that He was calling his name Israel in addition to Jacob, and that it would not be forbidden for him to be called Jacob." This is different from when Abraham and Sarah had their names changed, and the original names were discarded. The Talmud states that it is forbidden to refer to Abraham or Sarah by their former names, but not so with Jacob; it is permitted to call Israel by his earlier name Jacob.[17]

Hosea

The struggle with the angel is also mentioned in the book of Hosea (12:4–5):

> In the womb, he [Jacob] cheated his brother. Grown to manhood, he strove with a divinity; he strove with an angel and triumphed; the other did sweep and implore him. It was at Bethel that he met him, so there he invokes him by name! But Yahweh, the god of hosts, cannot be invoked but as Yahweh.

Three traditions are interwoven here: Jacob holding his brother's heel, the struggle with the angel, and the theophany at Bethel. Raddak, in his commentary on verse 4, points out that Jacob's holding the heel of Esau is a "miraculous phenomenon, since a fetus, while in the womb, has no power in

---

17. *b. Ber.* 13a.

any of his limbs. Surely, he has no strength to pierce the afterbirth and seize the other fetus by the heel." However, according to Raddak, this was a sign for posterity—that in the end, this is the heel: the sons of Jacob will rule over the sons of Esau. Hosea's condemnation of Jacob, that he cheated his brother in the womb, is harsher than Esua's accusations. In Genesis, Esau complains that Jacob cheated him twice in adulthood. Yet Hosea says that Jacob was a cheater before he was even born. It appears that one of Jacob's characteristics was grabbing and holding. He was holding his brother's heels in the womb, and according to the tradition of Peniel, he refused to let go of the man.[18]

According to Hosea, Jacob strove with God (Hos 12:4). The verb *śārāh* occurs only here and in Gen 32:29 in connection with the name Israel. The prophet mentions that Jacob struggled with God (Hos 12:4), while in the following verse 5, he struggles with an angel and prevails. Nevertheless, in no other place does Hosea mention angels. In Genesis, Jacob wrestles with a man instead of an angel. However, we should point out that the Hebrew word for "man" is a generic term, and it refers to both humans and divine beings who have the same appearance.[19] The verse in Hosea states that in his manhood he struggled with God. The Hebrew word for manhood is *'ôn*, and it has been suggested to interpret it as "wickedness" (*'āwen*).[20] This interpretation creates a parallelism to "deception," which is a key word in our chapter (Hos 12:1, 8). Indeed, Hosea's nickname for Bethel is *bêt 'āwen* (4:15; 10:5). This critical view of Bethel is also found in Jeremiah: ". . . as the House of Israel were shamed because of Bethel, on whom they relied" (Jer 48:13). What is strange here is that Jacob overpowered the divine being, but nevertheless, the shrine is not to Yahweh, but to a lesser god called Bethel. He invoked Bethel by name instead of calling him Yahweh.[21] To describe Jacob's success against the angel, the narrator uses the verb *yākōl* (to succeed). The usage of this verb further shows the link between Genesis and Hosea (see Gen 32:26; Hos 12:5).

In the story of Jacob's encounter at Jabbok, it is not clear who won. In Hosea, we read that the angel wept and beseeched Jacob to let him go. This detail is not mentioned in the Torah. However, the subjects and the objects of Hos 12:5 are not clear; the medieval commentators, such as Rashi,

18. Andersen and Freedman, *Hosea*, 607.
19. Ibid., 608.
20. Macintosh, *Hosea*, 481.
21. Ginsberg, "Hosea's Ephraim," 343.

Ibn Ezra (1089–1164), and Raddak, interpret it as the angel who cried, while according to Wolf and Mays it was Jacob who cried.[22] In the two encounters at Bethel and Peniel, Jacob did not cry. On the other hand, Jacob did cry on two occasions: when he met Rachel (Gen 29:11), and when he reconciled with his brother Esau (33:4). It is possible that we have here an allusion to cultic traditions that involve rituals of weeping at Bethel, which is mentioned in Gen 35:8, Judg 2:1–5, and Hos 7:14.[23] The events in Hos 12:5 do not appear according to a chronological order. The sequence of Bethel and Jabbok is reversed. It has been suggested that Hosea reversed it deliberately. The mention of Bethel probably refers to Jacob's second encounter with God. This is where, on his way home, God confirmed the angel's renaming of Jacob as Israel. It is also possible that Hosea did not know the exact details of the story. Hosea, in his chapter, describes how deceit characterized Israel from the start. To illustrate it, he mentions Jacob, who, in the womb, was a supplanter. This trait of deceit is shared by Jacob's descendants. Hosea describes the sinfulness of Judah and Ephraim. Since God gave Jacob the strength to overcome the angel, the question is why Israel turned to foreign powers for help instead of turning to God. Besides verses 4–5, the chapter alludes to Jacob's past in several verses (vv. 9, 12, 13, 14). The biblical narrator mentions episodes from Jacob's past in order to create similarities between the fathers and the sons—"the deeds of the fathers are lessons to the sons."

In conclusion, angles are mentioned at important junctions in Jacob's life and are one of the main characteristics of the Jacob cycle. The angels appear to be guardian angels who accompanied Jacob during his travel. They are the fulfillment of God's promise to Jacob: "Remember, I am with you: I will protect you wherever you go and will bring you back to this land" (28:15). The story of Jacob wrestling with a mysterious being evidently has several layers, which include mythical imagery. The biblical narrator transformed it and describes Jacob as wrestling with a divine being. This divine being changed Jacob's name to Israel. The changing of the name signals a new beginning and is a form of blessing.

There are many similarities between the dream at Bethel (Gen 28) and the Peniel story (Gen 32). More so, Gen 35:10 contains another parallel tradition of God blessing and changing Jacob's name, which is similar to the Peniel story. What is common to the three chapters is the blessing that is

---

22. Wolff, *Hosea*, 213; Mays, *Hosea*, 163.
23. Hvidberg, *Weeping and Laughter in the Old Testament*, 98–146.

bestowed on Jacob. As with the appearance of angels, the motif of blessing is a recurring theme in the Jacob story. Another tradition of Jacob wrestling with a divine being is mentioned by the prophet Hosea. Some details in the story are different from our story in Genesis. Nevertheless, by mentioning Jacob's deception, the narrator wanted to create symmetry between Jacob, Judah, and Ephraim, who sinned like Jacob. The sins of the patriarch should serve as a lesson to his descendants.

Continuing with the theme of encounters with the divine, in chapter six we will examine the subject of dreams. In the ancient world, people believed that they received messages from deities. Therefore, we shall examine the phenomenon of dreams in the Jacob cycle.

6

Dreams

IN THE ANCIENT WORLD, dreams were perceived as channels of communication between human beings and external sources. In sleep they believed messages were conveyed to the unconscious mind. Messages, often related to the future, sometimes included clear and unambiguous announcements, advice, injunctions, or warnings. Several Akkadian sources referred to a "god of dreams," whose chief task was to send dreams to slumbering human beings. In some Mesopotamian sources, bad dreams and evil signs came from sorcerers who sought to harm a person, but charms and spells could be used to avert them.[1] It was also thought that the soul, or part of it, left the body of the sleeper and embarked on adventures and journeys. The content of the dream consisted of incidents and experiences of the soul during its wanderings.

The Greeks, too, believed in the external and passive origin of dreams. They thought that gods and spirits who brought dreams entered through the keyhole, stood alongside the bed of the sleeper, conveyed a message to him or her, and then departed the same way they came. Sometimes the gods stood in front of the dreamer and acted out the content of the dream. Classical mythology refers to the "people of dreams" or "tribes of dreams"[2] who lived in the entry way to the underworld—in caves or under trees—from whence they dispersed dreams throughout the world at night.[3] The Greeks also seemed to believe that the content of prophetic dreams depended not only on gods and spirits, but on the dreamer's psychological and physical condition as well: the hour, diet, age, and so forth.

1. Oppenheim, "Mantic Dreams," 346.
2. Hesiod, *Theogony*, 211.
3. Homer, *Od.* 24.11.

In the Hebrew Bible, however, with its monotheistic message of One God who rules the universe, there is no clear explanation as to why the Almighty would communicate with a sleeping person, rather than clearly and openly when the recipient was awake. Hence, it is possible that nocturnal dream theophanies are meant to express the distance between human beings and God. God appears in dreams in order to moderate the shock or danger of direct waking revelation. The dream represents a more refined and sophisticated state in the development of religion than that which is reflected in a direct encounter with the deity.[4]

Since dreams served as a mode of communication, we find that they are also mentioned in the Jacob cycle. God's first appearance to Jacob was in a dream that took place at Bethel (Gen 28). Later, at the house of Laban, the angle of God appeared to Jacob in a dream (Gen 31:10–13). A third dream is recorded to Laban who, while in hot pursuit of Jacob, was visited by God in a dream at night (Gen 31:24). Finally, Jacob, on his way down to Egypt, stopped at Beer Sheba to make sacrifices to God, and God appeared to him in the visions of the night (Gen 46:1–4). Hence, in this chapter, we will analyze the dreams in the Jacob cycle and try to understand what's behind the dreams and what they convey.

Bethel

Jacob's dream at Bethel is unique because its verbal message is complemented by a vision (28:12) to which the dreamer himself provides an interpretation (v. 17). It should, however, be emphasized that the link between the meaning of the vision (v. 17) and the verbal message (vv. 13b–15) is indirect. The narrator describes a ladder in the dream. Its top reaches to heaven, and angels of God are on it ascending and descending. There is a strong argument that the biblical author was influenced by multiple extra-biblical sources. The ladder reminds us of the Mesopotamian ziggurats, or sacred towers, which soared dozens of meters skyward and which were often described as having their tops in the heaven.[5]

Similarly, the angels' ascent and descent on the ladder in Jacob's dream parallels those of the Assyrian version of the myth of Nergal and Ereshkigal, where we read that the gods came down "the long stairway

---

4. For extensive study on the subject of biblical dreams, see Bar, *A Letter that Has Not Been Read*.

5. Speiser, *Genesis*, 219–220; Sarna, *Understanding Genesis*, 193.

(*simmiltu*) of heaven."[6] From an account of the angels ascending and descending the ladder (v. 12), the biblical author reports the appearance of the Lord, who "was standing beside him" (v. 13). The ladder and the angels are only stage props, whose main function is to lead up to the climax: the appearance of the Lord.

The promises to Jacob that constitute the heart of the dream (vv. 13–15) include a personal promise (v. 15) as well as others that have more national dimensions—possession of the land and the promise of offspring (vv. 13b–14). From the thematic perspective, God's promises are quite similar to those he made to Abraham in Gen 13:14–16. He will give land to Jacob and his children, who will be like the dust of the earth. When God promises the land to Jacob, the text emphasizes that the reference is to "the ground on which you are lying," which is appropriate to Jacob's present situation. Jacob is concerned that he may not see his homeland again; the Lord promises that not only will he do so, but it will become his permanent possession and his children's in the distant future. On the other hand, the personal promise at the end of the dream has more immediate implications: "Remember, I am with you: I will protect you wherever you go and will bring you back to this land. I will not leave you until I have done what I promised you" (Gen 28:15). This pledge is meant to encourage Jacob, who, totally indigent, is now fleeing Esau's rage and journeying to an unknown land, believing that God has abandoned him. It is obvious that the Lord's promise to Jacob is appropriate to his personal situation and will be realized in his own lifetime. It should be emphasized that the promise of returning "to this land" is a recurrent motif in Jacob's two other dreams (Gen 31:13 and 46:4) and highlights Jacob's bond to his birthplace. Just as the promise of a son is a recurrent motif in the Abraham cycle, the motif of divine assistance and protection is prominent in the stories of Jacob and Esau (Gen 26:3, 24; 28:15; 31:3; 32:10; 46:3; 48:15, 21; 50:24).

Jacob's dream in Bethel is marked by an emotional response—astonishment, which quickly gives way to fear. His uneasiness at Bethel stems only from his sense of the place and nearness to God—"You shall venerate my sanctuary, I am the Lord" (Lev 26:2). At this stage, Jacob's reaction has nothing to do with the verbal message addressed to him by God in the dream. This emotional reaction takes place during the night.

---

6. Millard, "The Celestial Ladder and the Gate of Heaven," 86–87; Gurney, "Nergal and Ereshkigal," 105.

Whereas the Bible assigns Jacob's dream a narrow meaning that relates exclusively to him, *Midrash Tanḥuma* goes beyond the confines of the story to give the dream a much broader significance, one that relates not merely to Jacob, who is leaving his country, but to the people of Israel wandering in exile from their homeland. As the midrash states:

> "And behold the angels of God descending and ascending": These are the princes of the heathen nations that God showed Jacob our father. The Prince of Babylon ascended seventy steps and descended; Media fifty-two and descended; Greece one hundred steps and descended; Edom ascended and no one knows how many! In that hour, Jacob was afraid and said: "Peradventure this one has no descent?" Said the Holy One blessed be He to him: "Therefore fear thou not, O my servant Jacob . . . neither be dismayed, O Israel" [Jer 30:10]. Even if thou seest him, so to speak, ascend and sit by Me, thence will I bring him down! As it is stated (Obad 1:4): "Though thou exalt thyself as the eagle and set thy nest among the stars, thence will I bring thee down, saith the Lord."[7]

The medieval exegete Obadiah ben Jacob Sforno (ca.1470-ca. 1550) explained the dream in accordance with the midrash:

> "Ascending and descending"—indeed ultimately, having gained ascendency, the Gentile princes will go down, and the Almighty who forever stands above will not forsake His people as He promised (Jer 30:11): "For I will make a full end of all the nations whither I scattered you, but I will not make a full end of you."

Thus, the *Tanḥuma* views the ladder as symbolizing history, and the angels as empires that rise and fall.[8]

The inspiration for this interpretation is probably the vision of the four kingdoms in the book of Daniel. The homilist saw before his eyes three empires that had ruled over the Jews and disappeared—namely, Babylonia, Media/Persia, and Greece. The fourth empire is Edom/Rome, which was still dominant in the time of the homilist. Jacob leaving Canaan represents the people of Israel, who are going into exile. Jacob's fright parallels the Jew's fear. Those who lived under Roman rule could not predict when Rome and its offspring—referred to in the rabbinic literature of Middle Ages as "Edom"—would lose their dominion. Therefore, he quotes from the prophecy of Obadiah (1:4), which confidently predicts the downfall of

---

7. Tanḥ. (Buber), *Vayetze* 2.
8. Leibowitz, *Studies in Bereshit*, 72–73.

Edom. Every ascent of the ladder depends on the descendent of someone else. Nor is it a ladder that has no end, for God stands at the top of it. It is the Lord who directs history. He raises up and lowers down, and he will bring low the Roman Empire too.

Modern scholars have a different interpretation as to the purpose of the Bethel story. Herman Gunkel, for example, sees the Bethel story as a ceremonial legend that accounts for the holiness attributed to the sanctuary and explains the origin of its associated rituals—for example, why the Israelites anointed stones with oil and gave tithes there.[9] In Genesis, we read about other sites of primitive ritual such as Peniel, Shechem, Beer Sheba, and Beer-lahai-roi. Here, the text notes the presence of sacred wells and trees where the patriarchs felt God's presence and worshiped.

Problems arose in the later period, however, when the Israelites no longer had a keen sense of the divine presence in these places and began to seek reasons for the rituals associated with them. In most cases, the standard answer was that God had appeared to the patriarchs there, and a particular ritual was conducted to commemorate that theophany. Gunkel notes that often in the history of religion, ritual and ceremonial legends appear and evolve as religious sentiments dim. In the case of Bethel, because God appeared to Jacob whose head lay on a stone when he beheld the celestial ladder, this site was sanctified, and the stone became a temple.[10]

Skinner agrees. According to him, the story comes to explain the anointing of the stone and giving of tithes. Like Gunkel, Skinner believes that sites such as Bethel were sacred even before the patriarchal age—going back to the primitive forms of Semitic religion within Canaanite culture. Hence, it is difficult to know to what extent the legends associated with them were transferred to the patriarchs and to what extent the patriarchs themselves developed these traditions.[11]

Von Rad also believes that the narrative is intended to clarify its association with the stone and to explain how Bethel became a famous cultic site.[12] According to the text, Jacob erected the pillar and anointed it with oil. Hence, it is possible that the pilgrims of later generations behaved similarly and anointed the stone. According to von Rad, ritual legends characteristically recount the first performance of the cultic act, by way of grounding

---

9. Gunkel, *Legend of Genesis*, 30–33.
10. Ibid., 33.
11. Skinner, *Genesis*, 12–13.
12. Rad, *Genesis*, 285.

its legitimacy. When the pilgrims brought their tithes to Bethel, they were participating in Jacob's vow and identified themselves with him (see Amos 4:4). Hence, Jacob indicates (1) the Lord's first appearance and directive to Jacob, (2) that it was Jacob who built the later altar, and (3) that it was Jacob who initiated the giving of tithes at this site.[13]

Sarna does not accept the association of the building of the sanctuary at Bethel with Jacob.[14] If the story focused on ritual, he argues, we might expect it to mention a prayer or altar. Neither of these elements appear in the text, nor in this context does the expression "house of God" (vv. 17 and 22) mean a temple. He also notes that whereas Abraham and Isaac built altars after God appeared to them, Jacob did not (although he did construct an altar after his return to Canaan from Haran, but this is not a temple). Nevertheless, the text clearly associated the original sanctity of Bethel with Jacob—a link that, as we shall see, endured for many centuries.

The later history of Bethel makes it clear that an ancient tradition was associated with the site. Although the sanctuary there was deemed holy for many generations, especially among the northern tribes, Bethel was first mentioned as a central, national, and religious site in the period of the judges. Because of the presence there of the ark of the Lord, tended by Phineas the grandson of Aaron (Judg 20:18–28), the Israelites were in the habit of going there to inquire of the oracle of the 'ûrîm (Judg 20:18, 27) and to pray, fast, and offer sacrifices (Judg 20:26 and 21:2–4). Bethel seems to have been important for both civilian and military reasons. Not only was it a major pilgrimage site (1 Sam 10:13), but the roads to Bethel are mentioned in stories from the period of the judges (Judg 20:30 and 21:9), and two-thirds of Saul's army bivouacked there (1 Sam 13:12).

Later, after Solomon built the temple in Jerusalem and made it the central sanctuary for all Israel, the importance of this site waned. When the kingdom split after Solomon's death, Jeroboam established cultic centers in Bethel and Dan to serve as alternatives to Jerusalem. Bethel was selected both for its traditional sanctity and for its geographic location, which made it easy to divert Jerusalem-bound pilgrims to it. In the period of Elijah, we read about the presence of a band of prophets there (2 Kgs 2:2–3). It is interesting that Elijah and Elisha, who fought against Baal worship, seemed to evince no opposition toward the shrine in Bethel. Nowhere in the Bible do we find any allusion to their displeasure with the place. Only the later

13. Ibid., 286.
14. Sarna, *Understanding Genesis*, 398.

tradition, reflecting the Deuteronomic centralization of the cult at a single location, reports the story of the man of God from Judah who came to rebuke Jeroboam as he was about to present an offering on the altar at Bethel (1 Kgs 13). The prophet Ahijah of Shiloh also rebuked Jeroboam, delivering the following message in the name of the Lord: "You have gone and made for yourself other gods and molten images to vex Me" (14:9).

In the eighth century BCE, Amos and Hosea issued a strong denunciation of Bethel. The latter referred to it as the house of delusion. Amos, who was active in the northern kingdom, directed his shafts against the cultic practices of its sanctuaries in general, and against Bethel in particular (Amos 3:14, 4:4, 5:5–6, and 9:1). Hosea's opposition was even fiercer; he rejected the Bethel cult as idolatrous, a treasonous breach of covenant between the Lord and Israel (Hos 4:15; 5:8; 8:5; 10:5–6, 8, 15; and 13:2).

Bethel had a long and ancient history predating the patriarchs. Originally a Canaanite holy site, it is identified with the village of Beitin, located about 10.5 miles north of Jerusalem at an elevation of 2,886 feet above sea level. Many archeological excavations in the area have revealed that there was an altar at the crest of the hill before 3,500 BCE and that a temple was built there in the nineteenth century BCE. Hence, there is no doubt that Bethel was a sacred Canaanite site before and during the patriarchal age.[15]

The name Bethel is also found in Ugaritic (*bt il*) and Akkadian (*bīt ili*). El was the chief god of the Canaanite pantheon. Thus, it represents the familiar form for temple names—the word בית (house) followed by the name of the deity honored there. We can compare Beth-Anath (Josh 19:38), Beth-Azmaveth (Ezra 2:24), Beth-Baal-Berith (Judg 9:4), as well as others. In all of these cases, the name of the sanctuary was applied to the nearly urban settlement.[16]

It is almost certain, however, that the Canaanites worshiped the head of their pantheon, who was named El, in the city of Luz, where they called his temple "Bethel" (the "House of El"), and this designation was transferred to the city. Hence, it is possible that the patriarchs and their descendants considered El-Bethel to be their own deity, who was Creator of Heaven and Earth—similar to El Elyon, the tutelary god of Shalem (Gen 14:18, 22)—and that they used "Bethel" as an epithet for the Lord. This is implied in the tradition that Abraham built an altar to the Lord there (Gen 12:8; 13:3), and additionally in the memory that Jacob erected a pillar

---

15. Kelso, *The Excavation of Bethel*.
16. Sarna, *Understanding Genesis*, 399.

there, where he vowed that it would become a house of God (28:15-22), and named the place Bethel (28:19). This site was already sacred to the Canaanites, and so remained holy to the Israelites.

If this was so, it seems that with the passage of time the traditions shared with the cults of the neighboring peoples blurred the uniquely Israelite lineaments of the site near Bethel. The ritual there acquired a form that was more appropriate to the ancient Canaanite tradition. This was particularly conspicuous when Jeroboam installed a golden calf there. A calf, after all, is a young bull, and in Ugaritic writings a bull is a totem of the Canaanite El.

From all this we may conclude that Jacob's dream at Bethel has two main objectives: to explain how Bethel came to be a holy site; and to rupture the Canaanite association with Bethel. Even though the area is referred to as "a place," which in fact means "a *sacred* place" (and indeed the place was sacred for the Canaanites), Jacob arrives there only by chance. He discerns no holiness at the site, as is attested by his reaction after the dream: "Surely the Lord is present in this place, and I did not know it!" (Gen 28:16).

The stone on which Jacob rests his head is unremarkable. It has no intrinsic sanctity or magical power. It has one purpose only—to serve as a marker of the divine revelation to Jacob. However, to sever all pagan association with Bethel, the author emphasizes the Tetragrammaton. It is YHWH who stands by Jacob and identifies himself as the God of his fathers. After the dream, Jacob himself also emphasizes the name YHWH. Furthermore, when Jacob returns from Mesopotamia, he instructs the members of his household to discard their foreign gods, purify themselves, and change their clothes before they approach the place (Gen 35:2). In short, the biblical author ignores the previous sanctity of the place. Therefore, the authentic holiness of Bethel is derived only from the theophany that Jacob experienced there.[17]

Jacob's Dream in the House of Laban

Another dream theophany visited on Jacob is described in Gen 31:10-13. The text as we have it is corrupt, but it is apparent that we are dealing with two separate experiences that have been merged.[18] One involves the

17. Sarna, *Understanding Genesis*, 400.
18. On the corruption of the text, see Sarna, *Understanding Genesis*, 214; Westermann, *Genesis 12-36*, p. 491.

stratagem by which Jacob made his flocks proliferate. This theophany took place in the narrative past and featured an angel of God,[19] with a visual element supplemented by the angel's words (v. 12). In the second theophany, however, the God of Bethel appears to Jacob and commands him to rise and leave Laban's house and return to the land of Canaan—a revelation that refers to the present and immediate future.[20] The message in the second theophany is verbal only. According to our text, the angel who told Jacob the secret of breeding the ewes now addresses him and tells him to go back to his homeland. But some time must have passed between the genetic counseling and the injunction to go back to his homeland. Further, verse 12 is almost a literal reprise of verse 10. The angel tells Jacob to lift up his eyes and see what he has already seen. For this reason, some have proposed inverting the order of the verses.[21]

Commentators disagree about whether this is a single or double dream. Nahmanides evidently sensed that there were two separate revelations here. In his commentary on v. 13, he writes, "This is not a single dream: Note well that 'lift up your eyes and see all the he-goats' was when the sheep were in the heat during one of the earlier years, but 'I am the God of Bethel' was spoken later, at the time of the journey, because after He told him to rise and leave this land he did not tarry any longer in Haran." S. D. Luzzatto (1800–1865), by contrast, in his commentary on verse 13, sees it all as a single dream in which the description of the he-goats is a flashback:

> "I am the God who has been with you until now and saw to it that the sheep bore speckled young. I am the one who tells you to rise and leave this land and I will help you." For it is all one dream that comes to him, now when the sheep were in heat that year.

Whether part of a single or double theophany, verse 13 is phrased as an imperative: "Arise and leave this land!"—and is evidently meant to encourage and reinforce Jacob, who is afraid of Laban. Laban has already deceived him several times, especially on his wedding night when

---

19. Some considered the verses that describe the proliferation of the sheep to be an expansion and supplement to Gen 30:28–43, where Jacob's method is explained. See Westermann, *Genesis 12–36*, p. 491.

20. Verses 11 and 13 are really an expansion of v. 3: "Then the Lord said to Jacob, 'Return to the land of your fathers where you were born, and I will be with you'" (Gen 31:3). Westermann argues that this verse stood in place of vv. 11 and 13 in the original text. See Westermann, *Genesis 12–36*, p. 492.

21. Ibid., 491.

he substituted Leah for Rachel. Jacob, though furious, could do nothing. When Laban overtakes the fugitive Jacob, he rebukes Jacob for what he has done. Jacob retorts, "I was afraid because I thought you would take your daughters from me by force" (Gen 31:33). Jacob has long been nursing his sense of being defrauded. His anger and frustration erupt in the serious charges with which he castigates Laban. The biblical author employs a flashback technique and quotes Jacob's complaint about past wrongs: Laban has repeatedly changed his terms of employment and has demanded that Jacob make good for animals eaten by predators. Jacob paid up even though he was not legally required to do so.[22] Jacob's wives share his sense of frustration. They tell him that they feel like alien women in their father's house because he has sold them and consumed their money.

In light of Laban's deceit, we can understand why the text recalls the revelation at Bethel, where God promised to protect Jacob and return him safe and sound to Canaan. Genesis 31:3 depends on the story of the dream at Bethel—whether by recalling God's promise to "bring [him] back to this land" (Gen 28:15) or by fulfilling Jacob's request in his vow that God return him in peace to his father's house. The instruction to Jacob to leave Laban's house has already appeared at the beginning of the chapter: "Then the Lord said to Jacob, 'Return to the land of your fathers where you were born'" (Gen 31:3). Because this verse does not refer to a dream, proponents of the documentary theory consider it to be a Yahwist version of the divine injunction for Jacob to return to his homeland. It seems at least as plausible that the verse is a précis of sorts, with the following verses merely filling in the details of the theophany.

Jacob's dream in the house of Laban incorporates a motif from daily life into its description of sheep mating. In it, the angel alludes to three different ram styles: the rams that are mounting the ewes are streaked, speckled, and finally mottled (31:12). In verse 8, however, Jacob mentions only two violations of the agreement by Laban, omitting the case of the spotted rams. That Laban did in fact breach their contract three times is indicated by the fact that Jacob mentions three instances of intervention by God: "But the God of my father has been with me" (v. 5); "God, however, would not let him do me harm" (v. 7); and "God has taken away your father's livestock and given it to me" (v. 9). Why did the angel reveal to Jacob the secret of

---

22. According to the Code of Hammurabi, as well as Exod 22:12, a hired shepherd was liable only for strayed or stolen lambs. See at length Loewenstamm "אנכי אחטנה" 69–70; Postgae, "Some Old Babylonian Shepherds," 1–21; Mabee, "Jacob and Laban," 192–207.

sheep breeding? According to the text, it is because God has "noted all that Laban has been doing to you" (v. 12). God is helping Jacob so as to redress the wrongs done to him by Laban. The dream makes no reference to the peeled rods of chapter 30; Jacob's prosperity is ascribed solely to God. For this reason, some believe that the tale of the rods (30:25–43) is a Yahwist version of the story, whereas the description in our chapter stems from the Elohist tradition (31:2, 4–16). Against this theory, however, there is a view that the stratagem Jacob employs to increase the number of sheep is not the result of a divine blessing and that the dream never, in fact, took place. Jacob does not want to humiliate Laban, so he tells his wives how their father has tricked him. He tells them that the multiplication of his own flock was the result of a divine revelation in which he was told what to do.[23]

After the dream, Jacob acts at once and without hesitation to implement the instructions he received in his sleep. He summons his wives from home and recounts how El Bethel has appeared to him in a dream and commanded him to return to his homeland. As Nahmanides reads the passage, Jacob is trying to persuade them to accompany him. Jacob could not take his wives away from their father's house without their consent because they were still part of that household. He describes his dream to them in order to emphasize that this abandonment of their paternal homestead is a divine imperative and that they have an obligation to come with him. Rachel and Leah's response, that they are like aliens in their father's house, is tantamount to their consenting to leave. After the conversation with his wives, Jacob sets out immediately (Gen 31:17). In other words, he does as he was told in the dream. Note that Rachel and Leah do not react to Jacob's dream vision of the rams, but only to the divine injunction to return to Canaan: "Now then, do just as the God has told you" (v. 16). This omission supports the argument made above that our text conflates what were originally two separate dreams.

Laban's Dream

Another dream found in the Jacob cycle is Laban's dream (Gen 31:24). When Jacob was a fugitive leaving his father's house, desperate and alone, he heard God's encouraging promises in a dream (Gen 28:15). Many years later, when Jacob was under the thumb of his father-in-law, who deceived and tricked him, a dream revealed how he could receive his due (Gen

23. Sarna, *Understanding Genesis*, 214.

31:10–13). Now, when Laban wants to harm Jacob, the Lord appears to him in a dream and warns him off, thus deterring him from acting.

The dream is described in a single verse: "But God appeared to Laban the Aramean in a dream by night and said to him, 'Watch yourself lest you say anything to Jacob, good or bad'" (Gen 31:24.) Unlike in Abimelech's dream, here the name of the patriarch is mentioned—perhaps because Jacob had spent two decades in Laban's household and they were intimately acquainted. Rashi, citing the Talmud (*b. Yebamot* 103a–b), explains "good or bad" as meaning "the bounty of the wicked is bad for the righteous." Nahmanides goes further and glosses the message as meaning, "Watch yourself, lest you say to him that you will treat him well if he returns with you from his way, and lest you frighten him that you will harm him if he does not come with you, because I have commanded him to return to his land." The phrase "good or bad" is also found in the response of Laban and Bethuel to Abraham's servant: "The matter was decreed by the Lord; we cannot speak to you bad or good" (Gen 24:50).[24] The expression is an example of merism, the expression of a whole by means of contraries (see Num 24:13; 2 Sam 13:22; Zeph 1:12; Jer 10:5). Accordingly, some maintain that here it means that Laban should not speak to Jacob at all.[25] Benno Jacob, by contrast, says that the phrase does not mean that Laban must refrain totally from interaction with Jacob, but only that he must not harm him and must not take anything from him or compel him to return to Haran.[26] In fact, according to verse 29, Laban does speak with Jacob and rebukes him for his conduct, while mentioning the warning he has received from God.

Incubation

People in the ancient world believed that dreams were messages from the gods. Therefore, not surprisingly, the Hebrew Bible portrays a type of dream that seems to be invited by the dreamer, who attempts to impose his will on God. In this variation, the dreamer goes to a sacred spot, offers sacrifices to God, and falls asleep hoping that God will visit him. The dream is supposed to provide advice and guidance. This type of dream is called an incubation

---

24. "Good" is missing from LXX and the Vulg., so that the phrase is the same as in verse 29.

25. Honeyman would render the phrase as "not any word at all" ("Merismus in Biblical Hebrew," 12).

26. Jacob, *First Book of the Bible*, 211.

dream. Incubation dreams are found in the Hebrew Bible and throughout the ancient Near East.

In Mesopotamia, incubation is a widespread phenomenon. The dreamers are usually kings and priests, and their dreams are preceded by prayer and sacrifice. In an Akkadian poem, we find an address to the goddess Mamu: "Reveal thyself unto me and let me see a favorable dream. May the dream that I dream be favorable, may the dream that I dream be true, may Mamu, the goddess of dreams, stand at my head; let me enter E-sagila, the temple of the gods, the house of life."[27]

In Egypt, incubation was practiced as an aid to diagnosing diseases and discovering remedies for them. One of the famous centers of incubation was the well-known temple in the city of Memphis. In the story of Satni, Mahituaskhit goes to the temple of Imuthes in Memphis to pray to the god. Afterward, she falls asleep in the temple where the god appears to her in a dream and gives her a recipe to cure her barrenness. Crying was also part of incubation rituals. It is found in the dream of Sethos in the temple of Hephaistos.[28] The king cries to his god in his sleep. The deity appears to him in a dream and promises him victory. In addition to traditional incubation practices, there were Egyptian magicians who could summon dreams by drawing magic pictures and repeating thaumaturgic names.

Our knowledge of incubation sanctuaries in Greece goes back to the fifth century BCE. The institution spread gradually, until sources from the second century CE report that there were more than 400 incubation centers throughout Greece and the Roman Empire. These temples were dedicated to various gods, some of them Egyptian and others Greek. As in Egypt, the main use of incubation was to find cures for disease. Consequently, many of the temples were dedicated to Asklepios.[29] Homer recounts his bravery and skill in medicine, which he learned from the centaur Cheiron. The temples dedicated to Asklepios became the best-known incubation sanctuaries. Asklepios's birthplace, Epidaurus, was especially prominent among such temples. Sufferers would sleep in the temple and then regain their health, thanks to dreams they had in the temple.[30]

---

27. Lutz, "An Omen Text," 146. Cf. Ehrlich, *Der Traum im Alten Testament*, 52; and Gnuse, *The Dream Theophany of Samuel*, 34.

28. Herodotus 2:114; Gnuse, *Dream Theophany*, 29.

29. Meier, "Dream in Ancient Greece," 303–19.

30. Strabo, 8.6, 15; Pausanias, 2.27.3.

Dreams

A good example of dream incubation from the Hebrew Bible is Solomon's dream at Gibeon (1 Kgs 3:4). According to the text, Solomon went to Gibeon because that was the site of the great high place. He offered a thousand animals on the altar there, and the Lord appeared to him in a dream. The sacrificial offerings seem to reflect the emotional need of human beings to honor their God, to placate him as a condition for receiving his bounty. Similarly, sleeping in sacred precincts was a way of drawing closer to God. Indeed, such places were consecrated because gods had appeared to mortals there. Accordingly, people who went back there believed that if the Lord appeared there once, he would do so again. We should also remember that it was only reasonable to expect that the gods would appear in temples built especially for them.

Dream incubation is already found in the book of Genesis. Jacob, on his journey to Egypt, stops at Beer Sheba and offers sacrifices, after which the Lord appears to him in a vision by night. The text does not explain why Jacob stopped to pray in Beer Sheba. Perhaps he was afraid to continue his journey because of his frailty and advanced age. Perhaps he was anxious about leaving Canaan to settle elsewhere, because his father Isaac had been forbidden to do so (Gen 26:2). More likely, Jacob stopped in Beer Sheba in order to seek divine blessing for his emigration. A closer reading of Genesis reveals that the patriarchs often interrupted their journeys in order to pray (Gen 12:8–9 and 28:18). Here, though, we read about a sacrifice to God. The fact that Jacob offered his sacrifice before the Lord appeared to him, rather than afterward, suggests that we have an incubation dream here. Jacob offered sacrifices and required divine assistance; as a result, the Lord appeared to him and encouraged him. Moreover, Jacob's arrival at the site of the revelation is not described as a matter of chance. It seems plausible that he was aware of the sanctity of the site. Josephus' description of the incident reinforces this view.

> Halting at the Well of the Oath, he there offered sacrifice to God; and fearing that the reason for prosperity prevalent in Egypt his sons would be so greatly enamored of settling there ... and furthermore that having taken his departure into Egypt without God's sanction his race might be annihilated; yet terrified withal that he might quit his life before setting eyes on Joseph-these were the thoughts which he had revolving in his mind when he sank to sleep. Then God appeared to him and called him twice by name

> ... Encouraged by this dream, Jacob with greater ardor departed for Egypt along with his sons and his sons' children.[31]

Several other biblical passages have been alleged to be incubation dreams but are less likely to be so. One of these occurred at Bethel, where Jacob went to sleep in a sacred place, and the Lord appeared to him in a prophetic dream. Jacob, however, arrived in Bethel purely by chance. He did not know that the place was holy—"Surely the Lord is present in this place, and I did not know it!" (Gen 28:16). In fact, the place became sacred only after Jacob's dream.

In conclusion, our examination of dreams in the Jacob cycle shows that dreams were prophetic and dealt with the future. The core of the dream is a verbal message, which sometimes is accompanied by visual scenes and often refers to the future. Each time Jacob sets out for another country, God appears to him in a dream and encourages him. Jacob's dream at Bethel and Beer Sheba are associated with a holy site. The format of all the various dreams is the same, beginning with God introducing himself and continuing with a message of encouragement. This is manifested by the phrase "Fear not," God's promise to remain with Jacob (28:15: 46:4), and the promise to return him to his homeland (28:15; 31:13; 46:4). Another dream that is found in the Jacob cycle is Laban's dream. This dream continues the theme of divine protection that is found in Jacob's dreams. Hence, God appeared to Laban in a dream and warned him not to harm Jacob.

In the next chapter we will examine the story of Dinah. Why was this story included in the Jacob cycle, and what kind of message did the narrator try to deliver? In addition, we will see how the Bible and later writers viewed the brothers' massacre of the inhabitance of Shechem.

---

31. Josephus, *Ant.* 2.170–176.

7

The Dinah Story

AFTER 20 YEARS IN Laban's house, Jacob returned home. He arrived in the vicinity of Shechem and pitched his tent there. He purchased a piece of land for one hundred *kĕśîṭâ* and set up an altar to God. At first glance, it appears as though Jacob found peace. All his fears came to an end after the hard life in the house of Laban, the struggle with the angel, and finally the meeting with his brother Esau. Unfortunately, this was only a short pause in Jacob's hard life. Soon we discover that Jacob suffered a major tragedy: his daughter was violated by Shechem, son of Hamor. This act was followed by Dinah's brothers, Simeon and Levi, retaliating by attacking the city of Shechem. They plundered the city to avenge the honor of the family. The existence of their clan was threatened as a result of their attack. The events narrated in chapter 34 detail the main story about Dinah. The birth of Dinah was mentioned already in Gen 30:21 and probably is inserted there to prepare the reader for our story. Dinah is also mentioned later, in the list of the people who descended to Egypt.

The rape of Dinah is the first in a list of calamities that befalls the patriarch following his arrival to Canaan. Jacob suffers for his own children, Reuben, Simeon, Levi, Joseph, and Judah. This signals the beginning of moral decline. Simeon and Levi massacred the inhabitants of Shechem; Reuben slept with Bilhah, his father's concubine (Gen 35:22); Joseph was then sold into slavery by his brothers (Gen 37); and Judah unknowingly slept with his daughter-in-law Tamar (Gen 38). Hence, we will examine the story of Dinah and try to understand the reason for its inclusion. In addition, we will see how the Bible and later writers viewed the brothers' massacre of the inhabitants of Shechem.

And Took Her and Lay With Her by Force

The dominant characters in the story of Dinah are portrayed in a negative light.[1] Despite being a victim of rape, Dinah does not appear so innocent. The description of her "going out to see the daughters of the land" is a condemnation of her behavior. Shechem is a rapist, but then he falls in love with his victim. Hamor, the father of Shechem, is a good father who tries to help his son and is, therefore, willing to share his land with strangers. However, from his address to his fellow citizens, we learn that he is not a truthful man. At first, the sons of Jacob receive the reader's sympathy; they are very angry and sad due to their sister's violation. But later, they massacre all the inhabitants of the town, thus shedding the blood of innocent people. Jacob is passive through the whole story and does not interfere. His only concern is the safety of his own clan. Jacob is afraid of the people of the land retaliating. Strangely, what is missing from our story is God. In the Jacob cycle, God is the main hero; he is the one who blesses Jacob by promising him the land and many descendants. He protects him and delivers him in times of stress. He guides Jacob, and Jacob turns to him for help in most cases, but not so in this story. There are no heroes in our story; Shechem raped Dinah, the brothers used guile in their negotiations with the Shechemites, and the Shechemites tried to deceive Jacob's sons. There is no good in our story, only evil. So what stands behind this story, and why did the author choose to include it in the Jacob cycle?

Scholars have pointed out that the story is not a monolithic text but includes several layers, reflecting multiple authors.[2] Zakovitch, for example, maintains that originally Dinah was not violated. Shechem fell in love with her and wanted to marry her. Since the brothers did not agree with Shechem, they tricked and massacred the Shechemites. The details about the rape were added to the text in order to justify the brothers' violence. The additions of these details were inspired by another story—that of Amnon and Tamar. Amnon, the son of King David, raped his sister Tamar. To avenge his sister's rape, her brother, Absalom, ordered his attendants to kill Amnon while he was drunk (2 Sam 13:26–29).[3] Still, it is not clear why the brothers had to kill all the males in the city of Shechem.

---

1. For a literary study, see Caspi, "The Story of Dinah," 236–55.
2. Zakovitch, *Jacob*, 122.
3. Ibid., 124.

The Dinah Story

Other scholars such as Fishbane, Fokkelman, Rendsburg, and Zakovitch comment on this story and chapter 26. According to Fishbane, chapter 26 balances chapter 34. More so, "The symmetry between Genesis 26 and 34, together with their parallel functions as interludes, thus preclude any assumption of haphazard editorial arrangement."[4] Both stories deal with the native people of the land—the Philistines in chapter 26, and the Shechemites in chapter 34. The motif of deception is integral to the stories. In chapter 26, Isaac deceives the Philistine king, Abimelech, at Gerar. In the second part of the chapter, Isaac charges the Philistines with deception. In our story, Simeon and Levi deceive the Hittites, while in turn it appears that the Shechmites also use guile and do not negotiate in good faith. There is the possibility of peril for Rebecca, who is almost taken by the Philistine king, while in 34:1–26 Shechem essentially takes Dinah. In the two stories, the patriarch displays fear; nevertheless, he escapes richer (26:31, 13; 34:28–29; 35:5). The similarity between the Dinah story and the stories of the patriarchs and their wives is also noted in the *Testament of Levi*, who transformed the story of Shechem, saying, "But I saw that the sentence of God was for the evil upon Shechem; for they sought to do to Sarah [and Rebecca] as they had done to Dinah our sister, but the Lord prevented them" (6:8). Although chapters 26 and 34 include motifs of deception and strife, there is a major difference between them: Isaac deceived Abimelech because he was afraid for his life. This is not the case with Simeon and Levi, who acted as a result of vengeance. The brothers deceived the Shechemites and then slew all the males in their city.

As for the story itself, it starts peacefully enough with Dinah going to visit the daughters of the land. Nevertheless, the verb $yṣ'$ (to go out), like the Akkadian and Aramaic cognate terms, connotes promiscuous conduct. When the expression "go out" refers to a woman, it is associated with "whoring."[5] Interestingly, in Gen 28, the same word is used of Jacob, but in the midrashim he is described as a righteous man. Not so with his daughter Dinah. According to the midrash, "This may be compared to one who was holding a pound of meat in his hand, and as soon as he exposed it a bird swooped down and snatched it away."[6] In the same way, Shechem, the son of Hamor, saw Dinah. According to R. Samuel b. Nahman, her arm became exposed. According to Rashi, she was a gadabout. He points out that she is

---

4. Fishbane, *Text and Texture*, 47.
5. Bechtel, "What if Dinah is Not Raped?," 31–32.
6. *Gen. Rab.* 80.5

referred to as "the daughter of Leah," and not the daughter of Jacob, because of her "going forth"—for Leah also was one who goes out, and it is stated, "and Leah went forth to greet him." Regarding this scenario, they introduced the proverb, "Like mother, like daughter" (Ezek 16:44). Alternatively, the author might have mentioned that she was the daughter of Leah to explain the role of Simeon and Levi, who were her full brothers.

Shechem, son of Hamor, saw her. The language "saw her" in the Bible usually refers to the appearance of a beautiful woman. However, as Ramban noted, "Scripture did not tell us about her beauty as it did for Sarah, Rebecca and Rachel, for it did not want to mention her beauty, being that it became a 'pitfall of sin for her.' Scripture speaks of beauty when it is a praise for these righteous women (Sarah, etc.), i.e., when it did not lead to sin, but not for this one (Dinah), whose beauty had tragic consequences."

To describe the severity of Shechem's action, the Bible uses three verbs "took," "lay," and "force." The verb "took" describes Shechem seizing Dinah unlawfully. It was a case of rape, which is expressed by the Hebrew word ʿnh that appears in two other instances (2 Sam 13:11–14; Judg 19:24). This interpretation was also given by the Ramban, who says, "But there is no need to say this, for any act of intimate relations that is carried against the will of a woman, even if she is not a maiden, is called 'affliction.'"[7] As for Dinah, not even a single word about her thoughts or feelings is mentioned in the text. This is in contrast to a later story about Amnon, who raped his sister Tamar and then hated her. The young man, Shechem, loved Dinah and petitioned his father to take the young girl for a wife. The word "take" appears here is in sharp contrast to verse 2, where the taking was done by force. Here, Shechem implores his father to take her legally. Dinah's name is not mentioned here; Shechem refers to her as "this girl," which sounds as though he belittles her. The word *yaldâ* (girl) appears only three times in the Hebrew Bible and points to her young age and her helplessness (Joel 4:3; Zech 8:5). It also reflects the lower status of women in the ancient world, who were used like commodities. Dinah does not have a say in the negotiating that pertains to her future. Shechem was not an ordinary guy; he was the son of Hamor the Hivite, the chief of the country. The city of Shechem was a city state that included a large territory, extending to Jerusalem and Gezer in the south and Megiddo in the north. As the custom in ancient

---

7. Weinfeld does not accept the interpretation that the story is about the rape of Dinah. According to him the Hebrew word ʿnh refers to sexual intercourse in general rather than rape. See *Deuteronomy*, 286.

times required, it was the parents who initiated marriages. Thus, Shechem asked his father to intercede on his behalf.

Jacob received the news that his daughter Dinah had been defiled. Although the reader knows it already, the passage comes to stress the relationship between the father and daughter and Jacob's responsibility and commitment to her. The severity of Shechem's act is described by the word *ṭimmēʾ* (defiled), which is repeated in this chapter several times (vv. 5, 13, 27). The verb refers to a moral and religious act, such as abuse of chastity or impurity. Despite hearing the news about the heinous crime that was perpetrated against his daughter, Jacob maintained his silence. He did not react. This is probably because he was waiting for the arrival of his sons, who at that time were in the fields. While this is understandable at this juncture, nevertheless, throughout the whole event, Jacob does not act and remains passive. King David, in a similar situation, upon hearing that his daughter was raped, became distressed and angry (2 Sam 13:21). Yet he did not punish Amnon for his act. Later, when Jacob received the bad news about Joseph, he tore his clothes and refused to be comforted by his sons.

In contrast to their father, Jacob's sons showed their emotions. When they returned home from the field and heard of the offense that was committed against their sister, "they felt grieved." The same reaction is also found in Gen 6:6, when God was grieved at the wickedness of the human race. In addition, the narrator tells us that the brothers were also very angry. The heinous crime is referred to as *něbālâ* (an outrage), which is an expression for transgression. It is usually linked to sexual crimes such as homosexuality (Judg 19:23), rape (2 Sam 13:12), or adultery (Jer 29:23). The verse states that Shechem committed an outrage in Israel. As pointed out by scholars, this is an anachronism since Israel did not exist yet. More so, the perpetrator was not an Israelite.[8]

At this stage of the story, Hamor made a speech to all the males in Jacob's family, which included a proposal. He proposed intermarriages between the two parties. In addition, he offered Jacob's family land to settle in his territory, which entailed economic advantages. Meanwhile, he did not mention the incident that involved his son and Dinah. More so, Dinah was still being held in Hamor's house. It is not clear if she was held against her will or if she stayed voluntarily. There is neither apology nor remorse in Hamor's speech. Here, Sarna raises legal questions regarding this situation.[9]

---

8. Sarna, *Understanding Genesis*, 234; Westermann, *Genesis 12–36*, p. 538.
9. Sarna, *Understanding Genesis*, 235.

He points to the Middle Assyrian laws, which deal with the rape of unbetrothed virgins, according to which the offender must pay a fixed amount of silver and gold, in addition to paying the bride price for the virgin to her father, and then it is up to the father to decide whether his daughter will marry the offender or not. This law is identical to the law in Exodus 22:15–16, which states that the offender must take his victim as a wife unless her father refuses. Nevertheless, he must pay the bride price for virgins. Still, the question remains: can Jacob, as an alien, the head of a small clan, raise any claims against the chief of the country?

Following his father's proposal, Shechem addresses Jacob and his sons. He is willing to pay whatever they want. More so, he urges them to ask for a high price as well as gifts. Our text mentions the bride price (*mōhar*) and gifts (*mattān*). In Akkadian, they are known as *terḥatum* and *biblum* respectively. The bride price (*terḥatum*) were meant to compensate for the bride's manual services and potential offspring—this is what the Hebrew Bible calls *mōhar* (Exod 22:16). The *biblum* were ceremonial marriage gifts to the bride's family. Giving gifts to the bride's family is also found in Genesis 24 in the story of Rebecca. Shechem was willing to give Jacob and his sons a *mattān* (voluntary gift) over and above the *mōhar* (bride price), on the condition that they would give him Dinah for a wife. The same ceremonial gifts appear in Gen 24:53 as well, there termed *migdānōt*.[10]

Jacob's sons respond to the speeches of Hamor and Shechem as Jacob still maintains his silence and does not take part in the negotiation. In the ancient world, and also currently in the Middle East, brothers are responsible for the honor of their sister. Ramban, on the other hand, gave another interpretation for Jacob's passivity, according to which "the elder [Jacob] did not respond to them at all, for his sons spoke in his place in this matter to protect his honor, because, since this incident was a matter of disgrace for them, they did not want [Jacob] to have open his mouth to speak about it at all."

The narrator mentions that the brothers spoke with deception, while reminding the reader of the heinous crime that was perpetrated against Dinah. The Hebrew word for deception, *mirmâ*, appeared already in the story of Jacob's deception of his father (27:35), and the root *r-m-y* is mentioned in the story of the deception of Jacob by Laban (29:25). Evidently, there is a link between these stories. Mentioning the crime against Dinah was the narrator's way of explaining the brother's behavior. The brothers agreed to

---

10. Bar, "What Did the Servant Give?," 565–72.

The Dinah Story

give their sister in marriage on the condition that every male Hamorite be circumcised. This, indeed, was a legitimate prerequisite since, according to Gen 17:9–14, circumcision was obligatory for males who wanted to be part of the Israelite community. More so, Exod 12:43–49 prohibits uncircumcised males to take part in the Passover sacrifice.

The brothers presented their proposal to Shechem and his father Hamor. It seems that they planned to attack Shechem in the aftermath of the mass circumcision. However, Ramban raises the question here about whether Jacob was aware of his sons' plan:

> There is a question that presents itself here: For it appears that [Jacobs sons] answered Shechem and Hamor with Jacob's approval and counsel, for they were in his presence when they spoke, and he knew concerning their response that they were speaking with deception. If so, why did he become angry at them for what they subsequently did? Furthermore, it is not credible that Jacob should have been willing to marry off his daughter to the Canaanite Shechem who defiled her.

The midrash also raises the question of Jacob's awareness regarding his sons' plan: "that the two sons of Jacob, Simeon and Levi, took each man his sword. Since it says, Simeon and Levi, do we not know that they were Jacob's sons? But 'sons of Jacob' teaches that they did not take counsel with Jacob."[11]

Another question that needs an answer is why the text first says the "sons of Jacob" (vv. 13–18), yet later we read that it was only Simeon and Levi who attacked the city and killed all the males. The LXX solved this problem by adding in v. 14 the words "Simeon and Levi, brothers of Dinah, sons of Leah." By this addition, the text removed the other brothers from the sin of deception. It is also not clear if the brothers believed that the Shechemites would accept their condition for circumcision. Ramban answered two questions:

> Now, all the brothers gave their deceptive response, although it was only Simeon and Levi who did the act of killing the Shechemites, yet the father cursed only their anger. The answer to all these question is that the deception that our verse speak was in that they told [the Shechemites] that all their males must be circumcised, because they thought that the people of the city would never do such a thing. And, they reasoned, if perhaps [the Shechemites] would

---

11. *Gen. Rab.* 80:10.

listen to their prince after all and would all undergo circumcision, [the brothers] would go to the city on the third day, when [the Shechemites] were in pain and would forcibly take their daughter (i.e., their sister-Dinah) from Shechem's house. This was the plan of all the brothers, and it was undertaken with the sanction of their father. Simeon and Levi, however, wanted to take vengeance against [the Shechemites] and they killed all the men of the city, although this was not part of the original plan.

The brothers ended their response with strong words, which included a hint about the future. If the Shechemites would not comply with their request, they say, they "will take [their] daughter and go" (v. 17). In other words, they are threatening them. We have here a hint of what eventually will occur. The brothers do not mention Shechem's sin, but it appears that there is an ironic insinuation here, implying that they did not forget what happens.

Shechem and Hamor agreed to the brothers' terms. We can't tell whether the brothers were surprised at their response, whether they thought perhaps that the Hamorites would reject the harsh conditions. Dismissal of their demands could have given the brothers an excuse for the use of force. It appears that Shechem had genuine feelings toward Dinah; he was infatuated with her. He wasted no time and was the first to circumcise himself. In his act, he served as a model for his townspeople who followed him. Still, there was a major hurdle that the father and son had to face. They had to convince their townspeople to follow their act. As the reader recalls, in their proposal to Jacob's sons, Dinah was not mentioned at all. Similarly, when they addressed their fellow citizens, there is no mention of Dinah or of Shechem's passion for Dinah and his violation of her. What they stressed was the economic aspect, the gains that they would have from the union with Jacob's clan. They will have more women, but more importantly, all the cattle and all their beasts would belong to them. More so, when they addressed Jacob's sons, they promised them that "they could acquire possessions in it" (v. 10). That is not the case, though, because in their proposal they suggested making Jacob's sons equal partners, where each side would give and take. Here it is only one side, the Shechemites, who would give and take. Evidently, Shechem and Hamor were dishonest from the start; they deceived Jacob and his sons and also tricked their fellow citizens. The mention of duplicity by Hamor and Shechem came to mitigate the brothers' final act, which ended the life of all the males in the city of Shechem. Ironically, "Their flocks, their possessions . . . will they not be ours?" (v. 23), which was the main bait, turned out to be, after several days, in the hands of the Israelites who plundered the town.[12]

The townspeople of Shechem did not need further persuasion; the promise of economic gain was a satisfactory reason for them. All the male citizens of the town were circumcised. In the Hebrew Bible, they are described as "all who go out at the gate of the city." Speiser pointed out that this phrase refers to the members of the community who were capable of bearing arms.[13] On the third day, when they were in pain, the brothers seized the moment. The third day after the operation was the most painful one—a day when they were unable to resist. On that day, Simeon and Levi came to town and slew all the males including Hamor and his son Shechem. Then the brothers took Dinah from the house of Shechem. Evidently, Dinah was held in the house of Shechem throughout the whole episode. To describe the brothers' act, the narrator uses chiasmus. As described, the brothers "took Dinah" and "went away," which is a reversal of the opening of our chapter were Dinah "was going out" and being "taken" (vv. 1–2). The other brothers also took part in the massacre and plunder of the city. It was greed that motivated them. Thus, they seized the flocks, herds, and asses along with all the wealth of the town, in addition to the children and the wives. Nevertheless, the narrator stresses the fact that this act was done because their sister had been defiled.

Only after the massacre of the town's males and the pillage of the town by the brothers did Jacob break his silence and rebuke Simeon and Levi. Still, there is no mention of the brothers' pillaging of the town. More importantly, Jacob does not address the moral issue of the brothers' killing innocent people for the crime of one person. For the moment, it appears that Jacob is more concerned with his own safety and the safety of his family. He is afraid that the action of the two brothers will unite the inhabitants of the land against him and destroy his clan. It is only later, on his death bed, that Jacob's true feelings about this incident will be revealed. Jacob uses harsh language against Simeon and Levi for their cruelty and violence (we will further analyze this message in chapter 9).

The last words in the chapter are the brothers' response: "Should our sister be treated like a whore?" (v. 31). The brothers stress the fact that Dinah was their full-blooded sister. Therefore, they were responsible for her. More so, by stressing that she was their sister, they indirectly refer to the

---

12. Wenham, *Genesis 16–50*, p. 315.
13. Speiser, *Genesis*, 265; and Speiser, "'Coming' and 'Going,'" 83–88.

tension that existed in the family, which is manifested in the Joseph story. They are not referring to her as Jacob's daughter. The statement "Should our sister be treated like a whore?" probably has a double meaning. It is addressed to Shechem, and possibly to Jacob as well, who did not act after the rape of Dinah and was willing to accept gifts.[14]

It is noteworthy that in the *Testament of Levi*, the Shechemites' punishment had nothing to do with Dinah's rape, which was only one in a series of crimes committed by them, going back many generations. More so, the verdict against them was ordered in heaven. It was a "divine will."

> But I saw that God's verdict upon Shechem was "Guilty"; for they had sought to do the same thing to Sarah and Rebecca as they [now] done to Dinah our sister, but the Lord had stopped them. And in the same way they had persecuted Abraham our father when he was a stranger, and they had acted against him to suppress his flocks when they were big with young; and they had mistreated Eblaen, his home born slave. And in this way they treated all strangers, taking their wives by force and banishing them. But the anger of the Lord against them had reached its term. So I said to my father: Do not be angry, Lord, because through you the Lord will reduce the Canaanites to nothing, and he will give their land to you and your seed after you. (*T. Levi* 6:8–7:1)

The fact that the verdict against the inhabitants of Shechem were ordered in heaven is also mentioned in the book of Jubilees:

> For the verdict was ordered in heaven against them, that they might annihilate with a sword all of the men of Shechem because they committed a disgrace in Israel. And the Lord handed them over to Jacob's sons, so they might exterminate them with the sword and carry out the punishment against them. (Jubilees 30:5–6)

Justifying the Brothers' Act

The story of Genesis 34 is mentioned briefly in the writings of Philo of Alexandria in his works *De migratione Abrahami* and *De mutatione nominum*, and by Pseudo-Philo in *Liber antiquitatum biblicarum*. Interestingly, Philo, in *De mig.* 34.224, praises the brothers, Simeon and Levi, for their

---

14. Wenham, *Genesis 16–50*, 317.

act. He describes them as: "the bearers and pupils of sound sense."[15] He continues, pointing out that they overthrew the Shechemites when they were "still occupied in pleasure-loving, passion-loving toil of the uncircumcised." The next time he mentions Genesis, in *De mutatione nominum*, Simon and Levi are "the champions who stand ready to repel such profane and impure ways of thinking."[16] Dinah's story is the only story from Jacob's life that is recounted by Pseudo-Philo, whose writings date to around 100 CE. The action of the brothers here is neither praised nor condemned.

The book of Jubilees justifies the use of trickery in order to kill the Shechemites. Not only was Hamor punished, but his father and all the males in the town:

> Jacob and his sons were angry at the men of Shechem because *they* defiled Dinah, their sister. So they spoke deceptively with them and acted in a crafty manner towards them and tricked them. Simeon and Levi entered Shechem unexpectedly and carried out punishment on all the Shechemites: they killed every man whom they found there and did not leave a single one alive. They killed them all painfully because *they* had dishonored their sister Dinah. (Jubilees 30:3–4)

According to the book of Jubilees, Jacob was aware of his sons' plan of deception and agreed with them. It is not clear, however, what the nature of the deception itself was, since the part about the circumcision was omitted. Since Jacob agreed with his sons' act, in his Testament to his sons he blesses Levi (vv. 18–19). Simeon is not mentioned, but receives the blessing with the other sons of Jacob (v. 23).

The book of Judith approves Simeon and Levi's act. According to the story, Judith is a descendant of Simeon's tribe (8:1), and she lived in Bethulia, which was part of the territory that belonged to the tribe of Simeon (Josh 19:4). She killed Holofernes, the commander of the Assyrian army. Before her arrival in the enemy camp, she prayed to God, mentioning Dinah's story:

> O Lord God of my ancestor Simeon, to whom you gave *a sword* to take revenge on those strangers who had torn off a virgin's clothing to defile her, and exposed her things to put her to shame, and polluted her womb to disgrace her . . . so you gave up their rulers

---

15. Philo, *De mig.* 34.224 (Colson and Whitaker, LCL).

16. Philo, *De mutatione nominum* 36.200 (Colson and Whitaker, LCL). On Philo's view, see Pummer, "Genesis 34 in Jewish Writings," 177–88.

> to be killed, and their bed, which was ashamed of the deceits they had practiced, was stained with blood, and you struck down slaves along with princes, and princes on their thrones. (9:2–3)

In her prayer, she ascribes the sin to all the townspeople in order to justify the destruction of the city of Shechem. Levi is not mentioned by name; thus, she creates a link between Simeon, heroism, and herself. Judith mentions the story of Dinah because she is afraid that she will suffer a similar fate. She does not identify with Dinah (her name is not mentioned at all) but rather with Simeon. Like Simeon, who fought for his sister's honor, so too did Judith fight for her own honor and the honor of her city. In contrast to the biblical story where God is not mentioned at all, here God is the hero of the story. As God gave Simeon the power to destroy the people of Shechem, Judith asked God to give her the strength to destroy her enemies.

As noted above, in the book of Judith it was God who gave Simeon *a sword* to take revenge against the strangers (Jdt 9:2). In the *Testament of Levi*, it was an angel who brought him a shield and sword to take revenge on Shechem because of Dinah (*T. Levi* 5:1–3).

Another story that justifies the brothers' actions is mentioned in the Joseph and Aseneth story, which dates to the first century CE and was written in Greek. The story tells us about the conversion of Aseneth from idolatry to monotheism, and about how she worshiped Joseph's God. Aseneth, who was a virgin, had rejected numerous worthy suitors but falls in love with Joseph, who was the vizier of Egypt. Joseph, on the other hand, rejects her because she is an idol worshipper. Only after she renounces her idolatry, confesses her sin, and embraces Joseph's God does he marry her. However, she was promised to Pharaoh's son. Since Pharaoh's son had heard of the brothers' bravery, he asks them to help him against Joseph with the promise of riches. Hence, we read that the two brothers drew their swords and said: "Do you see these swords? It was with them that the Lord God avenged the outrage on the sons of Israel, which the men of Schechem committed in the affair of our sister Dinah, whom Schechem, Hamor's son, defiled" (23:13). The story does not explain from where the swords came, but it was through them that God punished the Shechemites. More importantly, the actions of the brothers in the Dinah story are justified.

The Dinah Story

Jacob and Shechem

Following his promise that God would return the Israelites to the promised land, Jacob said to Joseph: "And now, I assign to you shechem, one more than your brothers, which I wrested from the Amorites with my sword and bow" (Gen 48:22). The Targum, Peshitta, and Vulgate do not render Shechem as a place name but as a noun. Thus, they avoided the conflict with the passage in Genesis, which describes Jacob as purchasing a parcel of land in Shechem. Instead, they interpreted it as Jacob giving Joseph a double share and elevating him to the status of firstborn, which is a tradition found in 1 Chr 5:1–2. This is based on the Hebrew word *šĕkem*, which means "shoulder." To measure the size of the land and to describe it's size, the Hebrews used parts of the human body. As we saw in the story of Dinah, Jacob had nothing to do with the conquest of the city; he opposed the brothers' attack against the city and condemned them for it. However, here we find a different tradition in which Jacob describes himself as taking part in the attack on Shechem. It is also possible that Jacob attributed the victory to himself for the simple fact that, in ancient times, heroic actions of the king's warriors were attributed to the king. Therefore, Jonathan's victory in Geba was attributed to his father, King Saul (1 Sam 13:3–4). However, we have to remember that in Genesis, the patriarchs resolved their conflicts with the local population, generally, in a peaceful manner. Only Abraham fought against Chedorlaomer and the kings because he had to rescue Lot. Nevertheless, we should point out that the reading as "one portion" is difficult and does not have philological support.

A different approach is found in *Targum Pseudo-Jonathan* compared to Gen 48:22, which tries to harmonize the two texts: "And I have given you the city of Shechem, one more portion than your brothers, who have taken it from the Amorites when I came there. And I have risen and helped them with my sword and bow." More so, the sages had difficulties with the story, which describes two people who attacked the city by themselves. Therefore, they stress the strength and heroism of Jacob. Although Jacob was against his sons' actions, he saw the danger that they faced. Hence, he came to their aid:

> And came upon the city confidently. Samuel asked Levi b. Sissi: What is the meaning of "and came upon the city confidently"? They felt confident in the strength of the patriarch, he replied. Now Jacob had not desired that his sons should act so, but when his sons did perpetrate that deed he said: Shall I let my sons fall

into the hands of the heathens? What did he do? He took his sword and bow and stood at the entrance to Shechem and exclaimed, "If the heathens come to attack my sons, I will fight them." It was to this that he alluded when he said to Joseph, *Which I took out of the hands of the Amorite with my sword and with my bow* (Gen 48: 22). And where do we find that our father Jacob took up his sword and bow?—In Shechem.[17]

Is it possible that we have a reference here to the ancient tradition that describes Jacob as taking part in attacking Shechem? In opposition to this tradition, we read in the book of Joshua that the conquest of Canaan was a result of God's involvement and ". . . not by your sword or by your bow" (24:12). These are the same words that were uttered by Jacob. More so, Joshua's speech was in the city of Shechem; therefore, it is possible that it was directed against the notion that Jacob was responsible for the capturing of the city. It appears that the narrator wanted to glorify Jacob and describe him as a hero who wrestled "with God and with men."[18] Hence, he added the verse in Gen 48:22, which describes Jacob as taking part in attacking Shechem. But as previously noted, this tradition was rejected by the mainstream ideologues and only appeared in one verse.[19] More so, if indeed, Jacob took part in attacking the city, why did he criticize his sons for their actions?

An Ancient Story

Some scholars have suggested that the story of Dinah is not an ancient one.[20] It is believed that the story was added later to the book of Genesis in order to explain the harsh criticism toward Simeon and Levi: "For when angry they slay men, and when pleased they main oxen" (Gen 49:6). The story originated from the period of the judges, when lawlessness and civil disorder existed everywhere. In other words, no rape occurred and no massacre was committed by Simeon and Levi. Indeed, in Jacob's rebuke of the brothers, there is no mention of killing the whole city. It speaks only of killing one man. There is no mention in the story of hamstringing an ox. More so, the text does not say a word about Dinah. In the original story, it was a large group of Israelites who negotiated with Shechem. A single family

17. *Gen. Rab.* 80:10.
18. Zakovitch, *Jacob*, 134–35.
19. Ibid., 134.
20. Van Seters, "The Silence of Dinah," 239–47.

The Dinah Story

joining the city would not be a burden. Indeed, the author used the term "Israel," which was used to describe the nation of Israel in the later period. The original story involved a large group of Israelites that attacked the city. Circumcision helped the attackers but was not the main reason for their success. When the story was added to the book of Genesis, the numbers of the attackers was reduced to two because only Simeon and Levi were condemned for the massacre. The editor who included the story was someone who was familiar with Deuteronomy or with its laws. The description of killing all the males and sparing the women and possessions follows Deut 20:10–14. However, this suggestion still does not answer the question: why were Simeon and Levi singled out, and why were they rebuked so harshly by Jacob if, indeed, there was no rape and no massacre was committed by Simeon and Levi?

The portrayal of Simeon and Levi in Genesis is different from that of later periods. The Levites did not participate in wars of conquest; their main function was guarding the tabernacle and its sancta. The tribe did not possess any territory and did not have an association with Simeon. Later, Simeon was the military partner of Judah and lived next to it, in the southern part of Canaan. No doubt this description of the brothers reinforces our assumption that the story is ancient one.

It is surprising that we don't have any traditions of the Israelites occupying Shechem by force. Shechem was a very important city because it was the capital of the central hill country. Reading the books of Joshua and Judges reveals that it was a prosperous town. The book of Joshua does not mention that the city was conquered, nor did the books of Joshua and Judges include Shechem among the unconquered cities. More so, archeological evidence does not support the notion that the city was destroyed. Undeniably, Joshua built an altar there and made a covenant with all the Israelite tribes there. Thus, the question arises, how was the city in the hands of the Israelites in Joshua's time? It was suggested that Shechem was taken slowly by peaceful infiltration. The story in the book of Judges points to a cooperative relationship between the Israelites and the Canaanites. It was only during the period of the judges that Abimelech destroyed the city. This leads us to believe that the story in Genesis is an authentic tradition, which dates to the preconquest times. It is not a retrojection of later events.[21]

---

21. Sarna, *Understanding Genesis*, 407.

Story Against Intermarriages

One possible explanation for including the story of Dinah is the biblical stance on the subject of intermarriages. In Genesis, there is no law that prohibits intermarriages. However, the patriarchs practiced endogamy within the family. Therefore, we read that Abraham married his half-sister, Sarah; Isaac married his cousin Rebecca; and Jacob married two sisters, Leah and Rachel, who were also his cousins. Esau married outside the clan when he married a Hittite woman, which was a source of bitterness for his father and mother (Gen 26:35). Later, in order to appease his parents, and in particular his father (28:8), he went to his uncle Ishmael and married his daughter Mahalath. The objection against intermarriages is mentioned again in the conversation between Rebecca and Isaac. When Rebecca feared that Esau might kill Jacob, she devised a plan to send her son, Jacob, away. To receive her husband's consent, she mentioned to him that Esau took foreign wives (v. 46). To prevent this from happening again, Jacob is sent to Mesopotamia. Furthermore, in Isaac's blessing to Jacob, he instructs him not to take a wife from among the Canaanites. He explicitly tells him to go to his uncle's house and marry one of his daughters. The reader may recall the patriarch's privilege to decide who his son would marry.

A law prohibiting intermarriages appears for the first time in the book of Exodus: "And when you take wives from among their daughters for your sons, their daughters will lust after their gods and will cause your sons to lust after their gods" (34:16). In addition, this prohibition appears twice in Deuteronomy (7:1–6; 23:4).

> You shall not make marriages with them, giving your daughters to their sons or taking their daughters for your sons . . . For you are a people holy to the Lord your God; the Lord your God has chosen you to be a people for his own possession, out of all the peoples that are on the face of the earth (Deut 7:3–6).

Later, the subject of intermarriage became a major concern, specifically after the return from exile. The book of Ezra describes in detail the intermarriages of officers, priests, and the Levites: "They have taken their daughters as wives for themselves and for their sons, so that the holy seed has intermingled with the people of the land and it is the officers and prefects who have taken the lead in this trespass" (9:2). It appears that the leaders themselves were among the offenders and apparently did not see intermarriages as sinful. When Ezra learned about this, he tore his clothes as

The Dinah Story

a sign of mourning. Ezra demanded the expulsion of the women. Did Ezra succeed? The Bible tells us that a commission of inquiry was appointed. The commission presented a list of intermarriages (Ezra 10:18–44). The end of the list states: "All these had married foreign women, among whom were some women who had borne children" (10:44). The text is ambiguous here, so we do not know if the expulsion of the women was successful.

Similarly, the book of Nehemiah deals with the subject of intermarriage. In chapter 13, Nehemiah writes: "In those days also I saw Jews who had married women of Ashdod, Ammon, and Moab; and half of their children spoke the language of various peoples" (Neh 13:23–24). Nehemiah recognized the importance of language for preserving the national identity and the importance of language to religion. Nehemiah reacts violently to intermarriage: "And I contended with them and cursed them and beat some of them and pulled out their hair . . ." (13:25). He also tried to convince the people of Israel not to marry foreigners. Thus, he mentions Solomon's sin caused by intermarriages. In contrast to Ezra, who demanded an immediate and cruel expulsion of foreign women, Nehemiah was more realistic and practical and asked the Israelites to abstain from intermarriages in the future.

This condemnation of intermarriage is also found in post-biblical texts, among them the book of Jubilees. The book recounts the history from the beginning until the exodus from Egypt and the Sabbath command that was given to Israel. Chapter 30 contains the story of Dinah, which started with the rape of Dinah and ends with the brothers' revenge. Most of the chapter deals with the question of intermarriage. Its goal is to condemn intermarriages with foreigners.

> And you, Moses, command the children of Israel and warn them not to give any of their daughters to foreigners and not to marry any foreign women, because that is abominable before the Lord. For this reason I have written for you in the words of the Torah everything that the Shechemites did to Dinah . . . Israel will not be free from uncleanness while it has one of the foreign women or if anyone has given one of his daughters to any foreign man. (Jubilees 30:11–14)

The book of Jubilees is so harsh in its condemnation of intermarriages that it mentions death as a punishment: "If there is a man in Israel who wishes to give his daughter or sister to any foreigner, he is to die. He is to be stoned because he has done something sinful and shameful within Israel" (Jubilees 30:7).

In conclusion, the story of the rape of Dinah is an ancient one. At the core of the story stands the question of intermarriage. Although in Genesis there is no law that prohibits intermarriage, the patriarchs practiced endogamous marriage within the family. Simeon and Levi, who were Dinah's full-blood brothers, took it upon themselves to prevent the undesirable marriage. In the biblical narrative, Jacob condemned the brothers' act because he feared that the actions of the two brothers would unite the inhabitants of the land against him and destroy his clan. Jacob was more concerned with his own safety and the safety of his family. Jacob did not address the moral issue of the brothers killing innocent people for the crime of one person. In contrast, justification for the brothers' act is mentioned in the writings of Philo and Pseudo-Philo, the book of Jubilees, the book of Judith, and the *Joseph and Aseneth* story. More so, according to the *Testament of Levi* and the book of Jubilees, the brothers' act was according to divine will. In Gen 48:22, there is a reference to the ancient tradition that describes Jacob as taking part in attacking Shechem. It appears that the narrator wanted to glorify Jacob and to describe him as a hero who wrestled both "with God and with men." But this tradition was rejected by the mainstream ideology.

In the next chapter, we will examine the final chapter of Jacob's life, which is intertwined with the Joseph story. It is primarily a story of family and the relationship dynamics that exist in it. The story contains elements of jealousy and hate, love, and forgiveness. Hence, we will look into the relationship between Jacob and his beloved son Joseph, and the relationship between Joseph and his brothers. We trust that this, in turn, will give us a better understanding of the life of Jacob.

8

Jacob and Joseph

CHAPTERS 37–50 IN THE book of Genesis are part of the so-called Joseph cycle.[1] These chapters describe the story of Joseph from his youth until his death at the age of 110 years. The story is a long one and is labeled a novella. There is a flow to the story, and most of the time there are smooth transitions between the chapters. This is in glaring contrast to the patriarchal narrative, which is fragmentary in nature. But the main difference between the story of Joseph and the patriarchal narrative is the figure of God. In the Joseph cycle, there is no theophany and God does not intervene, God is behind the scenes; nevertheless, his guiding hand is felt throughout the narrative. Intertwined within the Joseph cycle is the continuing story of Jacob and the description of his final years. From the sale of Joseph into slavery until Jacob's reunion with his son Joseph, we read about tribulations of hard life that Jacob endured. In this part of the book of Genesis, the patriarch Jacob is no longer the main character, instead he is shadowed by his son Joseph, and Jacob plays a secondary roll. Hence, the current chapter will describe Jacob's final years. We will examine the relationship between Jacob and his sons, focusing on Jacob's relationship with his favorite son, Joseph. In addition, we will scrutinize the relationships between Joseph and his brothers, which will help us see the dynamics that existed in Jacob's family.

The Sale of Joseph

Joseph is the hero of chapters 37–50. Predictably, chapter 37 starts with: "This, then, is the line of Jacob: At seventeen years of age, Joseph tended

1. For extensive study on the Joseph story, see Redford, *A Study of the Biblical Story of Joseph*; Vergote, *Joseph en Égypte*; Coats, *From Canaan to Egypt*.

the flocks with his brothers" (Gen 37:2). This is the first time that Joseph is mentioned, except for the earliest short note of his birth. This is typical to the biblical narrative, which passes over the life of its heroes many times with silence. Ironically, we read that Joseph tended flocks with his brothers and was a helper to the sons of his father's wives, Bilhah and Zilpah. Joseph, the son of Jacob's beloved wife Rachel, is found in an inferior position; therefore, he is ranked by the sons of these concubines. It is possible that the sons of the concubines treated him harshly. This might explain his motivation for bringing bad reports about them to his father. The first detail the reader sees about Jacob is: "And Israel loved Joseph more than all his sons, for he was the son of his old age" (v. 3). Jacob evidently repeated the same mistake committed by his parents; he showed favoritism to his son Joseph. It was the favoritism that his parents displayed—Isaac for Esau and Rebecca for Jacob—that accelerated the rivalry between the brothers. Now in his old age, Jacob does the same. More so, to show the parental preference, the biblical narrator says: "and he made him an ornamented tunic" (v. 3). This was not missed by his brothers; therefore, in the next verse we read, "And his brothers saw that their father loved him more than his brothers and they hated him and could not speak a friendly word to him" (v. 4).

The hatred of the brothers toward Joseph intensifies with Joseph's dreams. The dreams in the Joseph cycle appear in pairs. In chapter 37, there is a description of Joseph's two dreams. These dreams are symbolic, and God does not appear in them. In the first dream, which is a reflection of daily life, Joseph describes how he and his brothers were gathering sheaves in the fields when suddenly the sheaves of the brothers bowed down to his sheaves. Although the dream was a symbolic one, the brothers understood its meaning and did not need someone to interpret it. The dream was obvious and reflected Joseph's desire to dominate his brothers. What Joseph could not achieve in his daily life he dreamt about. Joseph's retelling of the dream was not prudent since it added fuel to the fire, and the brothers hated him more for his dream. Note that the biblical narrator mentions dreams in the plural while, so far, the Bible has mentioned only one dream. Hence, it might anticipate the second dream, or it is possible that this was one in a series of dreams that was narrated by Joseph. The narrator uses wordplay on Joseph's name *Yôsēp* by using the root *y-s-p* to say, "so they hated him even more."

The second dream is a repetition of the first one, but the symbols are changed. Here, in the dream, Joseph dreams of the sun, the moon, and eleven stars that bow to him. The dream has a celestial setting. The sun represents his father, and the moon his mother, whereas the eleven stars represent his brothers. The brothers are compared to the stars probably because Israel has been compared to the stars of heaven many times. In contrast to the first dream, Joseph's parents are also included in the second dream. They also bow to him. Just like with his first dream, Joseph recounted his dream to his brothers, but this time in the presence of his father. Upon hearing the dream, Jacob did not lose any time and rebuked Joseph—this probably came to ease the tension between Joseph and his brothers. According to Ramban, the father alone replied in the presence of the brothers to allow them to hear the rebuke. He further asked him, "Are we to come, I and your mother and your brothers, and bow low to you to the ground?" (v. 10). The fact that his mother is mentioned led the Rabbis to conclude that dreams also contain false things, since Joseph's mother, Rachel, was already dead. Another interpretation, however, is that the dream refers to Joseph's stepmother, Bilhah, who raised him. Most telling are the brothers' and father's reactions. The brothers, we are told, were angry with him. Evidently, they believed in the message of the dream—otherwise, why were they envious of Joseph? After all, Jacob "kept the matter in mind." Accordingly, he was waiting for the fulfillment of the dream. As mentioned before in chapter 6, people in the ancient world believed in dreams; they thought that dreams contained a message from God about the future.

In the next scene, Jacob sends his sons to pasture the flock at Shechem. The area of Shechem was known for its green pasture, which includes ample water supply and fertile soil. Joseph stays home with his father; why he did not join his brothers we are not told. It is only later that Jacob sends Joseph to see his brothers. Was Jacob not aware of the hatred of the brothers toward Joseph? He probably sent him in light of the previous episode, when his sons attacked the city of Shechem; Jacob was afraid of retaliatory actions from the local inhabitance of the land. To his father's request, Joseph responded with one word: *hinnēnî* (I am ready). This is the same word, and the only word, that Abraham uttered when God asked him to sacrifice his son Isaac. Joseph's response is surprising in light of the hatred the brothers harbored toward him. From Jacob's and Joseph's reactions, it appears that they did not suspect that the brothers had any malicious intentions. Hence, the brothers concealed their true intentions, keeping their feelings toward Joseph to themselves.

Joseph's arrival ignited the brothers' hatred. Just seeing him from afar, they conspired to kill him. Possibly, they recognized him from a distance because of his coat. The appearance of Joseph with the coat kindled their resentment and murderous plan. Using sarcasm, they referred to Joseph as a dreamer. Their plan was to kill him, to throw him into one of the pits, and then to say that he was devoured by an animal. The usage of the plural form, "let us kill him," shows that all the brothers took part in this plan to kill Joseph.

Only Reuben, the older brother, did not agree with his brothers' murderous plan. As the older brother, he had authority over his brothers. He tried to save Joseph, to rescue him. He suggested they throw him into the pit alive, but not kill him. His plan was probably to return to the pit and rescue Joseph, and then bring him back to his father. Why did Rueben come to Joseph's aid? Is it possible that because he lost his father's approval after the incident with Bilhah, he was now trying to restore his father's trust. More so, as the oldest son, he would be blamed for Joseph's misfortune. Reuben was sincere in his attempt to save Joseph. This is clear from his reaction when he returned to the pit and found it empty; he ripped his clothes as a sign of mourning. He did not know that the other brothers sold Joseph into slavery, so he thought that Joseph was dead. Later, when the brothers were incarcerated in Egypt for three days, they attributed their suffering to what they did to their brother Joseph. In a flashback, Reuben reminded the brothers that they did not listen to him: "Did I not tell, Do no wrong to the boy? But you paid no heed" (Gen 42:22).

When Joseph arrived, the brothers stripped him of his tunic. The coat of many colors, which was a symbol of status and showed Jacob's love for Joseph, was taken. Joseph was thrown into the pit. To convey the cruelty of the brothers, the narrator uses the verbs "stripped," "took," and "dumped." More so, while Joseph was pleading for his life (see Gen 42:21), the brothers were sitting and eating. Joseph was thrown to "an empty (*rēq*) pit" (Gen 37:24), which foreshadows the "seven empty (*hārēqôt*) years" (Gen 41:27). What saved Joseph from a certain death was Judah's idea to sell Joseph into slavery. Evidently, Judah had second thoughts about the plan to kill Joseph. Killing a person carries with it blood guilt. A murdered man's blood cries out from the ground for vengeance (Gen 4:10). Hence, to avoid blood guilt, Joseph was sold for 20 pieces of silver.

To deceive their father, the brothers took the coat of many colors and dipped it in the blood of a kid that they had slaughtered. The coat, which was a status symbol and showed Jacob's love for Joseph, now becomes the main tool of deception. More so, as mentioned in chapter 2, what we have here is measure for measure. When Jacob deceived his father Isaac, he did it with the aid of "skins of the kids" (27: 16); now, Jacob is deceived with Joseph's coat that is dipped in a kid's blood (37:31). From reading the Hebrew of verse 32, it is possible that the brothers sent the tunic to Jacob, but the second part of the verse implies that they brought the tunic themselves. The contradiction is solved by source division.[2] Conversely, as B. Jacob suggested, they sent and someone brought it to Jacob. More so, the Hebrew word conceals the sender. In other words, "Jacob will not know that the robe came from them and not even that Joseph had arrived at his destination."[3] This interpretation will solve the unlikely statement by the brothers—"your son's tunic," instead of "our brother's"—when they were speaking to Jacob about their brother. What is very clear is that the brothers were afraid of the encounter with their father, and they could not witness the grief they were causing him.

As the brothers had planned, the deception succeeded. Jacob recognized his son's garment. The word "recognize" is a key word in the Joseph narrative (v. 33; 38:25–26); the brothers failed to recognize Joseph, but he recognized them (Gen 42:7–8). The word appears first in Jacob's deception of his blind father. Isaac failed to recognize that it was Jacob whom he was blessing (Gen 27:23). Jacob's reaction is described in stages: At first he recognized the tunic. Then the bloody tunic leads him to conclude that a wild beast devoured his son. He expresses his horror by saying *ṭārōp tōrap Yosēp*. It has been suggested that this form and repetition of the verb points to a standard cry of lament when someone was attacked by an animal.[4] Since Jacob pronounces the death of his son, he rends his garment in an act of mourning and puts sackcloth on his loins. More so, he laments for his son for many days. He was probably feeling guilty for sending his son. This suffering of Jacob will last for 22 years until they are reunited (41:46; 41:3; 45:6). He refuses his children's consolation and wishes to go down and meet Joseph in Sheol. According to the Hebrew Bible, all the dead descend to a place named Sheol. The good and bad go to Sheol, and there is no return from there. In the Hebrew Bible, there is no heaven or hell—this concept will be developed only later. Interestingly, in the last part of v. 35, after Jacob

---

2. Westermann, *Genesis 37–50*, p. 43.
3. Jacob, *The First Book of the Bible*, 255.
4. Westermann, *Genesis 37–50*, p. 43.

expresses his wish to go down to Sheol, we read: "Thus his father bewailed him." The Hebrew language used here makes it possible that the reference is to Isaac, who wept for his son Jacob. Indeed, according to the biblical chronologies, Isaac lived another 12 years after the sale of Joseph.

Joseph and His Brothers

It will take more than 20 years for the brothers to meet Joseph. The 13 years that Joseph spent in slavery, in addition to the 7 years of plenty, had elapsed. While the Bible concentrates all this time on Joseph, there is not a single word about Jacob; for four chapters he is ignored. As Joseph had predicted, the years of famine arrived, now the scene shifts back to Canaan, Jacob, and his sons. Jacob hears that there is plenty of grain in Egypt. He criticizes his sons for lack of action and orders them to go down to procure rations. He asserts his authority as the old patriarch. The brothers were aware of the famine and they felt it. They probably even considered a trip to Egypt, which was known as the granary for the surrounding countries. It seems that they were reluctant to suggest this idea to their father because they did not know how to present it. Will their father let them go, or maybe it would remind him of their previous trip, which led to Joseph's "death."[5]

The rations in Egypt were based on per capita; therefore, ten brothers went down to Egypt. The brothers are referred to as Joseph's brothers in preparation for meeting with him. Previously, Jacob showed favoritism toward Joseph, now he shows it to Benjamin. The narrator mentions the fact that Benjamin is Joseph's brother, the second son of Jacob's beloved wife Rachel. Like Joseph, who enjoyed a special status, now it is Benjamin who replaces Joseph as his father's favorite. Since Benjamin was his favorite, Jacob is reluctant to send him to Egypt. He is afraid that another "accident" might happen to him. He uses an elusive term to describe it. Both Rachel and Joseph had encountered misfortune during a journey.

Jacob again is withdrawn to backstage when his sons went down to Egypt as he ordered them. In Egypt, they met the vizier of the land who is no other than their brother Joseph. Joseph recognized them, but they fail to recognize him. Seeing the brothers bowing down to him brought back memories of his boyhood dreams; his dreams are being fulfilled. Joseph treats his brothers harshly as he accuses them of spying. He probably did it because he wanted to get information about his father and brother who

---

5. Jacob, *The First Book of the Bible*, 283.

were left home in Canaan. In addition, he wanted to know whether the brothers felt any remorse and changed their evil inclination. This line of interrogation proved helpful and, thereby, Joseph discovered that his father and brother were still alive. To see if the brothers truly changed, he puts them through a series of tests. First, he suggests that one of them return to Canaan and bring their younger brother back while the rest are imprisoned. Joseph then changed his plan and incarcerated his brothers for three days. Why he confined them for three days we are not told. It is possible that Joseph wanted to exert psychological pressure on the brothers. Indeed, in the three days that they were held in prison, their feelings of guilt surfaced. The brothers felt that they were being punished on account of their brother, so they perceived it as divine retribution. Devising a new plan, Joseph allows all the brothers to return home, keeping Simeon behind in jail. Hearing that Reuben tried to save him, Joseph took Simeon into custody. He kept Simeon because he was the second son of Leah and was known for his cruelty. It is possible that he led the brothers into taking action against Joseph. The thought of how much suffering and pain he would inflict on his older father by detaining nine of his brothers probably caused Joseph to change his plan. Nevertheless, the scene of the brothers returning home with one less brother is reminiscent of the situation they faced many years earlier when they returned without Joseph.

Back in Canaan, the brothers had to face their old father Jacob. They reported to him about their meeting with "the man who is lord of the land." The man spoke to them harshly and accused them of spying. Hence, they protested and claimed to be honest men. It was the man's accusations that led them to divulge information about the family. They were twelve brothers once but no more. They did not want to mention the word dead. The younger brother is with his father in Canaan. The brothers omit the fact that they were incarcerated in Egypt for three days; more so, they did not even mention that Simeon was in custody. Instead, they say that the man told them: "leave one of your brothers with me" (v. 33). They also did not say a word about finding the money in their sacks. The hardest news they left for the end: The man asked them to bring their younger brother in order to prove that they were honest men and not spies. In exchange, the man promised to restore Simeon to them and promised that they could trade in the land. The promise of trade originates from the brothers own imagination. The brothers hoped this addition would soften Jacob. It might help to convince Jacob to see the gain, which would be the result of returning with

Benjamin. The threat that if they did not comply and return with Benjamin, he would kill them, is omitted. What the brothers are trying to do is to create a peaceful version of their trip to Egypt, to elevate their father's fears so he would agree to send Benjamin.

To delay and to increase the suspense of Jacob's reaction, the narrator describes the brothers as they are emptying their sacks and finding the money. The brothers had already found the money before they reached Canaan. Indeed, that is what they told Joseph on the next trip (43:21). However, it is their reaction and Jacob's reaction that are the keys here. From the moment that the brothers returned to Canaan, they are afraid of their father's reaction. There is a sense of tension in the text, which is expressed in verse 35 in a wordplay of "saw-dismayed" *wayyirʾû—wayyîrāʾû*. It is not only the brothers who are afraid, it is also Jacob who needs to face reality.

As what the brothers feared occurred and in an outbreak of emotion, Jacob complains that he is the one who suffers; it is his sons who disappear. He mentions Joseph who is no more, as well as Simeon. He compares Simeon's fate to Joseph's, and now they want to take Benjamin. It is here for the first time that Jacob blames his sons for the disappearance of Joseph. In chapter 37, there was no hint that Jacob was suspicious of his sons in committing a crime against Joseph. Jacob's harsh language prompted Reuben to respond. For the last time, Reuben assumes leadership. Although he knew that his father's accusations are valid, nevertheless, it was the fear of the famine that prompted him to reply. Reuben tries to convince his father to allow him to take Benjamin with him on the next journey to Egypt. He even offers to put his two sons to death if he does not return with Benjamin. Jacob remains steadfast and rejects Reuben's proposal, he does not even argue with him, he simply refused to accept any suggestion. He does not allow his son Benjamin to join the brothers. Interestingly, he refers to Benjamin here as "my son" and not "your brother." The sense that he rebukes them and the language "my son" are echoes of past events when the brothers sent the tunic to their father and said: "Is it your son's tunic?" (37:32).[6] He also changes the language, before he said that Joseph is no more; now he says that Joseph is dead. Finally, he says that if Benjamin meets a disaster on the journey, it will bring down his white head to the underworld in grief. Again there is a link to 37:55 where Jacob said: "No, I will go down mourning to my son in Sheol." The brothers do not respond because they know there is nothing they can say.

6. Sarna, *Understanding Genesis*, 297.

The next scene in chapter 43 is similar to chapter 42, as it opens with a statement about the severe famine and a discussion about a journey to Egypt to bring some food. In the first scene, when Jacob ordered his sons to go to Egypt, he asserted his authority as the patriarch. Here, for the second time, he tells them: "Go again and procure some food for us" (43:2). Jacob again tries to delay the inevitable; his sons must again go down to Egypt. But what is the meaning of "buy us a little food," as we are told that the famine is severe? Is it possible that by asking, little Jacob was hoping that they would not have to comply with the cruel conditions that the man set? But Judah removes any unrealistic thoughts from his father, and with all the cruelty, he reminds his father that the man warned them: "Do not let me see your face unless your brother with you" (v. 3). He leaves Jacob with no option but to say yes or no.

Jacob again tries to delay—to avoid making a hard decision. He blames his sons for saying too much, for divulging that they have another brother. But what can he gain now from his charges against his sons, these can't change the man's demands. Evidently, it shows how distressed Jacob was so he tries to stall. To their father's accusation, the brothers replied that the man asked them specifically about their family, about their father and brother. This account does correspond to the description of interrogation in chapter 42, where it appears that the brothers offered information freely. But, reading 44:19 shows that Joseph, indeed, asked the brothers if they had a father or brother.

From chapter 43 onward, Judah became the spokesman for the brothers, while Reuben is not heard from again. Like his brother Reuben, Judah tries to convince his father to send Benjamin with them. He repeats the words that his father previously uttered when he sent them down to Egypt: "that we may live and not die" (42:2). In addition, he adds the words "you and we and our children" (43:8). It is probably the word "children," which refers to the vulnerable young ones, that caused Jacob to agree with Judah. Not the incarceration of Simeon, who still waits for his release, or the begging of his son, or Reuben's speech, it was only the hunger of the young children that moved him. Indeed, the midrash deals with this question: In addition, Judah also pledges himself offering to stand as a guarantee for Benjamin. In other words, Jacob can demand Judah's life if he fails to bring Benjamin back home. While Reuben was willing to sacrifice the life of his two sons, Judah is prepared to sacrifice his own life. By offering himself,

Judah is now rebuking his father for procrastinating. If he had not delayed them, they could have been there and back twice.

With no other choice, Jacob places his trust in God, invoking God's mercy: "Take your brother too; and go back at once to the man. And may El Shaddai dispose the man to mercy toward you, that he may release to you your other brother, as well as Benjamin. As for me, if I am to be bereaved, I shall be bereaved." (43:13–14). Jacob ordered his sons to take a lavish gift to the man in order to soften him, which is a reminder of his own gift to his brother Esau. But the hardest of all he leaves for last, when he tells his sons to take Benjamin with them. In spite of putting his trust in God, he still utters: "If I am to be bereaved, I shall be bereaved," which is a cry of despair that expresses irrevocable fate. According to Rashi: "And as for me Until your return I shall be bereaved because of doubt. If I be bereaved of Joseph and Simeon, I am bereaved of Benjamin."

For a second time, the brothers made the trip to Egypt. Joseph sees the brothers with Benjamin but ignores them. Instead, he gave orders to send an invitation to them to go to his house where a meal was prepared for them. Because they are alone, away from all the buyers, and were taken to the man's house, the brothers were afraid that they would be enslaved. Joseph created this situation in order to have an opportunity to place a goblet into Benjamin's bag that he uses for divination. When the brothers left after dining with him, he sent men to pursue them. As planned, Joseph's goblet was found in Benjamin's bag and consequently he was accused of theft.

This act of trickery played by Joseph is very similar to what Rachel did to her father Laban, when she stole his idols. The stolen idols were used for divination as was the goblet "stolen" by Benjamin. In both stories, a group of fleeing people is pursued and caught (31:23, 25; 44:4, 6). Laban and Joseph accused the runways with theft even though they declared their innocence. The search starts with the least likely culprit. In Rachel's case, the idols that were stolen by her were not found, while with Benjamin who did not steal, the goblet was found.

The Rabbis noticed these similarities between the stories, and they added a conversation among the brothers after Benjamin was taken:

> They stand and hit Benjamin on his shoulders and say to him, "You are a thief, a son of a thief. You have shamed us. You are the son of your mother—who likewise shamed your father," "and Rachel stole the terafim (Gen 31:19)."[7]

---

7. Tanḥ. (Buber), *Mikets* 13.

When the goblet was found, the brothers ripped their clothes in horror. Death penalty was pronounced for the thief of the goblet. The brothers returned back to the city where they had to face the man. They throw themselves on the ground before him—they were desperate. The story reaches its climatic moment in the meeting between the brothers and the man. It is Judah who speaks at length to the man. This is the longest speech in the book of Genesis. The speech is divided into three parts. The first part (vv. 18–29) summarized the past events. For the first time, Joseph hears what took place at home when the brothers returned home without him. He learns of his father's lament, which still continues. Judah then goes on to explain the impact on their father if they return without Benjamin (vv. 30–32), and in the last part he offers to take Benjamin's place as a slave (vv. 33–34). The speech is a masterful one that's intended to appeal to the man's emotions and to his sense of fairness. Judah mentions the state of their aged father several times in order to evoke these emotions. He does not mention the theft of the goblet. When the brothers showed their devotion to their brother and old father, they implied that they considered the sale of Joseph a crime, and when Judah offers himself as a slave, Joseph realized that his brothers had changed. Judah's last words: "For how can I go back to my father unless the boy is with me? Let me not be witness to the woe that overtakes my father!" (v. 34). This emotional plea brings Joseph to tears and he reveals his identity (45:1–3).

It was Joseph's love for his father that caused him to reveal his true identity—he could not hold himself any more. Twice before he was overwhelmed and close to his breaking point. The first time was when Reuben reminded his brothers of the sale of Joseph (42:24); and then again when he saw Benjamin (43:30). Now, after the brothers showed their remorse and sincerity, he could not contain his feelings any more. He ordered all the people to go out. Then, he stood opposite his brothers without witness. According to Rashi: "he was unable to bear that Egyptians should stand by him and hear that his brothers are shamed when he would make himself known to them, I am Joseph whom you have sold etc." He wanted them to be respected in Egypt. He also tried to remove their fear when he no longer blamed them for having sold him into slavery. Thus, he told them that it is God who sent him ahead of them to ensure their survival. He used the verb "sent" three times to emphasize that it was God's will. He urged them to hurry back with their father.

Jacob's Migration to Egypt

The brothers return to Canaan with the news that Joseph is alive and the ruler of all Egypt (45:26). Upon hearing it, Jacob's heart went numb, he did not believe them. According to Rashi, he put it out of his mind skeptically; he did not pay attention to what he heard. Only after hearing Joseph's message and seeing the wagons that he sent, was Jacob convinced that his sons were not lying. The disbelief turned to joy; the good news revived his spirit. Interestingly, when the bad news about Joseph's disappearance arrived to him, he was called Jacob and he ripped his clothes (37:34). Now, when he receives the good news and his spirit is revived, he is called Israel. Israel is the name of the father of the brothers, who are now reconciled and united again.[8] Before, Jacob expressed his desire to go down to Sheol to meet his beloved son, now he expresses his wish to see his son in the land of the living.

On the way to Egypt, Jacob stopped at Beer Sheba and made sacrifices to the God of his father Isaac. He receives a nocturnal vision there. In the message that he received, God gave him permission to go down to Egypt. The divine promise of peoplehood is to be fulfilled in Egypt. The decent to Egypt is part of the divine plan as God told Abraham that his descendants would be strangers in a land not theirs, and they would be enslaved and oppressed for 400 years. To reassure Jacob, God told him that he would protect him in Egypt, like He protected him in Mesopotamia and Canaan. In addition, God promised that he would bring him back to Canaan. Indeed, later we read that Jacob's sons buried him in the cave of Machpelah (50:13). Finally, God's last words to Jacob: "and Joseph's hand shall close your eyes" (46:4). It is believed that this refers to the custom in which the eldest son or the nearest kin closes the eyes of the deceased.[9] Rashbam however, understood it differently and translates: "Joseph will take care of your affairs." In other words, you will live to an old age without worries.

After many years of separation, father and son are reunited. Joseph is eager to see his father, so he does not lose any time and goes to Goshen to meet him. He embraced his father around his neck and wept on his neck a good while, in other words, he wept more than is customary. When Jacob received the news that Joseph was "dead," he wept over Joseph, now it's Joseph's time to cry. Hence, we read that Jacob did not fall upon Joseph's neck and did not kiss him. Maybe it is because Jacob was overwhelmed by

---

8. Jacob, *The First Book of the Bible*, 307.
9. Sarna, *Understanding Genesis*, 313.

emotion. Now, after seeing his son, he declares that he is ready to die. There are no more questions about the faith of his beloved son.

After Joseph met with his father, he arranged for an audience of his brothers with Pharaoh (47:1–2). Accordingly, the brothers were presented before Pharaoh and requested residence in the region of Goshen. Their request was approved by Pharaoh, who further instructed Joseph to appoint some of his brothers as "keepers" of the royal holdings to be in charge of his livestock. What is interesting here is that for his father, he arranged a separate audience because the nature of this meeting was far different. The brothers appeared before Pharaoh as petitioners, but that's not the case with Jacob. He appeared as the old patriarch who blessed Pharaoh. The Hebrew word *bārak* can mean bless or greet. In the ancient world, there was a custom where people would wish the king a long life (2 Sam 16:16; 1 Kgs 1:31). In our text, it probably means "greet with blessing."[10] Later, the Rabbis formulated a special prayer for an appearance before a king: "Praised be who has given of his splendor to human beings."[11] In the meeting, Pharaoh asked Jacob his age. There is no particular reason for asking Jacob his age, unless he looked older than anyone Pharaoh had seen before. In Egypt, the ideal life span was 110, so Pharaoh wondered if Jacob exceeded it.[12] He reveals his age to be 130 years old, which he refers to as few and hard. According to the Ramban, he did not yet live nearly as long as Abraham or Isaac, but he aged due to a life filled with arduous hardship. The biblical account mentions that his father Isaac lived 180 years (Gen 35:28), and his grandfather Abraham 175 years (25:7). Indeed, as mentioned before, Jacob's life is one long struggle. He had to flee from his brother Esau to Haran, then he endured hardship in Laban's house. He had to deal with two jealous wives and the death of his beloved wife Rachel. His daughter Dinah was raped; he thought that his beloved son Joseph was dead. No reaction on Pharaoh's part—he does not respond. Jacob pronounces a second blessing on Pharaoh, and then he departs.

Jacob is the only patriarch who died in a foreign land. His demise is described in detail; he prepares to die (47:28–31). He lived 17 years in Egypt out of 140 years. In Egypt, he lived with Joseph for 17 years, which equals the number of years he lived with him in Canaan. Jacob does not want to be buried in Egypt, he wants to be buried in his ancestral grave.

---

10. McKenzie, "Jacob's Blessing," 390–95; Hamilton, *Genesis: Chapters 18–50*, p. 610
11. *b. Ber.* 58a.
12. Sarna, *Understanding Genesis*, 320.

The desire to be buried in one's own land is mentioned in other ancient Near East texts. In the story of Sinhue, for example, we read of an Egyptian official who fled from Egypt to Asia in spite of his success in exile, he says:

> Whichever god decreed this flight, have mercy, bring me home! Surely you will let me see the place in which my heart dwells! What is more important than that my corpse be buried in the land which I was born! Come to my aid![13]

Jacob asked Joseph to put his hand under his thigh. Putting the hand under the thigh was an integral part of oath-taking. Usually, people raised their hand or held a ritual object. The scene is very similar to the description of Genesis 24:1–9, where Abraham made a similar request from his servant. Jacob wanted to lie down with his fathers. It was believed that after death, people are reunited with their ancestors. Later, Joseph would make a similar request, he asked his brothers to bury him in the land of Canaan (50:25); this request was fulfilled at the time of the Exodus. In addition to putting the hand under the thigh, Jacob asked Joseph to take an oath: "swear to me." In the ancient world, taking an oath was a sacred act. The words "swear to me" are the same words that Jacob used many years earlier when he bought the birthright from his brother Esau (25:33). Joseph would mention his swearing to his father when he requested permission from Pharaoh to go and bury him. Indeed, Pharaoh would mention the oath when granting Joseph the permission. In reaction to Joseph swearing, Jacob bowed at the head of the bed. There is no explanation for this act. Hence, probably it was a sign of gratitude to Joseph or to God or also a prayer. The bowing is also fulfillment of Joseph's dream (37:9–10); where he dreamt that in addition to his brothers, his father and mother bowed to him.

In the next scene, Jacob is meeting with Joseph and his two sons, Manasseh and Ephraim. These two sons are promoted to the status of Israelite tribes as equal to Jacob's son. A parallel is made between Joseph's sons, Ephraim and Manasseh, with Jacob's oldest sons, Reuben and Simeon. By elevating Joseph's sons, Jacob is in effect adopting them as his own, in other words, he gave Joseph a double portion of the inheritance. Jacob also mentioned the younger son, Ephraim, first, in contrast to their order at birth; thus, we have here a hint about the forthcoming developments. It's noteworthy that in contrast to his father Isaac, who wanted to bless only

---

13. Lichtheim, *Ancient Egyptian Literature*, 1:228; Hamilton, *Genesis: Chapters 18–50*, p. 624 no. 15.

Esau, Jacob wanted to bless Joseph's two sons. However, he still wants to bless the younger brother over the older brother.

A puzzling question appears in verse 8. When Joseph's sons stood next him, Jacob asked, "Who are these?" This kind of question is possible only after Jacob's arrival to Egypt.[14] A possible solution is that the verses were artificially placed or the story of Joseph is made up from a different origin. Traditional commentators solved the problem by pointing to verse 10, where Jacob is described with poor vision. Jacob could still see, therefore, he saw two young men in front of him but could not recognize them. Mentioning the poor vision explains Joseph's reaction in the next scene. Interestingly, the description of Jacob's poor vision is similar to his father Isaac. The scene is patterned after chapter 27. Isaac, Jacob's father, also suffered from failing eyesight, which enabled Jacob to steal the blessing. However, Joseph, in contrast to Jacob, was a righteous man and did not use trickery to take advantage of his father.

Jacob kissed and embraced Joseph's sons. This act was part of the blessing ritual and similar to the scene where Isaac pronounced his blessing. What is missing here are the offerings of food and drink.[15] The two verbs "kissed and embraced" appear only in the Jacob cycle in 29:13 and 33:4, however, the order is reversed where embrace appears before the kiss. Jacob blessed his two grandsons so they would proliferate abundantly; this blessing is similar to the blessing that was given to the patriarchs (17:2; 22:17; 26:4; 35:11). The Hebrew word *weyidgû* describes proliferation, which comes from the word *dag* (fish), in other words: May they be like fish, which are fruitful and multiply. The root *d-g-y* is a synonym of *p-r-y* (to be fruitful), and this root is part of the name of Ephraim. Evidently, Jacob planned to give the larger part of the blessing to Ephraim. When Joseph saw that his father placed his right hand on Ephraim's head and his left hand on Manasseh's, he realized that his father was planning to pass over the older son. Thus, when Joseph tries to remove Jacob's hand from Ephraim's head to Manasseh's, he thought that the poor vision of his father caused him to mix the two. Manasseh is like the other firstborn in Genesis that were passed by for different reason like Cain, Ishmael, Esau, Reuben, and Zerah. No reason is given for Jacob passing over Manasseh. Jacob insists on blessing Ephraim, he saw into the future, he spoke like a person that possessed a prophetic spirit. Indeed, in the ancient world, it was believed that the dying

---

14. Rad, *Genesis*, 415.
15. Westermann, *Genesis 37–50*, p. 187.

could see into the future, therefore, great importance was attributed to what they said before their death.[16] The difference in the blessing is quantities—to the elder he promised to become a people and to be great, but the younger brother would be more numerous fathering a group of nations. This was true at least in the beginning where, according to census results, Ephraim numbered 45,000 descendants, while Manasseh had 32,000 (Num 1:32–33 and 34–35). Later, however, the numbers were reversed and Manasseh had more descendants 52,700 to Ephraim's 32,500 (Num 26:34, 37). However, this again was changed. Joshua, the leader of Israel, belonged to the tribe of Ephraim and important places such as Shechem and Shiloh were in his territory. In the time of the Judges and with the divided monarchy, Ephraim was the leading tribe of the "House of Joseph" and represented the whole north in contrast to Judah to the south.[17]

Jacob blessed his grandsons once more after Joseph's interruption. He blesses them with a single blessing: "God make you like Ephraim and Manasseh" (Gen 48:20). As before, he puts Ephraim before Manasseh, hence, he reaffirms Ephraim's precedence over Manasseh. The blessing is for fruitfulness, and it follows a similar blessing in Genesis (12:3b; 18:18; 26:4; 28:14). Their blessing became an object of reference, and anyone who wishes to bless someone is to use this form of blessing. The blessing attests to the greatness of these two tribes. This form of blessing existed in ancient Israel as we read in the book of Ruth: "May the Lord make the woman who is coming into your house like Rachel and Leah, both of whom built up the House of Israel . . . And may your house be like the house of Perez whom Tamar bore to Judah . . ." (Ruth 4:11–12). On the other hand, a negative formula is used by Jeremiah: "And the whole community of Judah in Babylonia shall use a curse derived from their fate: 'May God make you like Zedekiah and Ahab whom the king of Babylon consigned to the flames!—because they did vile things in Israel" (Jer 29:22). To this day, Jacob's words are used when a Jewish parent blesses their sons on Shabbat eve, they say: "May God make you like Ephraim and Manasseh." When they bless their daughter they say: "May God make you like Sarah, Rebecca, Rachel, and Leah."

In conclusion, like the previous chapters of the book of Genesis (25–35), which describe the adversity and tribulations that Jacob endured throughout life, the same theme is found in the Joseph cycle. Jacob's life is a long journey of hardship. We would expect Jacob to learn from his mistakes

---

16. Gaster, *Myth, Legend, and Customs*, 214.
17. Delitzsch, *Genesis*, 2:362; and Dillmann, *Genesis*, 2:438–39.

in the past and to learn from past experiences. However, this is not the case here. Jacob made the same errors that his parents made. He showed favoritism toward his son Joseph, who was the son of his beloved wife. This, in turn, led to the animosity that Jacob's sons harbored toward Joseph. The brothers' hatred toward Joseph intensifies with Joseph's dreams, which eventually led to Joseph's sale into slavery. Like his father Isaac, who was not aware of the rivalry between his sons Jacob and Esau, similarly, Jacob did not suspect that his sons had any malicious intentions toward Joseph. Hence, the brothers concealed their true intentions and kept their feelings toward Joseph to themselves. The brothers were consumed with so much hatred that it appears they did not give much thought to their actions and the pain that they inflict upon their father.

The suffering of Jacob would last for 22 years until he reunited with Joseph. As for the brothers, it would take more than 20 years for them to meet Joseph. In those meetings, Joseph would put his brothers through tough tests. At the same time, his old father Jacob was waiting in Canaan for the return of his sons from Egypt. Did Joseph not have any mercy on his father? It appears that Joseph tested his brothers in order to see if they had changed their evil thoughts and showed remorse. The tests, indeed, proved the brothers felt remorse and had a change of heart. Jacob lived with Joseph in Egypt for 17 years, which is the same number of years they lived together in Canaan. In Jacob's meeting with Pharaoh, he refers to the years of his life as few and hard. Like other firstborn in Genesis that were passed by for different reasons, Jacob passes over Manasseh and blesses Ephraim; no reason is given for this. This continues the theme of the Jacob cycle where the younger surpasses the older.

Following the theme of blessings, our next chapter will examine the Testament of Jacob. Before his death, Jacob spoke his last words to his sons, which include the blessing he bestowed upon them.

9

The Testament of Jacob

Genesis 49:1–28 is the first long poem in the Hebrew Bible. Before his death, Jacob calls his sons and tells them their future as well as the future of the twelve tribes. In verse 1, Jacob's sayings are characterized as predictions. They appear in the form of commands and wishes expressed by Jacob. The testament includes ten of Jacob's sayings, which are addressed to each son individually. Simeon and Levi are mentioned together. The poem ends with the words, "All these were the tribes of Israel, twelve in number, and this is what their father said to them as he bade them farewell, addressing to each a parting word appropriate to him" (v. 28). Though Gen 49:1–28 is often called the "Blessing of Jacob," close examination shows otherwise. It contains curses in addition to praises along with geographical and historical details. Ibn Ezra wrote:

> Those who say these are blessings, on the grounds that the passage concludes with the words "and he blessed them," are mistaken; where are the blessings to Reuben, Simeon and Levi? And so far as the conclusion "and this is what their father said to them" (49:28) "and afterwards he blessed them," [this is true] but Scripture does not mention what the blessing was.

In other words, what came before are not blessings. Therefore, titles such as "The Last Words of Jacob" or "The Testament of Jacob" are more appropriate. In this chapter, we will discuss Jacob's words to his sons and see what's behind them. The maxims are a collection of independent sayings that refer to different events and different situations. Some refer to the past, while others allude to events 100 years in the future. Hence, we will try to identify those events and see if they indeed match our knowledge of the earlier period of the patriarch Jacob and see if some of his predictions ring true in light of the later biblical text.

The Maxims' Period

In verse 1, Jacob tells his sons, "Come together that I may tell you what is to befall you in days to come." It is comprised of a collection of maxims about the different tribes and their future. However, there is a problem with this assumption because some of the details do not refer to the future. Instead, they describe events from the present and past. The sages noted, "Jacob wished to reveal to his sons the end of the withdrawal of God's right hand from the battle against the enemies of the Jewish people, but the divine Presence departed from him and he was unable to do so."[1]

Modern scholars have not reached a consensus on the dating of the Testament of Jacob. It is possible that verses 23–24 allude to the wars between Israel and Aram in the seventh century BCE. Therefore, the composition is from a later periods. Because verse 10 speaks of the hegemony of Judah over the other tribes, there might be a case for later composition. Hence, "the scepter shall not depart from Judah" was understood as a prophecy for the rise of the Davidic dynasty or the Messiah. Thus, it is possible that this part was composed during the time of David or Solomon. An earlier period of composition can be surmised from the tribes' places of habitat, Zebulon (v. 13) and possibly Issachar (vv. 14–15), the scattering of Simeon and Levi (vv. 5–7), and the power of the tribes of Judah (vv. 8–12) and Joseph (vv. 22–26). These descriptions of the tribes suit the period of the judges. In this period, the tribe of Levi was scattered in the Levitical cities and became a priestly tribe of which there is no hint in Genesis. The tribe of Simeon was in the process of being absorbed by Judah. According to Josh 19:10–16, the tribe of Zebulun occupied inland territory and was blocked from the sea by the tribe of Asher. Not so in Genesis, where Zebulun dwells by the seashore.

The geographical and historical conditions mentioned in the poem make it possible to date the poem to the judges' period with some revisions in the tenth century BCE. Dillmann points out that the poem was remote from Jacob's era, yet it was written before the dissolution of the tribal organization under the monarchy/monarchial period. He maintains that the date of composition belongs to the period of the judges.[2] Seebas

---

1. *b. Pesaḥ.* 56a.
2. Dillmann, *Genesis*, 2:447.

has a similar view, and according to him, apart from a few glosses (vv. 7b, 8b–9, 18), the poem predates the Song of Deborah and probably originated in the twelfth century BCE.[3] Alternatively, Delitzsch argued that the poem originated with Jacob. He pointed out the inconsistencies with the descriptions of the tribes following their settlement and the vision described in the poem. In particular, he stressed the irrelevance of the condemnation of Reuben, Simeon, and Levi, which are only conceivable from a pre-Mosaic standpoint. The saying concerning Zebulun's territory was never realized in the time of Joshua or under the kings. And the sayings concerning Issachar are different from the Song of Deborah. Verse 23 can also be understood without being a reflection of Syrian warfare.[4] On the other hand, Gunkel maintains that the sayings of Gen 49 belong to various eras. According to him, "Next to Judg 5, Gen 49 is the most important chapter in the OT for the earliest history of the tribes."[5]

Deuteronomy 33 shows that during the holidays when the Israelites would gather, the priests would bless the tribes' representatives before they returned home. The similarity between Gen 49, Deut 33, and some details in the Song of Deborah proves that there was a tradition to bless the tribes. The content of the blessing varied from tribe to tribe and was changed with the passing of time and according to the changing circumstances. This custom, according to which each tribe received his own particular blessing, suits the judges' period. In that period, the fate of each tribe was different, and many times it had to do with its relationship with the surrounding nations. Thus, blessings could not exist in the monarchial period. It is possible that the roots of this tradition originate from the time of Moses, or even from an earlier period, which included memories of the time of the patriarchs. It is most likely that Moses blessed the Israelites before his death, and likewise the patriarch Jacob did the same. The fact is, there are two versions of blessings—one attributed to Moses and the other to Jacob, which points to the antiquity of this custom. Since the blessings are connected to the earlier period of the patriarchs, it is possible that the content of the blessing was linked to the deeds of the tribe's founder. In other words, the destiny of the tribe was a reward or punishment that is based on the behavior of its founder.

Upon examination of Jacob's sayings, we find that there is no connection between them. The Testament of Jacob is a collection of independent

3. Seebass, "Die Stämmessprüche," 333–50.
4. Delitzsch, *Genesis*, 2:367.
5. Gunkel, *Genesis*, 453.

sayings that refer to different events and different situations. Indeed, some refer to the past while others allude to events hundreds of years into the future. Nevertheless, there is still a connection between the Testament and the earlier parts of Genesis. The order of the maxims from Rueben to Benjamin corresponds to the order of the births of Jacob's sons, which are narrated in Gen 29:32–34; 35:18. Jacob's condemnations of Reuben and later of Simeon and Levi, refer to episodes that are mentioned in chapters 34 and 35:22.

The six sons of Leah are addressed first, and Rachel's two sons last. In between, the sons of the maidservants are mentioned. Here the tribal order does not coincide with the birth stories narrated in chapters 29–30. It has been suggested that they were arranged in chiastic order: Dan son of Bilhah, Gad son of Zilpah, Asher son of Zilpah, and Naphtali son of Bilhah.[6] Each group is mentioned in descending order of rank. The only exception is Issachar and Zebulun, which is reversed because of historical reasons. Dillmann suggests that the order of the tribes reflects their settlement from the north, Dan (Josh 19:40–48), Gad (Num 32:33–36), Asher (Josh 19:24–31), and Naphtali (Josh 19:32–39).[7]

The saying about Reuben, Levi, Simeon, Judah, and Joseph are lengthy ones, while the sayings of the other tribes are short ones. The two tribes of Joseph and Judah dominate this poem; there are five verses devoted to each of these 2 tribes, which means 10 of 24 lines in this poem. This is not a coincidence, because they are the main characters of the Joseph cycle. More so, Judah is the ancestor of the Davidic kingdom of Judah, and Joseph's tribes' progeny, in particular Ephraim, represent the future kingdom of Israel. In contrast to the blessing of Moses, Jacob reprimanded some of the tribes such as Reuben, Simeon, and Levi. The aim was to explain their fate, which was a result of their wrongdoing. This resulted in a small territory, and therefore, Rueben had a small territory compared to Judah, Simeon's territory was within Judah's, and Levi had only scattered cities. Dan, Gad, and Benjamin are described as fighting for their survival, while the tribes of Issachar, Zebulun, Asher, and Napthali are portrayed as serving others. A similar narrative is also found in Judg 1, which describes the settlement of the tribes in Canaan. Judah marches first and leads the attack against the Canaanites (vv. 1–20). Next to Judah is the House of Joseph, who captures Bethel with trickery (vv. 22–26). The other tribes fail to dispossess the

6. Sarna, *Understanding Genesis*, 331.
7. Dillmann, *Genesis*, 2:445.

inhabitants of the land. They are required to perform forced hard labor for them and are pressured by them. Evidently, the aim of Gen 49 and Judg 1 is to praise and glorify the tribe of Judah above all the other tribes.

Reuben

Reuben was the firstborn son; therefore, Jacob addresses him first. Reuben is criticized for his moral failing because he slept with his father's concubine, Bilhah (Gen 35: 22). Reuben abused his power as head of the tribes. In all the genealogies, he appears as the firstborn. In Joseph's sale into slavery, Reuben plays a prominent role. He appears mindful of his position. The loss of leadership reflects an early period since there is no testimony that alludes to the hegemony of this tribe. There is no conceivable reason for inventing a story about Reuben as a firstborn. The fact that we have here an early tradition about Reuben stems from the fact that, in an earlier period, the patriarch still had the authority to transfer the birthright. This is in contrast to the later period, which is attested to in the legislation of Deuteronomy (21:15–17). Reuben joined the list of eldest sons in Genesis who lost their privileged position, such as Cain, Ishmael, Esau, and Er.

In verse 3, Reuben receives praises for his position as the firstborn; in verse 4, he is degraded from it. Reuben is called the "first product" of Jacob's manly strength and power. As the firstborn, he should have preeminence over his brothers in position and power. However, Reuben is described as unstable as water; a reckless person. This motif of water, which refers to human character, is mentioned in Isaiah: "But the wicked are like troubled sea / Which cannot rest / Whose waters toss up mire and mud" (57:20). Jacob turns from addressing Reuben directly and uses the third person form of speech. He refers to Reuben's sexual act, which is also recorded in the book of Chronicles: "Reuben the first-born of Israel. He was the firstborn; but when he defiled his father's bed, his birthright was given to the son of Joseph, son of Israel" (5:1). The Chronicler explains Reuben's loss of his birthright as a punishment for a sin that is recorded in Gen 35:22. According to the Chronicler, the birthright was transferred to Joseph, but in reality, the leadership of the tribes was transferred to Judah, who became the strongest among his brothers. Jacob used harsh language to describe Reuben's act—"you brought disgrace." The Hebrew root *h-l-l*, which means "to pollute, defile, profane" is used to describe sexual immorality. The third person form of speech also appears in the last part of verse 4, when Jacob describes Reuben's action he says, "my couch he mounted." Evidently, Jacob addresses all his sons here.

Reuben is mentioned in the tribal blessings of Moses: "May Reuben live and not die" (Deut 33:6). This represents a period in time where the tribe's existence was threatened. Although, we should point out that in the censuses of Num 1 and 26, Reuben's numbers are not so small. But in the monarchial period from David on we read only of a Moabite-Ammonite region, not of Reuben's territory, which points to the tribe's decline. One explanation is that Reuben's population and territory were assimilated by Gad. Another theory suggests that it was threatened because it was slow to become sedentary. The Reubenites remained seminomadic, pastoralist people who were inadequately organized, which invited attacks from the neighboring non-Israelite tribes.[8] In the post-Mosaic era, there is no testimony from any source attributing importance to the tribe. Thus, no judge, king, or prophet was designated as a Reubenite.

Simeon and Levi

Jacob's second and third sons, Simeon and Levi, are addressed next. The brothers are linked together because of their joint attack against the city of Shechem, which is mentioned in chapter 34. It was their cruelty that received their father's rebuke. At first, Jacob rebuked the brothers because he was afraid: "You have brought trouble on me, making me odious among the inhabitants of the land, the Canaanites and Perizzites; my men are few in numbers, so if they unite against me and attack me, I and my house will be destroyed" (v. 30). Jacob ignored the moral question here, that the brothers had killed innocent people who were punished for the crime of one man. It is only with the passage of time that Jacob relates to the moral act of the brothers. Jacob mentions that they are brothers—indeed, they are brothers from the same parents, but also brothers in crime. It is because they were blood brothers of Dinah that they were so outraged at her defilement. Their weapons are tools of lawlessness. The Hebrew language is difficult. Various interpretations have been offered, which appear to be guesswork.[9] After the opening statement about the brothers, Jacob dissociated himself from them. He did not want to be linked with them because of their violence. The rea-

---

8. Tigay, *Deuteronomy*, 323 no. 50.

9. For a summary of the different suggestions, see: Hamilton, *Genesis: Chapters 18–50*, pp. 648–47 no. 4.

son for their repudiation is because they slew men and maimed oxen when they were angry. It was pointed out that the language in the Hebrew Bible denotes laming large animals, and similar expressions are found in Greek and Arabic, where it is connected to animal sacrifice.[10] However, examination of Gen 34:28 shows that the cattle in Shechem were not mutilated but taken by the brothers as spoils. Therefore, this suggests that Jacob's rebuke refers to another act of cruelty that was carried out by the two brothers. Indeed, the Targums, Aquila, Symmachus, and Peshitta, including medieval commentators such as Ibn Ezra and Ramban, explain the Hebrew word *shôr* (ox) as *shûr* (wall), referring to the act of tearing down of city walls.

Another difficulty is that according to Gen 34:25, the brothers Simeon and Levi killed all the males. Meanwhile, according to Jacob's blessing, each of them killed one single man. An interesting interpretation is found in the *Testament of Levi*, which is different from the biblical version: "And I killed Shechem first, and Simeon [killed] Hamor. And after that the brothers came and smote the city with the edge of the sword . . ." (*T. Levi* 6:4–5).

Jacob curses his sons using the same words used by God in Gen 3:14 and 4:11, and later by Noah, who curses his son in 9:25. Noah's curse and Jacob's curse are similar. Something immoral was perpetuated by a son who put his father in a precarious situation. Although Jacob curses the anger of his sons, he really curses them. Their punishment is division and dispersion. Indeed, their descendants did not obtain a distinct land region. In the first census, the tribe of Simeon numbered 59,300 (Num 1:23); then by the end of the wandering period, it numbered only 22,200 (Num 26:14). Simeon lost two-thirds of his territory, which reflects the historical situation of the settlement. This is when Simeon's land was absorbed by the tribe of Judah (Judg 1:3; Josh 19:1). The cities of Simeon were within the territory of Judah (Josh 19:1–9; 15) and later, the descendants of Simeon looked for new dwelling places outside the land of Canaan (1 Chr 4:38). Simeon is not mentioned in the blessing of Moses (Deut 33) or the Song of Deborah (Judg 5) and disappeared after disruption of the kingdom.

Levi did not receive territory, so the Levites were dispersed among all the tribes, and they received 48 cities (Num 35:1–8). In other words, they lived in cities belonging to other tribes. They carried the ark of the Lord and were supported by income from the sanctuaries (Deut 10:8–9; 18:1–2). During the conquest and settlement times, the Levites did not take part in the wars and play only a sacral role. Evidently, Jacob's address to the Levites

---

10. Krebs, ". . . sie haben Stiere gelähmt" (359–61).

points to an early pre-conquest tradition. In contrast to Simeon, who is not mentioned in the Blessing of Moses, Levi is praised. Accordingly, Moses prays that God will grant Levi prosperity and protection. In addition, he mentioned their priestly functions, which included teaching the laws and instructions in ritual and civil matters.

Judah

In contrast to his previous statements, Jacob now blesses and praises Judah. It is the second longest speech when compared to Joseph's oracle. Judah's strength is compared to a young lion. Although Judah sinned against Joseph and Tamar, there are some mitigating circumstances. Judah wanted to sell Joseph, not kill him. He was hesitant to give his third son to Tamar since his first two sons were dead. As for sleeping with Tamar, he thought that she was a harlot. Judah's rise to prominence is one of the motifs in the Joseph story. It was Judah who suggested selling Joseph; he became the spokesman for the brothers to their father (43:3–5); he represents the brothers in Egypt (44:14–16); and he negotiated the release of the youngest brother (44:18–34). Judah is the one who leads the family migration to Egypt (46:28). This rise to prominence received its full recognition here, in the blessing of Jacob.

Judah's population during the wandering period was the largest as indicated by the census of Num 1:26; 26:22. His tribe encamps in front of the Tent of Meetings and was the first to march and lead the Israelites (Num 2:3, 9; 10:14). The heads of Judah's clan were the first to bring gifts to the Tabernacle (7:12). At the time of the conquest of Canaan, he took a leading role in the wars with the Canaanites. Caleb, the son of Jephunneh from the tribe of Judah, is mentioned first in the list for the apportionment of the land, which included the names of the chieftains (34:19).[11] The tribe of Judah was unimportant during the judges' period and is ignored in the Song of Deborah. It is only during the time of King David that the tribe gained hegemony over all of Israel. The power and successes, which are praised in Jacob's address, can only be applied to a later period. The early Jewish interpretation perceived the passage about Judah as a reference to the Jewish Messiah, while Christians point to this as a prophecy about Jesus Christ.[12]

---

11. Sarna, *Understanding Genesis*, 335.
12. 4Q252; *Gen. Rab.* 98:8; *b. Sanh.* 98b; Sheridan, *Ancient Christian*, 325–35.

Judah is praised as a mighty conqueror. Not only do the sons of Leah pay homage to him, but all the kindred tribes praise him as well. They bow to him and acknowledge his leadership and supremacy. This is similar to the blessing Isaac bestowed on Jacob: "And let your mother's sons bow to you" (Gen 27:29). There is wordplay here of "shall praise you" (*yôdûkā*) and the name "Judah" (*Yĕhûdâ*). This kind of expression could only be materialized during the time of David. For a long period, the tribe was isolated and separated from the northern tribes by heathen territory. The tribe of Judah was surrounded by the Philistines to the west, the Amalekites to the south, and on the east by the Edomites. The Amalekites, who were nomadic tribes, raided the Negev region, making war against them inevitable. It was King Saul who came to Judah's aid. He defeated the Amalekites, and by doing so, incorporated an important tribe into the emerging monarchy. It was during the time of David that the tribe of Judah gained its hegemony.

Judah is portrayed as a lion whelp, which is metaphor for strength. The scripture repeats the lion theme three times. The lion is considered as the strongest and most powerful beast of prey (Prov 30:30); so this is Judah. Interestingly, in the Moses blessing, Gad and Dan are also compared to a lion. In the Balaam blessing, the whole nation of Israel is compared to a lion. The lion as a symbol of royalty was well known in the ancient world including Israel (Ezek 19:1–9; Zeph 3:3; Solomon's throne 1 Kgs 10:18–20). As a metaphor for strength, it is used everywhere and even in countries that don't have lions such as the designation "Richard the Lion–hearted."[13] The lion became associated with messianic expectations (Rev 5:5; 4 Ezra 11:37; *Gen. Rab.* 98:7).

The next description of Judah is of a ruler who is bearing the king's "scepter." In other words, Judah will enjoy hegemony over the other tribes. The kingdom will not depart from Judah and will remain under his power as it was promised in Nathan's oracle (2 Sam 7:15; Ps 89:33–37). This will take place in the future when "tribute shall come to him." In Hebrew, it is expressed by the words *yābō' šîlōh*, which is obscure. There is no consensus among scholars for its meaning. One possibility is that it refers to the city of Shiloh and refers to northern Israel. It alludes to the time when the Davidic kingdom of Judah will include the northern tribes.[14] An interesting interpretation was offered by Rashi, who suggested that Shiloh is a combination

---

13. Westermann, *Genesis 37–50*, p. 229.

14. Lindblom, "The Political Background of the Shiloh Oracle," 78–87; and Becker, *Messianic Expectations*, 35–36.

of two Hebrew words *šāy* (tribute) and *lô* (to him), as it is stated: "Let them bring presents unto him that is to be feared" (Ps 76:12). The homage will be given to him by the people. This can mean the other tribes or it can refer to foreign people who were subject to the Davidic empire.

The Qumran community gave Gen 49:10 a messianic interpretation:

> A ruler shall not depart from the tribe of Judah while Israel has dominion. There will not be cut off a king in it belonging to David. For the staff is the covenant of the kingship; the thousands of Israel are the feet, until the coming of the Messiah of the Righteousness, the branch of David, for to him and to his seed has been given the covenant of kingship over his people for everlasting generations.[15]

From the image of Judah the warrior and conqueror, the author portrays an idyllic and peaceful situation. Judah is now riding on his ass, which was the beast of burden in pre-Davidic times. In ancient times, nobility rode donkeys, and in Zechariah 9:9, the messiah rides an ass. Mules are mentioned with the elevation of Solomon as a king (1 Kgs 1:33–35, 38–40). The land of Judah would be fertile and produce wine like a fountain. So abundant would be the wine that he will wash his garments in wine. Substituting wine for laundry water points to his successes. More so, the image of a donkey harnessed to a vine expresses the idea of successful harvests. Alternatively, a donkey that is tied to the vine indicates the owner's wealth.[16] In addition, it was suggested that it is possible that we have a reference here to a guild of linen workers.[17] According to 1 Chr 4:21, some members of Judah's tribe were engaged in weaving and dyeing. Archeological excavations at Tell Beit Mirsim, which is situated in the territory of Judah, reveal that a center for the dyeing and weaving industry existed there. In other words, wine is used in the text as a poetic term for red-colored dye, or it was used as an ingredient of dyestuff.[18] The theme of prosperity continues in verse 12, where it says that wine and milk would be in abundance. This would be manifested by the redness of the eyes because this is the nature of those who drink wine—to have the whites of the eyes turn red. The teeth would be white with milk because the land of Judah would be good pasture

---

15. Quoted in Hamilton, *The Book of Genesis*, 660. Cf. Burrows, *More Light on the Dead Sea Scrolls*, 401; Allegro, "Further Messianic References in Qumran Literature," 174–76; Vermes, *Scripture and Tradition in Judaism*, 53.

16. Mathew, *Genesis 11:27–50:26*, p. 896.

17. Sarna, *Understanding Genesis*, 337.

18. Ibid.

terrain for the herds of sheep. Indeed, the territory of Judah had suitable conditions for cultivating vines, especially the areas of Hebron and En Gedi (Num 13:23; Song of Songs 1:14). The land was also known for cattle breeding because it was excellent pasture land.

Good and Carmichael suggest that the blessings on Judah are referring to earlier episodes in Judah's life.[19] Hence, Judah's description as a lion (v. 9) is the wild beast that devoured Joseph (37:33). The staff (v. 10) is the one he pledged to Tamar (38:18, 25), and ass (עיר v. 11) stands for Er (ער 7-38:6). As for Judah washing his garments in the "blood of grapes" (v. 12), this refers to dipping Joseph's coat of many colors in blood (37:31). Although this allegorical interpretation sounds interesting, the symbolic equivalent is not so close, more so, Jacob's maxim came to praise Judah and not to criticize him.

Zebulun

Zebulun is the sixth son of Leah and next to receive Jacob's blessing. His brother, Issachar, was born before him, making him the fifth son of Leah. Nevertheless, the order is reversed and Zebulun appears before his older brother for Jacob's blessing, as well as for the blessing from Moses. It was suggested that this description reflects a time when the tribe of Zebulun was in ascendancy.[20] The Song of Deborah mentions him before his brother and praises him (Judg 5:14, 18. Cf. 4:6, 10). He took part in Gideon's battle against the Midianites (Judg 6:35). Later, during the time of David, he contributed the largest military aid among the western tribes (1 Chr 12:33). Another reason for the placement of Zebulun in the fifth place is to suggest a parallel with Dan who was the fifth son of Jacob in Gen 29-30. More so, Zebulun and Dan both have a connection with the sea.[21] However, there is a problem with the description of Zebulun, who will dwell by the seashore. This is also evident in the blessing of Moses where Zebulun and Issachar are described as gaining their wealth from maritime resources (Deut 33:19). Josh 19:10-16 reveals that at no time did the tribe of Zebulun have any access to the coast of the Mediterranean, nor did it border Sidon. Zebulun was a land-locked tribe because it was blocked from the sea by the tribe of

---

19. Good, "Blessing on Judah," 427-32; Carmichael, "Some Sayings in Gen 49," 435-44.

20. Sarna, *Understanding Genesis*, 338.

21. Sasson, "A Genealogical 'Convention' in Biblical Chronography?" 183-84.

Asher. The description of living by the sea side with its border extended to Sidon is more appropriate to Asher. Indeed, in the Song of Deborah, Asher is located "at the seacoast . . . at his harbors" (Judg 5:17). Several tribes are mentioned with the sea, which suggests that the Philistines and the Phoenicians employed Israelite labor. In other words, those Israelites gained their wealth from servicing ships and commerce (2 Sam 24:6–7). It is noteworthy that in the testament of Zebulun (6:1–8), there is a description of Zebulun making a boat to sail upon the sea. He caught fish for five years and gave them to every man he saw as well as to all the houses of his father.[22]

Issachar

Issachar is mentioned after his younger brother Zebulun. He dwelt along the Jordan River to Lake Tiberias and in the plains of Jezreel. His land was very fertile, and caravan routes from the Mediterranean to Betshean crossed his territory. In the Song of Deborah, highest praises are given to the tribe. Their officers stood by Deborah and were loyal to Barak. However, in Jacob's address, Issachar is rebuked for seeking comfort, and he predicts that the tribe will be enslaved by the Canaanites. This is the opposite of Joshua because of what was written in 16:10, where Israel made the Canaanites serve them. It is also ironic that his name means "pay," but here, Issachar is not a hired man but a slave. It's hard to know when this actually occurred. It was pointed out that among the El-Amarna letters, the king of Megiddo, in a letter to the Egyptian pharaoh Amenhotep III, he asks the pharaoh to make sure that the land of *Šunama* was being cultivated by "men of the corvée" from the towns of Yapu and Nuribta.[23] According to Josh 19:18, Shunem was part of Issachar's territory and Yapu part of Zebulun territory (19:12). Thus, it was de Vaux who suggested: "the eastern part of the plains of Jezreel must therefore have been colonized by groups of people coming from Zebulun, who chose to live as serfs on good land rather than as shepherds or herdsmen in a poorer district."[24] While according to Sarna, until the time of Deborah, the tribe of Issachar preferred to serve the local overlord in exchange for a peaceful existence.[25]

---

22. Charles, *The Testament of the Twelve Patriarchs*, 118.
23. Moran, *Amarna Letters*, EA 365, p. 363.
24. Vaux, *The Early History of Israel*, 664.
25. Sarna, *Understanding Genesis*, 340.

The animal metaphor used to describe Issachar was an ass: "Issachar is a large-boned ass." In other words, he is as strong as a donkey. This interpretation is based on linking *gerem* with the Aramaic *gram* (bone). Conversely, the Samaritan reads *ḥamôr gerîm* ("an ass of foreigners")—in other words, one who serves alien people. Issachar is described as lying down because he needs his rest from carrying a heavy load. Although, at first resting seems to be good and pleasant, he submits to servitude. His shoulder/back carries the load of cargo. Evidently, the metaphor here describes the hardship that Issachar suffered from submitting to Canaanite lordship. This coincided with the description in Judges 1 where Issachar is not mentioned as receiving territory. This hardship lasted until the overthrow of the Canaanite city states at the time of Deborah.

It is noteworthy that the interpretation of Issachar's tribe as serfs to the local Canaanites stems from the last part of v. 15, *lĕmas-ʿōbēd*, which Mendelsohn and other scholars interpret as "a slave at forced labor."[26] The phrase appears here for the first time in the Hebrew Bible, and according to Heck, it is archaic. The meaning "a slave at forced labor" is a later development.[27] We have to remember there is no mention in the Hebrew Bible of the subjugation of the Issacharites by the Canaanite overlords. Hence, not surprisingly, the LXX translated "and he became a farmer." In light of this translation and examination of the portrayal of Issachar, Heck arrived at the conclusion that the blessing of Issachar is a statement about the good, hardworking character of Issachar.[28] We should point out that the hard work of Issachar is also mentioned in the *Testament of Issachar* where we read: "Therefore, when I was thirty-five years old, I took to myself a wife, for my labor wore away my strength, and I never thought upon pleasure with woman; but owing to my toil, sleep overcame me" (3:5).[29]

Dan

Dan is the first son of the handmaid who is blessed. He was the first son of Bilhah. He is the only one of the handmaid tribes who settled among the tribes of Leah and Rachel. His territory bordered on Ephraim's, Benjamin's, and Judah's regions. At first, his territory was limited to the area between

26. Mendelsohn, "State Slavery," 14–17.
27. Heck, "Issachar," 394.
28. Ibid., 385–96.
29. Charles, *Testaments of the Twelve Patriarchs*, 104–5.

Zorah and Eshtaol (Judg 13:25). There are two sayings about Dan in verses 16 and 17, and they are independent of each other. One is a wordplay on the name Dan, and the second is an animal metaphor. Both verses praise Dan. Besides Judah and Joseph, Dan is the only tribe who received two separate blessings.

In his address, Jacob refers to Dan "like one of the tribes of Israel," which is puzzling. This led to some speculation as to the origin of the tribe. Gordon and Yadin suggested that the tribe of Dan joined the other tribes after the formation of the tribal confederation.[30] According to Yadin, the tribe of Dan had close relations with the Sea People. The tribe was an ancient tribe and did not have any connections with the confederacy of tribes. Through the years, the tribe got closer to the tribes of Israel until it became one of them. Its place of habitat was along the coast near Jaffa. Yadin points out the connections between the tribe of Dan and the tribe of Danaoi. This tribe's members were seafarers worshipping the sun where they lived by the eastern Mediterranean coast and the Jaffa area. The similarities between the two groups led Yadin to the identification of the two. However, the similarities between the two groups can be explained as an outcome of contact and influence.

Historically, the tribe was pressed by the Amorites on the west (Judg 1:34); and possibly by the house of Joseph on the east (1:35); and possibly it was pressured by Judah (15:11). As a result of these pressures, the tribe moved northward to conquer Laish and settle there under the name Dan. Samson, the biblical hero who fought bravely against the Philistines, belonged to the tribe of Dan and lived in the original territory. And de Vaux suggested that Dan was originally part of the tribe of Benjamin.[31] After the tribe of Dan moved north, the tribe was separated from the tribe of Benjamin and became autonomous. This might explain the phrase that Dan judged his people "as any other of the tribes of Israel."

Dan is mentioned in the blessing of Moses (Deut 33) and the Song of Deborah. In the Song of Deborah, the tribe is rebuked for not participating in the war against the Canaanites. In the blessing of Moses, Dan is blessed with lion-like strength. This simile was used for the tribe of Judah (Gen 49:9). It is possible that this inspired the name *Laish*, which was the new place of habitation for Dan, which also means lion. Jacob's blessing of Dan

---

30. Gordon, "Mediterranean Factor," 21–22; Yadin, "Why Did He Remain in Ships?," 9–23.

31. Vaux, *The Early History of Israel*, 775–83.

appears to refer to the earliest period of the Danites. It describes a tribe that fights for recognition and acceptance by the other tribes (49:16). In the next verse, he is described as fighting for survival against foes. Jacob uses here an animal metaphor to describe it. Dan is like a serpent who is lurking by the road. He strikes a passing horse in his heel, so his rider is thrown back from the horse. Furthermore, Dan is "like a viper by the path." The word viper appears only here in the Hebrew Bible and is probably the equivalent of the Akkadian *šippu/ šibbu*, which is a type of serpent. It appears as the name of a deity and also in some parables. In one inscription, the speed of the Assyrian king Tiglath Pilesar I (1077–1115 BCE), who went to battle against his foes, is compared to the speed of a serpent.[32] In contrast to Judah (the lion), who is powerful, it is Dan the weaker against the stronger; he is dangerous yet succeeds in his battle. Medieval commentators believed that this prophecy referred to Samson, who, through his strength and tricks, defeated the Philistines on several occasions. Hence according to Rashi:

> "Dan shall judge his people"—avenge his people of the Philistines . . . "as one of the tribes of Israel"—all Israel will be united with him and he will judge them all—this message he prophesized concerning Samson.
>
> "Which bites the horses heel"—so that his rider is thrown backward who it (i.e., the snake), did not touch. A parallel is to be found in Samson (Judg 16, 28) when he grasped hold of the pillars and those on the roof died.
>
> "For Thy salvation do I wait O Lord"—he prophesied that the Philistines would pluck out his eyes and that he was destined to say: "O Lord God, remember me and strengthen me, only this once . . ."

However, it is more likely that the prophecy refers to the period of the settlement, since it describes Dan as one who attacks caravans that pass through his territory. During that period, the tribe controlled an important junction that led to the mountains and plains area. The Amarna letters mention the king of Jerusalem, ʿAbdi-Ḫeba, who reports that his caravan on his way to the king of Egypt was robbed in the field of Ayyaluna (Aijalon).[33] In another letter, the two sons of the governor of Gezer almost

---

32. *AKA* 45 ii, 76–77; for the translation "quick as a viper," see *CAD* Š/2, 375.
33. Moran, *Amarna Letters*, EA. 287, 328.

died by the ʿApiru in Aijalon and in Ṣarḫa (Zorah).[34] Aijalon and Zorah were settlements in the territory of Dan (Josh 19: 41–42) that were strategically located in the area that served a passage way from the mountain area to the plains.

Gad

Zilpah, the maidservant of Leah, gave birth to Gad. His tribe included seven large families. According to the blessing of Jacob: "Gad shall be raided by raiders; but he shall overcome last" (Gen 49:19). The saying consists of wordplay on the name. Four of the six words are from the root *g-d-d*. According to Rashi, all these words denote troops. He further explains:

> For they will cross the Jordan with their brethren, to wage war, everyone armed, until the land will be conquered. All his troops will return upon their way to their inheritance which they took in Transjordan, and not one man of them will be missing.

Historically, the tribe of Gad settled east of the Jordan. When Transjordan was conquered by Israel during the time of Moses, they requested, along with the Reubenites and half of Manasseh, to settle there because of their abundant cattle. Moses accepted their request on the condition that they would cross the Jordan to participate in the conquest of the land of Canaan. Geographically, Gad was sandwiched between the Moabites to the south, the Ammonites to the east, and the Arameans to the northeast. Thus, they had to fight against the Ammonites and Moabites. During the Judges period, the Gileadites were saved from the Ammonites by Jephthah and later by Saul. Thus, Ramban suggests that our passage is probably alluding to the wars of the Ammonites against Jephtah the Gileadite (Judg 11:33). The Ammonites occasionally raided the Gilead, and the reference is to the time of Jephtah, who won a victory over them and their cities. Later, King Mesha of Moab, rebelled against Israel and dealt harshly with the Gadites. In the famous Moabite Stone from the mid-ninth century BCE, he claims: "Now the men of Gad had always dwelt in the land of Ataroth, and the king of Israel had built Ataroth for them; but I fought against the town and took it and slew all the people of the town as satiation for Chemosh and Moab."[35]

---

34. Ibid, *EA*. 273, 318.
35. "Moabite Stone," In *ANET*, 320.

The adage of Jacob predicts Gad's frequent involvement in war. Gad will be able to fight back against those who would seek to destroy him. In the blessing of Moses, this image of the warrior is repeated, and he is compared to a ferocious lion (Deut 33:20). Later, in the era of the monarchy, Gad is described as an "expert in war," having faces "like the faces of lions," and as being "as swift as gazelles upon the mountains" (1 Chr 5:18; 12:9). In the Song of Deborah (Judg 5:17), the tribe is rebuked for remaining on the other side of the Jordan river and not coming to aid his brothers on the west side of the Jordan river. But it is possible that this was a result of Gad being occupied with his own wars.

Asher

Asher was Zilpah's second son. There is wordplay with the name Asher, which means "good fortune." Joshua 19:24–31, 34 defines Asher's territory, which was located in the western hills of Galilee, from Mount Carmel in the south, along the coastal plain of Akko, to the hinterland of Phoenician Tyre and Sidon, and in the westernmost part of the valley of Jezreel. With the passing of time, the boundaries of Asher had been changed. Part of his territory was annexed by the tribe of Zebulun after the Israelites defeated Sisera (Judg 4–5). Later, during Solomon's reign, the king gave some of Asher's territory "twenty cities in the land of Galilee" (1 Kgs 9:11–13) to the king of Tyre as payment for material for the construction of the temple.

Asher is blessed with the fertility of its land. Besides feeding himself, he would provide oil to kings. His fertile land yielded corn, wine, and oil. Moses similarly blessed him: "May he dip his foot in oil" (Deut 33:24). The highlands of Galilee were famous for plentiful olive oil. In the Talmud we read: "that one time the people of Laodicea were in need of oil; they appointed an agent and instructed him, 'Go and purchase for us a hundred myriad worth of oil.'"[36] After looking for it in several places, they were able to obtain it only in Asher. The export of oil from Israel is also mentioned in Ezekiel 27:17, which states it was sent to Phoenicia. Oil was used as a present for kings and also as a form of taxation: "Now oil is carried to Egypt" (Hos 12:2). The Amarna letters detail a request made to Pharaoh by king Alashiya, who wrote: "and send me my brother, 2 *kukkubu*-containers of sweet oil."[37] Judges 1:32 speaks of Asher dwelling among the Canaanites as

---

36. *b. Menaḥ.* 85b.
37. Moran, *Amarna Letters*, EA 35, 107.

the tribe failed to capture the important cities in his territory. Evidently, the testament refers to the period of Judges before the defeat of the Canaanites. The Song of Deborah rebukes Asher for not aiding his brothers because he preferred beaches and harbors (Judg 5:17). Asher is the only tribe who did not have a national leader in the period of the Judges.

Naphtali

Naphtali is Bilhah's second son and the sixth son of Jacob. The fact that he was Bilhah's son testifies to his lower status. This is also evident in the listings of Jacob's sons, where he appears ninth (Deut 33:23). The saying about him appears in one verse that has two parts. In the first part, Naphtali is referred as ʾayyālâ. Scholars have debated the meaning of this Hebrew word; does it mean "hind" (Speiser, Dahood, O'Connor, Westermann, and Sarna)[38] or "terebinth" (Cross and Freedman, Stuart)[39]? We should point out that the midrash (b. Soṭah 11b) records that there were only animal metaphors. Naphtali is the only tribe compared to a female animal. This was to allude to the prophetess Deborah, who was his female descendant. The comparison with the hind may refer to the heroes of this tribe (Ps 18:34).

The second part of verse 21 is a reference to the Song of Deborah; the words ʾimrê šāper were interpreted by Onqelos and Rashi as "who gives off beautiful words." This poem alludes to Barak from the tribe of Naphtali, who is praised for his glorious victory against Sisera. Another possibility would be that Naphtali was quick to pay the tribute of sheep to the Canaanite overlords. This interpretation is based on the word ʾimr, which means "lamb" in many Semitic languages.[40] A third interpretation would be that the tribe is compared to a terebinth with spreading branches. This is based on the reading of the LXX, where the second part of the verse reads "giving beauty by its fruit." This interpretation was based on the understanding of the Hebrew word ʾayyālâ as terebinth.

Not much is said about Naphtali. The tribe was blessed with fertile territory. Its territory included the upper Galilee, which was rich with fruit

---

38. Speiser, *Genesis*, 363, 367; Dahood, "Northwest Semitic," 81–82; O'Connor, *Hebrew Verse Scripture*, 176; Westermann, *Genesis 37–50*, p. 218; Sarna, *Understanding Genesis*, 342.

39. Cross and Freedman, *Studies in Ancient Yahwistic Poetry*, 89; Stuart, *Studies in Early Hebrew Meter*, 145, 150 no. 40.

40. Ugar. ʾimr; Phoen. ʾmr; Aram. ʾimmar; Akk. immeru—"lamb, fawn, sheep, ram."

trees and vegetation, in addition to the western and southern shores of Lake Tiberias. Therefore, it is possible that the tribe fished the lake as mentioned by *Targum Jonathan* and Talmudic sources.[41] At the beginning of the judges' period, they were living among the Canaanites and were subject to them. It was in the war against Sisera that they played a major role. Barak, the son of Abinoam from the tribe of Naphtali, led the Israelites in their rebellion where his tribesmen risked their lives (Judg 5:18). High praises given to the Naphtali tribe are found in both Jacob's and Moses' blessings, which refer to the period of the judges.

Joseph

Joseph's testament is a lengthy one, spanning verses 22–26. Joseph was the favorite son of Jacob, so he is blessed even more the Judah. The language is enigmatic and more ancient than the other utterances, except vv. 3–4. The poet's use of the ancient, older, divine name "Mighty One of Jacob" (v. 24), is an indication of an ancient language. Although the blessings were given to Joseph, they are for his two sons, Ephraim and Manasseh. This is the only blessing that did not include the name of the tribe. We have to remember that the territory that belonged to Joseph became the territory of his sons, Ephraim and Manasseh. More so, later, the name Joseph is attached to the territories of his sons (Josh 17:1). The narrator begins by glorifying the territories of Joseph before describing what happened to Joseph. Hence, he is alluding to the reason why Jacob did not bless Joseph with eternal kingship, which was given to Judah. Ephraim and Manasseh are not mentioned here like in Moses' blessing where they appear together with Joseph (Deut 33:17). This is because in the previous chapter (Gen 48), when Jacob blessed the sons of Joseph he said: "By you (Joseph) shall Israel invoke blessings, saying: God make you like Ephraim and Manasseh (v. 20)."

The blessing starts with the name Joseph "*ben pōrāt Yôsēp*," which is used for two tribes of Ephraim and Manasseh. This is rare. The name Joseph is mostly used for the northern kingdom of Israel. Joseph is compared to a wine or wild ass. The first suggestion is based on the word פֹּרָת *pōrāt*, which is a participle of פָּרָה *pārāh*, which means fruitfulness. The Hebrew *ben pōrāt* is probably a wordplay on the name Ephraim, which is the more important of the two Joseph tribes. In the Bible, the image of a righteous man flourishing like a tree appears many times (Ps 1:3; Jer 17:8). Joseph is

---

41. *t. B. Qam.* 8:18; *b. B. Qam* 81a–b.

like a young fruit tree by the spring. Its branches climbed over the wall, or alternatively, the branches spread to a source of water. It has been suggested that the Hebrew word *šûr* has the meaning of "source of water," and it possibly refers to a canal of water that runs parallel to the eastern part of the Nile.

The second interpretation of Joseph as a wild ass by a spring follows the previous pattern of Judah the lion, Issachar the bony ass, Dan the serpent, Naphtali the hind, and Benjamin the wolf. Speiser pointed out that *pōrāt* is the feminine of פֶּרֶא *pere'* (wild ass). More so, the next line, *bānôt ṣāʿădâ*, was suggested to be an equivalent to the Arabic "wild asses." In Genesis, Ishmael is referred to as a wild ass (16:24). Additionally, the words *ʿayin* and *šûr*, which appear in the blessing, are also mentioned in the birth narrative of Ishmael. Therefore, we have a wordplay that refers to the Ishmaelites who sold Joseph into slavery. The next two verses speak about the archers, and Ishmael who was known as a "bowman" (21:20).

It is not clear if the attacks that are mentioned in verse 23 refer to Joseph or to the tribes of Ephraim and Manasseh. It is striking that the text does not name the enemies. Nowhere is there any mention of attacks on Joseph by the archers. Therefore, medieval commentators understood the verse as an allusion to the trials that Joseph endured and the opposition he faced from the Ishmaelites, the hostility of Joseph's brothers, and the malicious accusations of Potiphar's wife. Alternatively, this was a prophetic saying that refers to the future attacks on the tribes of Manasseh and Ephraim, which are mentioned in the book of Judges 6:3. It is more likely that the enemies who attacked Joseph were the brothers who made Joseph's life bitter. Indeed, the term *śāṭam* (bore a grudge), describes what the brothers sought to do to Joseph (Gen 49:23) and appears later when the brothers feared what he would do to them (Gen 50:15). More so, since the narrative deals with Joseph, it would be logical and appropriate to have some saying about him.

Although Joseph was attacked, the assault failed because of divine assistance. God gave Joseph the strength, and he prevailed. Verse 24 speaks of "his bow, his hands," in the singular, which strengthens the argument that the verse refers to Joseph. Joseph's bow remained firm; the bow symbolized military strength, therefore, breaking one's bow meant defeat, but this is not the case with Joseph. It was the Mighty One of Jacob who protected him. This divine title appears only four times and in poetic text, which points to its antiquity (Ps 132:2, 5; Isa 49:26; 60:16). This ancient epithet of God corresponds to the Akkadian divine title *bēl abāri* ("endowed with strength"). The other description of God that is mentioned in the verse is "the shepherd, the stone of Israel." In the Hebrew Bible, God is compared to a shepherd (Ps 80:2) and Rock of Israel (2 Sam 23:3; Isa 30:29), which is similar to "stone of Israel." The divine help that is described here is similar to the description in Psalms 18:35, which speaks of the hand and bow of the warrior. Furthermore, the God who assisted the warrior is referred to as the Rock of Israel, which is parallel to the stone of Israel in our verse.

God's protection and what He did to Joseph's enemies has been described so far. Now the next two verses 25–26 describe what God will do for Joseph. The blessing of prosperity and fertility of the land is given. More so, Joseph's blessing will surpass what he (Jacob) received from his ancestors. The trait of "God as a personal God" who helps and blesses Joseph underlies the passage. To show continuity between the past and the present, the author used the names *God of your father* and *Shaddai*. These two epithets are associated with blessing, and El Shaddai specifically with Jacob (28:3; 35:11; 43:14; 48:3). The blessing included rain and dew from above and spring from the deep, which symbolizes agricultural blessings. This is similar to the blessing that Moses gave Joseph: "Blessed of the Lord be his land with the bounty of dews from heaven, And the deep that couches below" (Deut 33:13). In addition, Joseph received the blessing of breast and womb, which is a sign of many descendants. These blessings Joseph received would rest on his head and on the brow of the elect (*nāzîr*) of his brothers. The Hebrew word *nāzîr* cannot be referring to the king but probably refers to "the one who is consecrated to a special act 'among his brothers.'"[42] Another interpretation understands *nāzîr* as the one who was exiled from his brothers. Joseph was separated from his family first during his 20 years of isolation and then by virtue of his duties in the palace. Ralbag (acronym for Rabbi Levi ben Gershom, known as Gersonides 1248–1334) interpreted: "the most obstinate of his brothers, that is, the brother who exercised the greatest control over his emotions and abstained from sin under the most trying circumstances."

Benjamin

Benjamin, Jacob's youngest son, receives the last blessing. Continuing with the pattern of animal metaphors, he is compared to a "ravenous wolf." Nowhere in the Hebrew Bible is the wolf described in a positive manner. The

---

42. Westermann, *Genesis 37–50*, p. 241.

description of a fierce wolf, in contrast to his portrayal as the defenseless son of Jacob, points primarily to the future. Indeed, according to the book of Judges, it was Ehud the Benjaminite who delivered the Israelites from the oppression of the Moabites (3:15–30). The army of the Benjaminite tribe participated in the war against Sisera (5:14). In the civil war against the other tribes, they fought back although they were outnumbered (20:14–21). The Benjaminites were known as "mighty warriors, bowmen" (1 Chr 8:40; 12:2). Saul, the first king of Israel, came from the tribe of Benjamin (1 Sam 9:1). Geographically, the tribe was situated between Judah to the south and the hill country of Ephraim to the north, controlling the north-south central highway, in addition to the east-west road leading to Transjordan. The description of a ravenous wolf who consumes foes in the morning and in the evening divides the spoils, probably reflects the Benjaminites activity when they attacked caravans that passed through the trade routes in their territory.[43] The fact that there is no mention of kingship in the saying suggests that it is pre-monarchial and suits the judges' period.

In conclusion, Jacob's maxims were a collection of independent sayings that refer to different events and different situations. Many refer to the past while others allude to events hundreds of years in the future. It contains curses as well as praises. Jacob reprimanded some of the tribes such as Reuben's, Simeon's, and Levi's. The aim was to explain their fate, which was a result of their wrongdoing. This resulted in smaller territories, therefore, Rueben had a small territory compared to Judah; Simeon's territory was within Judah; and Levi had only scattered cities.

The two tribes of Joseph and Judah dominate the poem; this is not a coincidence since they are the main characters of the Joseph cycle. More so, Judah is the ancestor of the Davidic kingdom of Judah, and Joseph's tribe, in particular Ephraim, represents the future kingdom of Israel. Hence, Judah and Joseph are praised and blessed. Dan, Gad, and Benjamin are described as fighting for their survival. Meanwhile, the tribes Issachar, Zebulun, Asher, and Napthali are described as serving others. There is colorful animal imagery used in the sayings. Therefore, Judah is portrayed as a lion, Issachar a lazy ass, Dan a cunning serpent, Naphtali a lovely hind, and Benjamin a wolf. These metaphors came to explain the manner in which the tribes acted in self-defense or conquest. Tribal economic features are also noted in the poem. Judah is known for his fertile land. Asher produces food for kings. Naphtali's land is productive. Zebulun supplies crews to

---

43. Sarna, *Understanding Genesis*, 345.

Canaanite-Phoenician ships. Joseph's place of habitat is the richest region of the land. In light of the similarity between Genesis 49, Deuteronomy 33, and in some details to the Song of Deborah, it is more than likely that there was a tradition to bless the tribes. The content of the blessing varied from tribe to tribe and was changed with the passing of time and according to the changing circumstances. Our examination of Jacob's maxims shows that they suit the Judges period. This was when the tribes were different from each other and had to fight for their own survival.

Conclusion

JACOB HAS THE MOST colorful personality in the book of Genesis. He is characterized as clever, deceitful, a manipulator, lover, husband and father—all displayed in a vivid way. No other story in the patriarchal narrative is dominated by the character of the man himself. In contrast to the patriarchal stories where God acts directly, in the Jacob's stories God is present but also behind the scenes. His guiding hand is felt. The story of Jacob is a long journey of suffering and struggle. The hard life that Jacob endured is a direct result of his deception of his brother Esau. He went into exile and stayed for 20 years at his uncle's home. Later, he joined his son Joseph in Egypt for a second exile and stayed there for 17 years. Still, before Jacob is to be exiled the first time from the land of Israel, God tells him: "Remember, I am with you: I will protect you wherever you go and I will bring you back to this land. I will not leave you until I have done what I have promised you" (Gen 28:15). God gave similar promises of protection and many descendants to Jacob as well, before he went down to Egypt (46:3). There is a continuous bond between God and Jacob. The promises of nationhood and posterity, which were given to Abraham and Isaac, are given to Jacob. The long journey of a hard life that Jacob endured made him ready and worthy to be the father of a nation. Although, at first the unity of the text is not obvious, reading the story shows that there is a flow to the stories. Each story leads to the next. Furthermore, many details in the Jacob stories are similar to past events in the lives of the patriarchs. In addition, some foreshadow the future. All of this is done in order to create similarities between the fathers and the sons—"the deeds of the fathers are lessons to the sons."

The Jacob story is a story of continuous struggle. Therefore, the first detail that is mentioned is the struggle between the twin brothers, Jacob and Esau, which started in the womb. It is a struggle for hegemony. This description forecasts the future relationship between the nations of Israel and Edom. Similarly, the story of the birth of Zerah and Perez stresses the rivalry between the two brothers, where each one wants the priority of birth. Just as the story of Jacob and Esau foretells the rivalry between the Edomites and Israel, so too does the story of Zerah and Perez. In the book of Genesis, the narrator's sympathy is with Esau, where the narrator describes his wild and bitter sobbing. However, this sympathy will change in later generations and in the prophetic books, where Esau will be described as a wicked person. In these books, there is a description of Esau that is not found earlier. This is the result of hostilities that existed between Israel and Edom.

Trickery and deception is one of the main motifs that characterizes the Jacob cycle. Therefore, all the protagonists—Jacob, Laban, Rachel, Simeon and Levi, Hamor and his son Shechem, Jacob's sons, and Tamar, Judah's daughter-in-law—deceived each other. These heroes use tricks, but they themselves are also tricked by others. The aim of these deceptions is to gain the advantage of being in control. However, the Hebrew Bible does not approve of this kind of action. Therefore, not surprisingly, each person is punished for his deception. In particular, Jacob was punished severely for his acts of deception. Although he was elected by God, Jacob was impatient and tried to "speed" his predestined right to be Isaac's heir. Jacob paid heavily for his impatience.

The Jacob stories feature an extended family that included two wives, two handmaids, and twelve sons, which contrasts the stories with those of Abraham and Isaac. Fierce rivalry existed between the two sisters, Rachel and Leah, who were competing for Jacob's love and the desire to give him many offspring, but still there is no hatred between the two sisters. This is in contrast to the intense hatred that is displayed in the book of Genesis among brothers. Not so with Rachel and Leah. Although the handmaids were lower in status, Rachel and Leah did not abandon the children of the handmaids; they accepted them as their own sons. The sisters were devoted to their children as well as to the children of the handmaids, and this is likely why in the blessing that was bestowed on Ruth, we read: "The Lord make the women who has gone into thy house like Rachel and like Leah" (Ruth 4:11).

Conclusion

In matters of religion, few details are given. This is not surprising, since the laws were given to the Israelites at the covenant in Sinai. Nevertheless, there are some religious practices that are mentioned already in the book of Genesis. Jacob, like the previous patriarchs, built altars to God as a form of worship and invoked his name. Sacrifices are mentioned as a form of fraternization. Prayers are simple, spontaneous outpourings of the heart and are not connected to a site or a cult. Setting up pillar stones is mentioned several times. The setting up of pillars was forbidden in the later periods as they were considered illegitimate (Deut 16:22). Not so in the Jacob cycle; the legitimacy of the pillar is not called into question. There is one religious prohibition from Jacob's time that lasted to current times: The prohibition is not to eat the thigh muscle. It is not part of the later Jewish law. By not eating this sinew, the Israelites were reminded of Jacob's wrestling with the divine being and the promise of victory and blessings he received. The first mention of tension between the God of Israel and that of alien gods appears in Jacob's return to Bethel. Jacob orders the people of his household to rid themselves of the alien gods. Still, there is no mention of conflict with idolatry, which will appear in later periods. As for the different divine names that are mentioned in the Jacob cycle, they do not point to different gods worshiped by Jacob. On the contrary, the different names for God point to different attributes of God. Examination of the Jacob cycle shows no regular patterns of worship. Liturgical calendars and specific places for worship did not exist yet. Religion developed as a reaction to a developing situation. There were no temples and no priests. It is only later, after the covenant at Sinai, that we find the Israelites on one side of the world and the gentiles on the other side.

What we witness in Genesis is an echo of primitive tales—human beings who are confronted directly by God, where he walks and talks among people. These tales were widespread in the ancient world. Later, the Hebrew scribes tempered this concept by interjecting an angel and also described God's appearance in the form of a dream. Angels appear predominately in the Jacob cycle. Later, in the Hebrew Bible, the angels no longer appear to humans but are seen in visions. The angels that are mentioned in the Jacob cycle appear to be guardian angels who accompanied Jacob during his travels. In Jacob's third encounter with an angel, he was wrestling with him. Evidently, the story has several layers, which include mythical imagery. The biblical narrator transformed it and described Jacob as wrestling with a divine being. The story is a reflection of Jacob's life and his struggles with people and God. The story is a combination of psychological and theological elements. Jacob will enter the promised land as the father of the Hebrew nation. His old name, Jacob, is connected to deceit, therefore, his name is changed to Israel. Chapter 35:10 contains another parallel tradition where God blessed and changed Jacob's name, which is similar to the Peniel story. A later tradition is mentioned in the book of Hosea, where Jacob was wrestling with a divine being. Some details in the story are different from our story in Genesis. What the prophet Hosea tried to convey is that the sins of the patriarch should serve as a lesson to his descendants.

Another way that God communicated with Jacob was through dreams. God appeared to Jacob three times in a dream (Gen 28:12–18; 31:10–13; 46:2–4). The phenomenon of dreams is one of the characteristics of the Jacob cycle. Examination of dreams in the Jacob cycle shows that dreams were prophetic and dealt with the future. The messages in the dreams were about the future and came to encourage Jacob. Indeed, each time Jacob sets out for another country, God appears to him in a dream and encourages him. This is manifested by the phrase "Fear not," which is God's promise to remain with Jacob (28:15: 46:4), and the promise to return him to his homeland (28:15; 31:13; 46:4). Hence, not surprisingly, when Laban was in hot pursuit after Jacob, God appeared to him in a dream and warned him not to harm Jacob. In all cases, the dreamer's reactions indicate that they believed that God is the source of their dreams.

Following the hard life in the house of Laban and the struggle with the angel, we read about a tragedy in Jacob's household. Dinah, Jacob's daughter, was raped and her brothers, Simeon and Levi, attacked the city of Shechem and massacred its inhabitants. We believe that the story is an ancient one and is a warning against intermarriages. In the biblical narrative, Jacob condemned his sons' acts because he feared that their actions would unite the inhabitants of the land against him and destroy his clan. In contrast, justification for the brothers' actions is mentioned in the writings of Philo and Pseudo-Philo, the book of Jubilees, the *Testament of Levi*, the book of Judith, and the Joseph and Aseneth story. A different version of our story is mentioned in Genesis 48:22, where it describes Jacob as taking part in attacking Shechem. However, it's more likely that the narrator wanted to glorify Jacob describing him as a hero who wrestled both "with God and with men."

The last part of Jacob's life is interwoven with the Joseph story. In this part of the narrative, Jacob is shadowed by his son Joseph. Jacob's

Conclusion

continuous hard life, from the sale of Joseph into slavery until Jacob's reunion with his son Joseph, is described. It is a classic story of a family and the dynamics that exist within. Jacob made the same errors that his parents made; he showed favoritism to his son Joseph and later to Benjamin. It is this preferential treatment that contributed to the hatred between the brothers that led to the sale of Joseph into slavery. Joseph himself was not so innocent, and his dreams about dominating his brothers intensified his brothers' hatred toward him. The brothers were consumed with so much hatred that it appears they did not give much thought to their actions and the pain that they inflicted upon their father. Thinking that his son Joseph was dead, Jacob would suffer for twenty-two years until he reunited with Joseph. Joseph put his brothers through a series of tests to see if they had changed their evil thoughts and showed remorse. Only after they passed those tests was there reconciliation between the brothers and Joseph, and it was then possible for the story to end on a good note.

The final chapter of the patriarch Jacob's life ended in Egypt where he spent his final years. Before his death, Jacob summoned his sons to tell them their future and the future of the twelve tribes. Jacob's maxims were a collection of independent sayings that refers to different events and different situations. Some refer to the past while others allude to events hundreds of years in the future. It contains curses in addition to praises. There is colorful animal imagery in the saying. In addition, tribal economic features are also noted in the poem. The content of the blessings varied from tribe to tribe and was changed with the passing of time and according to changing circumstances. Jacob's maxims show that they suit the Judges period. This was when the tribes were different from each other and had to fight for their own survival.

Jacob's words to Pharaoh that summarize the life of the third patriarch Jacob and the father of the twelve tribes of Israel, describe a life of misfortune and suffering: "... Few and hard have been the years of my life ..." (Gen 47:9).

Bibliography

Aḥituv, S. *Canaanite Toponyms in Ancient Egyptian Documents*. Jerusalem: Magnes, 1984.
Albright, W. F., trans. "The Moabite Stone." In *ANET*, 320–21.
———. "The North-Canaanite Poems of Al ʾêân Baʿal and the 'Gracious Gods.'" *JPOS* 14 (1934) 101–40.
Allegro, J. M. "Further Messianic References in Qumran Literature." *JBL* 75 (1956) 174–87.
Allen, C. G. "On Me Be the Curse, My Son!" In *Encounter with the Text: Form and History in the Hebrew Bible*, edited by Martin J. Buss, 159–172. Philadelphia: Fortress; Missoula, MT: Scholars, 1979.
Alter, R. *The Art of Biblical Narrative*. New York: Basic Books, 1981.
Andersen, F. I. "Note on Genesis 30:8." *JBL* 88 (1969) 200.
Andersen, F. I. and David Noel Freedman. *Amos*. AB 24A. New York: Doubleday, 1989.
———. *Hosea*. AB 24. Garden City, NY: Doubleday, 1980.
The Babylonian Talmud. Edited by I. Epstein and translated by M. Simon. 30 vols. London: Soncino, 1987.
Bar, S. *A Letter that Has Not Been Read: Dreams in the Hebrew Bible*. Cincinnati: Hebrew Union College Press, 2001.
———. "What Did the Servant Give to Rebecca's Brother and Mother?" *Bib* 94 (2013) 565–72.
Bauer, H. " Die hebräischen Eigennamen als sprachliche." *ZAW* 48 (1930) 73–80.
Bechtel, L. M. "What If Dinah Is Not Raped? (Genesis 34)." *JSOT* 62 (1994)19–36.
Becker, J. *Messianic Expectations in the Old Testament*. Translated by. D. E. Green. Philadelphia: Fortress, 1980.
Ben-Reuben, S. "Buying Mandrakes as Retribution for Buying the Birthright." *BethM* 28 (1982/83) 230–231. (Hebrew)
Blum, E. *Die Komposition der Vätergeschichte*. WMANT 57. Neukirchen-Vluyn: Neukirchener, 1984.
Brenner, A. "Female Social Behavior: Two Descriptive Patterns within the 'Birth of the Hero' Paradigm." *VT* 36 (1986) 257–73.
Buber, Salomon. *Midrash Tanḥuma*. Translated by John T. Townsend. Jersey City, NJ: Ktav, 1989.
Burrows, M. *More Light on the Dead Sea Scrolls*. New York: Viking, 1985.
Carmichael, C. M. "Some Sayings in Gen 49." *JBL* 88 (1969) 435–44.

Caspi, M. "The story of Dinah." *BethM* 94 (1983) 236–55. (Hebrew)
Charles, R. H., trans. *The Testament of the Twelve Patriarchs*. London: Black, 1908.
Coats, G. W. *From Canaan to Egypt: Structural and Theological Context for the Joseph Story*. CBQMS 4. Washington, DC: Catholic Biblical Association, 1976.
Cohen, N. "Sibling Rivalry in Genesis." *Judaism* 32 (1983) 331–42
Philo, of Alexandria. *Philo*. Translated by F. H. Colson and G. H. Whitaker. 12 vols. Loeb Classical Library. London: Heinemann, 1932.
Cowley, A. E., ed. and trans. *Aramaic Papyri of the Fifth Century B.C.* Oxford: Clarendon, 1976.
Cross, F. M., and D. N. Freedman, *Studies in Ancient Yahwistic Poetry*. SBLDS 21. Missoula, MT: Scholars Press, 1975.
Dahood, M. J. "Northwest Semitic Notes on Genesis." *Bib* 55 (1974) 76–82.
Delitzsch, F. *A New Commentary on Genesis*. Translated by Sophia Taylor. 2 vols. New York: Scribner & Welford, 1889.
Dillmann, A. *Genesis*. Translated by W. B. Stevenson. 2 vols. Edinburgh: T. & T. Clark, 1897.
Draffkorn, A. "Ilani/Elohim." *JBL* 6 (1957) 216–24.
Ehrlich, E. L. *Der Traum im Alten Testament*. BZAW 73. Berlin: Töpelmann, 1953.
Eitan, I. *A Contribution to Biblical Lexicography*. New York: Columbia University Press, 1924.
Farmer, A. K. "The Trickster Genre in the Old Testament." PhD diss., Southern Methodist University, 1978.
Finkelstein, J. J., and Moshe Greenberg, eds. *Oriental and Biblical Studies: Collected Writings of E. A. Speiser*. Philadelphia: University of Pennsylvania Press, 1967.
Fishbane, M. "Composition and Structure in the Jacob Cycle (Gen. 25:19—35:22)." *JJS* 26 (1975) 15–38.
———. *Text and Texture: Close Reading of Selected Biblical Texts*. New York: Schocken, 1979.
Fitzmyer, J. A. *The Aramaic Inscriptions of Sefire*. BibOr 19. Rome: Pontifical Biblical Institute, 1967.
Fokkelman, J. P. *Narrative Art in Genesis*. Assen: Van Gorcum, 1975.
Frazer, J. C. *Folklore in the Old Testament*. 3 vols. London: Macmillan, 1919.
Freedman, D. N. "The Original Name of Jacob." *IEJ* 13 (1963) 125–26.
Gaster, T. H. *Myth, Legend, and Customs in the Old Testament: A Comparative Study with Chapters from Sir James G. Frazer's Folklore in the Old Testament*. New York: Harper & Row, 1969.
Geršom, ben Levi (Ralbag). *Perušehi ha-torah le-rabbenue Levi ben Geršom (Ralbag)*. Edited by Jacob Leib Levy. Jerusalem: Mossad HaRav Kook, 1992. (Hebrew)
Gevaryahu, H. M. "In Clarification of the Nature of the Terafim in the Bible." *BethM* 15 (1963) 81–86. (Hebrew)
Gevritz, S. "Of Patriarchs and Puns: Joseph at the Fountain, Jacob at the Ford." *HUCA* 46 (1975) 33–54.
Ginsberg, H. L. "Hosea's Ephraim, More Fool than Knave: A New Interpretation of Hosea 12:1–4." *JBL* 80 (1961) 339–47.
———. *The Ugaritic Texts*. Jerusalem: Vaad Halashon, 1936. (Hebrew)
Giveon, R. *Les Bédouins Shosou des documents égyptiens*. Leiden: Brill, 1971.
Gnuse, R. K. *The Dream Theophany of Samuel*. Lanham, MD: University Press of America, 1984.

Bibliography

Good, E. M. "The Blessing on Judah, Gen 49:8–12." *JBL* 82 (1963) 427–32.
Gordon, C. H. "Biblical Customs and the Nuzu Tablets." *BA* 3 (1940) 1–12.
———. "The Mediterranean Factor in the Old Testament." In *Congress Volume: Bonn 1962*, edited by G. W. Anderson et al., 19–31. VTSup 9. Leiden: Brill, 1962.
Greenberg, M. "Another Look at Rachel's Theft of the Teraphim." *JBL* 81 (1962) 239–48.
———. *Biblical Prose Prayer*. Berkeley: University of California Press, 1983.
Gunkel, H. *Genesis*. Translated by Mark E. Biddle. Macon, GA: Mercer University Press, 1997.
———. *The Legends of Genesis*. Translated by W. H. Carruth. New York: Schocken, 1964.
Gurney, O. R. "The Myth of Nergal and Ereshkigal." *AnSt* 10 (1960) 105–31.
Hamilton, V. P. *The Book of Genesis: Chapters 18–50*. Grand Rapids: Eerdmans, 1995.
Haran, M. "The Religion of the Patriarchs: An Attempt at a Synthesis." *ASTI* 4 (1965) 30–55.
Heck, J. D. "Issachar: Slave or Freeman? (Gen 49:14–15)." *JETS* 29 (1986) 385–96.
Hendel, R. S. *The Epic of the Patriarch: The Jacob Cycle and the Narrative Traditions of Canaan and Israel*. Atlanta: Scholars, 1987.
Hesiod and Theogonis. Translated by D. Wender. London: Penguin, 1973.
Hoftizer, J. *Die Verheissungen an die drei Erzväter*. Leiden: Brill, 1956.
Homer. *The Iliad*. Translated by M. Hammond. London: Penguin, 1987.
Honeyman, A. M. "Merismus in Biblical Hebrew." *JBL* 71 (1952) 11–18.
Houtman, C. "Jacob at Mahanaim: Some Remarks on Genesis 32:2–3." *VT* 28 (1978) 37–44.
———. "What Did Jacob See in His Dream at Bethel? Some Remarks on Genesis 28:10–22." *VT* 27 (1977) 337–51.
Hvidberg, F. F. *Weeping and Laughter in the Old Testament*. Leiden: Brill, 1962.
Hyatt, J. P. "The Deity Bethel and the Old Testament." *JAOS* 59 (1939) 81–98.
———. "A Neo-Babylonian Parallel to Bethel-Sar-Eṣer, Zech 7:2." *JBL* 56 (1937) 387–94.
———. "Yahweh as 'The God of My Father.'" *VT* 5 (1955) 130–136.
Ibn Ezra, Abraham. *Ibn Ezra's Commentary on the Pentateuch: Genesis*. Translated by H. Norman Strickman and Arthur M. Silver. New York: Menorah, 1988.
Isbell, C. D. "Initial ʾAlef-Yod Interchange and Selected Biblical Passages." *JNES* 37 (1978) 227–36.
Jacob, B. *The First Book of The Bible: Genesis*. Abridged, edited, and translated by E. J. Jacob and W. Jacob. New York: Ktav, 1974.
Jubilees. In *The Old Testament Pseudepigrapha*, edited by James H. Charlesworth, vol. 2:11–82 Garden City, NY: Doubleday, 1985.
"Judith." In *The Old Testament Pseudepigrapha*, edited by James H. Charlesworth, vol. 1:248–67. Garden City, NY: Doubleday, 1985.
Keel, O. "Das Vergraben der 'Fremden Götter' in Genesis XXXV 4b." *VT* 23 (1973) 305–36.
Kellerman, D. "טָמַן." In *TDOT*, 5:342–44.
Kelso, J., et al. *The Excavation of Bethel (1934-1960)*. AASOR 39. Cambridge, MA: American School of Oriental Research, 1968.
Kempinski, A. "Jacob in History." *BAR* 14 no.1 (1988) 42–47.
Kodell, J. "Jacob Wrestles with Esau (Gen 32:23–32)." *BTB* 10 (1980) 65–70.
Krebs, W. "'. . . sie haben Stiere gelähmt' (Gen 49:6)." *ZAW* 78 (1966) 359–61.
Kugel, J. L. *How to Read the Bible: A Guide to Scripture, Then and Now*. New York: Free Press, 2007.

BIBLIOGRAPHY

———. *The Ladder of Jacob*. Princeton: Princeton University Press, 2006.

Leibowitz, N. *Studies in Bereshit (Genesis)*. Translated by Aryeh Newman. 4th rev. ed. Jerusalem: World Zionist Organization, 1981.

Lewy, J. Les textes paléo-assyriens et l'Ancien Testament." *RHR* 110 (1934) 29–65.

Lichtheim, M. *Ancient Egyptian Literature*. 3 vols. Berkeley: University of California Press, 1973–1982.

Lindblom, J. "The Political Background of the Shiloh Oracle." in *Congress Volume: Copenhagen, 1953*, 78–87. VTSup 1. Leiden: Brill, 1953.

Loewenstamm, S. E. "אנכי אחטנה," *Leshonenu* 29 (1965) 69–70. (Hebrew)

Luckenbill, D. D. *The Annals of Sennacherib*. Chicago: University of Chicago Press, 1924.

Lutz, H. F. "An Omen Text Referring to the Action of a Dreamer." *AJSL* 35 (1918–1919) 145–57.

Luzzatto. *The Book of Genesis: A Commentary by Shadal*. Translated by Daniel A. Klein. Northvale, NJ: Aronson, 1998.

Lycophron. *Lycophronis Alexandra*. Edited by Eduard Sheer. 2 vols. Berlin: Weidman, 1958.

Mabee, C. "Jacob and Laban: The Structure of Judicial Proceedings (Genesis XXXI 25–42)." *VT* 30 (1980) 192–207.

Macintosh, A. A. *Hosea*. ICC. Edinburgh: T. & T. Clark, 1997.

Maimonides, M (Rambam). *The Guide of the Perplexed*. Translated by M. Friedländer. New York: Hebrew Publishing, 1881.

Mason, R. *The Books of Haggai, Zechariah and Malachi*. London: Cambridge University Press, 1977.

Mathews, K. A. *Genesis 11:27—50:26*. Nashville: Broadman & Holmen, 2005.

Mays, J. L. *Hosea*. Philadelphia: Westminster, 1969.

Mazar, B. "The Historical Background of the Book of Genesis." *JNES* 28 (1975) 73–83.

McCarter, K. P., and Ronald S. Hendel, "The Patriarchal Age: Abraham, Isaac and Jacob." In *Ancient Israel*, edited by Hershel Shanks, 1–31. Washington, DC: The Biblical Archeology Society, 1999.

McCarthy, D. J. "Three Covenants in Genesis." *CBQ* 26 (1964) 179–89.

McKenzie, B. A. "Jacob's Blessing on Pharaoh: An Interpretation of Gen 46:31—47:26." *WTJ* 45 (1983) 386–99.

McKenzie, J. L. "Jacob at Peniel: Gen 32:24–32." *CBQ* 25 (1963) 71–76.

Meier, C. A. "The Dream in Ancient Greece and its Use in Temple Cures." In *The Dream and Human Societies*, edited by G. E. von Grunebaum and Roger Caillois, 303–19. Berkeley: University of California Press, 1966.

Mendelsohn, I. "State Slavery in Ancient Palestine." *BASOR* 85 (1942) 14–17.

Margulies, M., ed. *Midrash Haggadol*. Jerusalem: Mossad HaRav Kook, 1947.

Midrash Leqaḥ Tov. Edited by S. Buber. Vilna: Wittwe & Geruder Roman, 1884.

Midrash Rabbah. Edited by H. Freedman and M. Simon. 10 vols. London: Soncino, 1939.

Millard, A. R. "The Celestial Ladder and the Gate of Heaven (Genesis xxviii.12, 17)." *ExpTim* 78 (1966/67) 86–87.

Moran, W. L., ed. and trans. *The Amarna Letters*. Baltimore: Johns Hopkins University Press, 1992.

Nachmanides (Ramban). *Commentary on the Torah*. Translated by Yaakob Blinder, with Yoseph Kamenetsky and Yehudah Bulman. New York: Mesorah, 2005.

Nielsen, B. "The Burial of Foreign Gods." *ST* 8 (1954/55) 103–22.

BIBLIOGRAPHY

Noth, M. *A History of Pentateuchal Traditions*. Translated by Bernhard W. Anderson. Englewood Cliffs, NJ: Prentice Hall, 1972.

———. *Die israelitischen Personennamen im Rahmen der gemeinsemitischen Namengebung*. Hildesheim, DE: Georg Olms, 1966.

Nougayrol, J. "Documents du Ḫabur." *Syria* 37 (1960) 205–14.

O'Connor, M. *Hebrew Verse Scripture*. Winona Lake, IN: Eisenbrauns, 1980.

Oppenheim, A. L. "Mantic Dreams in the Ancient Near East." In *The Dream and Human Societies*, edited by Gustave E. von Grunebaum and Roger Caillois, 341–350. Berkeley: University of California Press, 1966.

Pagolu, A. *The Religion of the Patriarchs*. JSOTSup 277. Sheffield: Sheffield Academic, 1998.

Philo of Alexandria. *Philo*. Translated by F. H. Colson and G. H. Whitaker. 10 vols. LCL. Cambridge, MA: Harvard University Press, 1958–1962.

Plautus, Titus Maccius. *Amphitryon*. Translated by Paul Nixon. Cambridge, MA: Harvard University Press, 1916–1938.

Pope, M. H. *El in the Ugaritic Texts*. VTSup 2. Leiden: Brill, 1955.

Postgae, J. N. "Some Old Babylonian Shepherds and Their Flocks." *JSS* 20 (1975) 1–21.

Pummer, R. "Genesis 34 in Jewish Writings of the Hellenistic and Roman Periods." *HTR* 75 (1982) 177–88.

Pury, A. de. *Promesse divine et légende cultuelle dans le cycle de Jacob: Gen 28 et les traditions patriarcales*. Ètudes bibliques. Paris: Gabalda, 1975.

Rad, G. van. *Genesis: A Commentary*. Translated by John H. Marks. Philadelphia: Westminster, 1972.

Rambam. (See Maimonides, M.)

Ramban. (See Nachmanides)

Rashi. *The Pentateuch and Rashi's Commentary*. Translated by Abraham ben Isaiah and Benjamin Sharfman. Brooklyn: S. S. & R., 1949.

Rast, W. E. *Tradition history and the Old Testament*. Philadelphia: Fortress, 1972.

Recker, C. *Die Erzählungen vom Patriarchen Jakob—ein Beitrag zur mehrperspektivischen Bibelauslegung*. Münster: Lit Verlag, 2000.

Redford, D. B. *A Study of the Biblical Story of Joseph*. VTSup 20. Leiden: Brill, 1970.

Reiner, E., trans. "Treaty of Esarhaddon with Baal of Tyre." In *ANET*, 533–34.

Rendsburg, G. A. *The Redaction of Genesis*. Winnoa Lake, IN: Eisenbrauns, 1986.

Rendtorff, R. *The Problem of the Process of Transmission in the Pentateuch*. JSOTSup 89. Sheffield: JSOT Press, 1990.

Ritner, R. K., trans. "The Legend of Isis and the Name of Re (1:22)." In *COS*, 1:33–34.

Sarna, N. M. *Exploring Exodus: The Heritage of Biblical Israel*. New York: Schocken, 1986.

———. *The JPS Torah Commentary: Genesis*. Philadelphia: The Jewish Publication Society, 1989.

———. *Understanding Genesis*. New York: Schocken, 1966.

Sasson, J. M. "A Genealogical 'Convention' in Biblical Chronography?" *ZAW* 90 (1978) 171–85.

Seebass, V. H. "Die Stämmesprüche Gen 49:3–27." *ZAW* 96 (1984) 333–50.

Segal, M. H. "The Religion of Israel before Sinai." *Tarbiz* 30 (1961) 215–30. (Hebrew)

Selman, M. J. "Comparative Customs and the Patriarchal Age." In *Essays on the Patriarchal Narratives*, edited by A. R. Millard and D. J. Wiseman, 91–139. Winona Lake, IN: Eisenbrauns, 1983.

Sforno, Obadiah ben Jacob. *Commentary on the Torah*. Translated by Raphael Pelcovitz. New York: Mesorah, 1987.

Skinner, J. *A Critical and Exegetical Commentary on Genesis*. ICC. New York: Scribner, 1910.

Soller, M. "Why No Message From Joseph to His Father?" *JBQ* 26:3 (1998) 158–67.

Sommer, B. D. *The Bodies of God and the World of Ancient Israel*. New York: Cambridge University Press, 2009.

Speiser, E. A. "'Coming' and 'Going' at the City Gate." In *Oriental and Biblical Studies*, edited by J. J. Finkelstein and Moshe Greenberg, 83–88. Philadelphia: University of Pennsylvania Press, 1967.

———. *Genesis*. AB 1. Garden City, NY: Doubleday, 1982.

Sperling, S. D. *The Original Torah*. New York: New York University Press, 1998.

Steinsaltz, A. *Biblical Images*. Translated by Yehuda Hanegbi and Yehudit Keshet. New York: Basic Books, 1984.

Strange, J. "Geography and Tradition in the Patriarchal Narratives." *SJOT* 11 (1997) 210–22.

Stuart, D. K. *Studies in Early Hebrew Meter*. HSM 13. Missoula, MT: Scholars, 1976.

Targum Neofiti 1: Genesis. Translated by Martin McNamara. Collegeville, MI: Liturgical, 1992.

Targum Onqelos. Translated by Israel Drazin and Stanley M. Wagner. Jerusalem: Gefen, 2012.

Taschner, J. *Verheissung und Erfüllung in der Jakoberzählung (Gen 25,19—33,17): Eine Analyse Ihres Spunnungsbogens*. Herders Biblische Studien 27. Freiburg: Herder, 2000.

Testament of Levi. In *The Old Testament Pseudepigrapha*. Edited by James H. Charlesworth, vol. 2:304–15. Garden City, NY: Doubleday, 1985.

Testament of Reuben. In *The Old Testament Pseudepigrapha*. Edited by James H. Charlesworth, vol. 2:296–300. Garden City, NY: Doubleday, 1985.

Thompson, T. L. *Historicity of the Patriarchal Narrative: The Quest for the Historical Abraham*. BZAW 133. Berlin: de Gruyter, 1974.

Tigay, J. H. *The JPS Torah Commentary: Deuteronomy*. Philadelphia: The Jewish Publication Society, 1996.

Tsevat, M. "בְּכוֹר." In *TDOT*, 2:121–27

Van Seters, J. *Abraham in History and Tradition*. New Haven, CT: Yale University Press, 1975.

———. "Jacob's Marriages and the Ancient Near East Customs." *HTR* 62 (1969) 377–95.

———. "The Silence of Dinah (Genesis 34)." In *Jacob: Commentaire à plusieurs voix de Gen 25–36; Mélanges offerts à Albert de Pury*, edited by Jean-Daniel Macchi and Thomas Römer, 239–47. Geneva: Labor et Fides, 2001.

Vawter, B. *On Genesis: A New Reading*. Garden City, NY: Doubleday, 1977.

Vaux, R. de. *The Early History of Israel*. Translated by D. Smith. Philadelphia: Westminster, 1978.

Vergote, J. *Joseph en Égypte: Genèse chap. 37–50, a la lumière des études Egyptologiques récentes*. Louvain: Publications Universitaires, 1959.

Vermes, G. *Scripture and Tradition in Judaism*. Leiden: Brill, 1961.

Vrolijk, P. D. *Jacob's Wealth: An Examination into the Nature and Role of Material Possessions in the Jacob-cycle (Gen 25:19—35:29)*. Leiden: Brill, 2011.

Bibliography

Walton, K. *Thou Traveller Unknown: The Presence and Absence of God in the Jacob Narrative*. Carlisle, United Kingdom: Paternoster, 2003.

Weinfeld, M. *Deuteronomy and the Deuteronomic School*. Oxford: Clarendon, 1972.

Weippert, M. *The Settlement of the Israelite Tribes in Palestine: A Critical Survey of Recent Scholarly Debate*. Translated by James D. Martin. Naperville, IL: Allenson, 1971.

Wellhausen, J. *Prolegomena to the History of Israel*. Translated by J. Sutherland and Allan Menzies. Edinburgh: Black, 1885.

Wenham, G. J. *Genesis 16–50*. WBC. Nashville: Nelson, 2000.

———. "The Religion of the Patriarchs." In *Essays on the Patriarchal Narratives*, edited by A. R. Millard and D. J. Wiseman, 161–95. Winona Lake, IN: Eisenbrauns, 1983.

Westermann, C. *Genesis 12–36: A Commentary*. Translated by J. J. Scullion. Minneapolis: Augsburg, 1985.

———. *Genesis 37–50: A Commentary*. Translated by J. J. Scullion. Minneapolis: Augsburg, 1986.

Wilson, J., trans. "List of Asiatic Countries Under the Egyptian Empire." In *ANET*, 242–43.

Wolf, H. W. *Hosea*. Translated by Gary Stansell. Philadelphia: Fortress, 1974.

———. *Joel and Amos*. Translated by Waldemar Janzen, S. Dean McBride, Jr and Charles A. Muenchow. Philadelphia: Fortress, 1977.

Yadin, Y. "And Dan, Why Did He Remain in Ships?" *AJBA* 2 (1968) 9–23.

Yeivin, S. "Y'qob'el." *JEA* 45 (1959) 16–18.

Yaron, R. "Aramaic Marriage Contracts from Elephantine." *JSS* 2 (1958) 1–39.

Zakovitch, Y. *Jacob: Unexpected Patriarch*. New Haven: Yale University Press, 2012.

Index

Hebrew Bible

Genesis

10:6	69	27:44–45	13
10:9	11	28:1–4	49
12:2–3	20	28:3	60
12:6–7	50	28:12	66
12:8	86	28:13	60, 62, 63
12:8–9	93	28:15	69, 78
13:15	20	28:15–22	87
14:18	86	28:16	87, 94
15:1	62n46	28:18	50, 52, 53, 93
15:7–8	20	28:19	87
16:7–8	67	29:11	78
17:1	20	29:18, 20	35
22:13	49	29:31, 33	30
22:17	20	29:32–34	133
24:7	20	30:1	36, 44
24:50	91	30:8	36n4, 73
25:3	17	30:23–24	37
25:7	125	31:3	56, 82, 88–89
25:34	17	31:5	63
26:2	93	31:10–13	xxiv, 81, 87, 90–91, 156
26:3–4	20	31:11–12	24
26:30	51	31:13	60–62, 82, 94, 156
26:35	110	31:15	35
27:4	19	31:17	90
27:29	138	31:19	57, 122
27:34	18	31:24	81, 90, 91
27:36	8	31:33	89
27:40	4	31:38–42	24–25

Genesis (continued)

31:45–54	52, 64
31:53	56
31:54	50, 51
32:2	xxiii, 66, 68, 75
32:4	7, 67
32:23–32	161
32:24	70
32:25	xx, 75
33:20	49, 60, 62
34:4–16	40
35:2	57, 59, 65, 87
35:4	59
35:7	49–50, 60, 61, 62
35:10	72, 75, 78, 156
35:20	53, 160
35:22	44, 46, 95, 133, 134, 160
35:28	125
36:13	10
36:17	10
37:2	113–114
37:14	59
39:6	35
42:21	116
42:21–22	32
42:22	116
44:9	28
44:27	35
48	148
48:20	128
48:22	xvii, 107–108, 112, 156
49:1–28	xxiv, 130
49:3	16, 49, 163
49:6	108, 161
49:7	9
49:9	143
49:14–15	161
49:16	144
49:19	145

Exodus

2:16	34
3:2	67
3:6	63, 64n50
13:21	67
15:6	38
17:15	49
19:10	58
20:3	57
20:7	33
21:17	18
22:12	25, 89n22
22:28	16, 49
24:4	54
24:5–11	50n4
32:2–4	57
33:20	71, 73
34:13	52
28–29	49
40:9–13	52

Leviticus

8:10–12	52
11:47	58–59
15:19	26
18:18	23, 43
19:14	17–18
26:2	82

Numbers

1:23	136
1:32–33	128
2:3, 9	137
7:1	52
7:12	137
8:2–26	49
13:23	140
24:5	9
24:13	91
26:34, 37	128
27:7–11	25n21
32:33–36	133
35:1–8	136

Index

Deuteronomy

7:3–6	110
7:5	52
10:8–9	136
16:22	13, 54, 64, 155
21:17	16
23:8	5
27:6–7	50n4
27:18	18
33	132, 136, 143, 152
33:10	9
33:13	150
33:17	148
33:19	140
33:20	146
33:23	147
33:24	146
33:28	8

Joshua

3:5	58
17:1	148
19:1	136
19:1–9	136
19:4	105
19:24–31	133, 146
19:32–39	133
19:38	86
19:41–42	145
19:40–48	133
24:14	57, 59
24:23	59
24:26	59
24:27	52

Judges

1:3	136
1:34	143
5	132, 136
5:14, 18	140
5:17	141, 146, 147
5:18	148
6:11	67
6:24	49
6:35	140
8:24	57
9:4	86
10:16	57, 59
11:30–31	54
11:33	145
13:17–18	72
18:14	27
19:23	99
19:24	98
20:18–28	85
20:30	85

1 Samuel

1:2	37
1:3	37
1:11	54
7:3–4	57
9:1	151
10:3	61n39
13:3–4	107
13:12	85
16:12	7
17:14	7

2 Samuel

3:7–8	46
7:15	138
8:14	4
11	46
13:11–14	98
13:12	99
13:21	99
13:22	91
13:26–29	96
16:8	54
16:16	125
18:18	53
23:3	150
24:6–7	141

Index

1 Kings

1:31	125
1:33–35	139
2:13–25	46
3:4	93
9:11–13	146
10:18–20	138
12:25	60
13	86
14:9	86

2 Kings

2:2–3	85
8:20–22	4
14:7	4
16:6	4, 20

Isaiah

1:24	62n47
9:7	9
19:8	64
30:29	150
49:26; 60:16	62n47, 149
65:11	47

Jeremiah

9:3	8, 19, 21
10:5	91
17:8	148
29:22	128
29:23	99
30:10	83
30:11	83
31:15	39
31:16	42

Ezekiel

19:1–9	138

Hosea

2:15	57
4:15	77, 86
7:14	78
10:1	52
10:8	61n39
12:2	146
12:4	8, 19, 70, 72, 77
12:4–5	xvii, 76

Joel

4:3	98

Amos

3:14	61n39, 86

Obadiah

1:4	83–84

Micah

5:12	52

Zephaniah

1:12	91
3:3	138

Haggai

1:13	67

Zechariah

7:12	61n39
8:5	98

Index

Malachi

1:2–3	12
2:7	67

Psalms

1:3	148
5:6	13
11:5	13
13:2, 5	62n47
18:34	147
37:37	11
76:12	138–139
80:2	150
89:33–37	138
91:9–11	68
129:5	13
132:2, 5	149

Proverbs

29:10	11
30:30	138

Job

1:1, 8	11
8:20	11

Song of Songs

1:14	140

Ruth

4:11	39, 47, 154
4:11–12	128
4:12	10–11
4:18–22	10

Esther

2:6	69
4:1	18

Apocrypha

Jubilees

19:13–15	12
30:3–4	105
30:5–6	104
30:7	111–112
30:11–14	111

Testament of Levi

6:4–5	136
6:8–7:1	104
5:1–3	106

Judith

9:2	106

New Testament

Romans

9:10–13	14

Revelation

5:5	138

www.ingramcontent.com/pod-product-compliance
Lightning Source LLC
Chambersburg PA
CBHW062043220426
43662CB00010B/1627